The Lady
With No Name

Fergus Dunlop

First published in Guernsey by Hollenden House 2021

ISBN 978-1-8383663-0-8 (hardback)
     978-1-8383663-1-5 (ebook)

www.fd.gg

author@fd.gg

Cover photograph © Fergus Dunlop

Typeset by www.ShakspeareEditorial.org

Contents

Photographs

To my mother
who never gave up

Preface

Sometimes you start writing and you don't quite know why. Maybe you are angry. Or things get weird, and bang, you jot them down. Then normality returns. Your notes were an indulgence and come to nothing. *The Lady With No Name* began like that.

In September 1988 I was a bachelor turned thirty. The girl I loved had junked my plan for a romantic break from our respective jobs in London. To be fair, she had never quite agreed to it. Anyway, instead of flying to meet me in Tuscany, she pleaded pressure of work. I drove south from Florence all night, alone, disgusted with myself as much as with her.

By dawn I was passing a volcano, and the idea formed to watch the sunrise from the top. I scrambled to the summit. The sun came up across the opposite rim of the crater and I did what anyone might do. I grabbed a pen and this log began.

My plan for that fortnight had been to bounce between friends from southern France down to western Turkey. A decade before, as a twenty-year-old, I had driven from the UK to Spain, then across Italy, out through the old Yugoslavia to Greece, and thence home. That was in the 1970s. This time, the border crossings would be easier. Greece had joined the European Economic Community in 1981, and Spain in 1986. The one trepidation was getting into Turkey.

If I had not put pen to paper at the top of Mount Vesuvius, the spark of writing a travel journal might never have caught. Entering Syria six months later, when Mediterranean encirclement became a real possibility, would have been too late to start.

The record lacks an opening chapter, Ibiza to Naples via a barn in the Luberon. The Bentley does not cruise along the French corniche, windows down, trailing the violins of Mancini's 'The Greatest Gift' on the scented breeze. Nor do I claim an overland circumnavigation of the Mediterranean. For that, I would have had to thread through Thrace to the Bosphorus. Instead I took the boat from southeast Italy to western Greece, another to Chios and a landing craft to Asia Minor.

So, I did not plan this. Had anyone suggested on 24th September 1988, as the day broke over Vesuvius, that my jottings would one day become a book, I would have laughed in their face.

The Lady was a 1950s Bentley S-Type 4.9 litre. I had found her that summer among the classified ads in *The Sunday Times*. She captured me at first sight: those irreproachable hindquarters backing out of a lock-up in Littlehampton; and the pennons on the radiator badge, from World War I aero-engine days.

The Bentley's continent-crushing potential was evident the moment I took her helm. Yet there was something sad about her. Sprayed white to carry the brides of West Sussex to and from church, she simmered with indignation, if not like an exiled queen, then at least a noblewoman disfigured. If a bear with a chain through its nose should look you in the eye, or a lioness, perish the thought, regard you through the bars of a cage, you would sense what I sensed.

Quite how to restore the S-Type's self-esteem I knew not, but I could try. I commiserated. The old wedding car and I were the same, wasting our potential.

I wanted to get married, but my girlfriend was unsure – gorgeous but indecisive, a deadly combination.

*

Most things happen slowly for me. I am slow to form a plan and slow to give one up. I tell myself there is plenty of time for everything. However, being slow, I have also learnt that time runs out.

Rarely does time evaporate, vanish into thin air, faster than when I am Driving. Hours can feel like minutes. For holidays I would leave my wristwatch at home. Why let time dominate? And once behind the wheel, it didn't – none of the vehicles in this book had a working clock. I might go a weekend without food and wonder why I was hungry.

This effortless, total focus was once called being in the groove. Now I believe the phrase is 'hacking the flow'. Computer gamers will understand.

Driving in the flow began for me with a Mk.1 Ford Fiesta. It was Calypso Green, a shocking 1970s sap colour, repeated just twice in the four decades since, and never quite as bright. That car had the 957cc block with high-compression cylinder head. Almost a motorcycle engine, it revved way beyond its design spec. Staying in the power band was an art in itself. But the Ford was agile. The tyres were skinny and the body was light. You could place those early Fiestas on a sixpence.

Position, momentum and balance are the essence of driving fast. The dynamics must be perfect for a high-speed run – it is also true of sports such as sailing and skeleton bob. To drive at full tilt on an unknown road, wet or dry, alert to what lies ahead, traffic thin, windscreen clean, tyres warm, grip understood, fuel tank a quarter full, sparse luggage and no passenger, what little weight there is located on the camber, revs in the power band, ready for the next gear, the 'stick held low for a shorter travel, coming onto the brakes, outside edge of the right foot hovering over the throttle, blipping the down-change, that is sport.

After a while, you and the car fuse. You understand each motion, every inch. On a muddy track, with snow tyres on the front, my Fiesta could pull a handbrake turn within its own wheelbase. I did it once by moonlight, on top of an earth dam, too narrow for a three-point manoeuvre, too dark to reverse back up. I know the exact spot. Miles from anywhere, in France. It was forty years ago but I could take you back there now.

The sport of driving also allows long hours. It rewards the latent quality of youth – reaction times and concentration – rather than stamina and brute strength. A car is less physically sapping than a bicycle or horse. It transcends weather, distance and night in a way that track and field cannot. It is more flexible than glamping and comes closer to nature than inter-railing.

Motorbikes also do the job, until it rains, but that is another story.

Driving is a way to engage with the world.

My green, British-registered Fiesta drove the length and breadth of France in 1977, the summer before uni. Like a tethered hornet, it diced the air around Dijon, while I completed an engineering internship at a French metal-basher, Vallourec, in Montbard. The solo runs were, by UK standards, ridiculous – 500 miles each way: La Ciotat to Vendoeuvres par Buzançais without motorways; La Rochelle to Val d'Isère in one daylight blast, again without motorways – to win a bet with a comtesse who said I could not post her a card from France's western and eastern frontiers with the same date stamp; Montbard to Monaco for the Grand Prix – Autoroute du Soleil – leaving the factory gates on the Friday evening, back on the assembly line by 07:00 on Monday – a 1,000-mile round trip.

At the time I must have thought I was invisible to the police. Only now do I close my eyes and see the Gallic fists shaking as my GB sticker disappeared up the road in a cloud of dust and rubber, and wince.

The next summer holiday, 1978, was a long one, the Elysium of the undergraduate, scarcely marred by the fact that I would have to resit my exams at the end of it. I earned money in July on a telephone sales desk and spent it driving that UK–Spain–Yugoslavia–Greece–UK circuit. From Athens to Bristol remains my marathon personal best – 2,100 miles inside two days, mostly on B roads, and all in a four-speed 957cc buzz-box. I arrived the day before the resit. (The miracle of that first borderline pass, and of a similar re-take for my second degree at Oxford, the violent death of the green Fiesta and the adventures of its red double, followed by the Blonde Bombshell, are also stories for another day.)

Thinking of those ferocious drives still sets my pulse racing.

To write while in the flow is best done by hand. A keyboard might serve back home. But the pen is immediate. Simple, neutral. It is also discreet. Rarely, even now, can technology do better. Keyboard entry in broad daylight, in public, makes one unapproachable in a way that writing by hand does not.

Much worse is voice recording. A weirdo chatting into his microphone on a park bench, nowadays with hands-free Bluetooth earpiece, will repel. People don't want to overhear you, or even seem to try. A speech recorder, like a selfie stick, has the world veering away. Besides, too much drivel spills out.

Pen and paper are what do it for me, hunkered down on a hilltop, or curled up against the cold in a cot. That is my style.

Best of all is writing as a break from driving. I am happiest pulled onto the grass after fifty miles of open road, turned away from the steering wheel, catching the after-flashes with words, trying to distil a second flow from the first.

So, gentle reader, if my pen occasionally intrudes into our story, please humour me. It was often my next best friend, after my wheels. And the vehicle speaks for herself.

*

Publishing three decades on has several big advantages. With my parents sadly dead, they and my grandparents can be recalled without embarassment. Other names can be named. No one will be shamed or sacked or shot for having bent the rules all those years ago. None of the cast will be heartbroken. Or sue, I hope. The text needs no changes to protect the innocent, myself included.

When I was thirty-something I was building a life. That was the real drama, not some road trip. The question was, what to do with me? Would my life work out? Would it amount to a hill of beans in this crazy world? Could I earn enough? Might my house be a home for a lasting love? What about kids? And school fees? And if it didn't, couldn't, then what did I bring to the party? Would I be remembered as a great colleague? A helpful neighbour? An amiable host?

Protecting my innocent self proved the right approach. I stayed gainfully employed. The City firm whose company car I drove to Cairo, frequently culled its staff to bring on younger blood. I was only as good as my last product idea or client win. Yet I worked for another dozen years with those bosses at Mercury Asset Management (MAM), now BlackRock. Of all their offices around the globe today, the one I modelled and helped start in Frankfurt is now their third-biggest money earner, after New York and London, I'm told. And with Brexit, who knows, soon to be their second?

My abuse of MAM's lax company car policy may have resulted in slow promotions, but I did not embarrass them by telling the world. When they eventually did make me redundant, after 9/11, this log, and others, were still under wraps. I had not blotted my copybook. In job interviews, my expertise was the topic. No one took cheap shots about the *Wacky Races*. I stayed employable.

I also feared the critics. As a schoolchild, English was the lesson I loved. But in my teens the teachers made clear that my writing was sub-par. That hurt, and I dropped the subject as soon as I could. Maybe my literary skin is a little thicker now, but not much. I expect this prose to be pilloried.

Life does not unfold like a novel. Drudgery surrounds surprise. This tale is beset with hapless repetition – but that is the point. Life without false starts is not actually life. Soldiers say that war is ninety per cent boredom. So is the open road. Repairs and more repairs. Any resemblance in these travels to a structure, a rhythm of crescendos and turning points, is purely coincidental.

A thirty-year delay carries other risks. I may pass the young reader by. Driving as a sport? You must be joking – kids would prefer self-driving cars. Fewer people nowadays take their driving test as teenagers. The average age for passing in Switzerland is twenty-five.

However, the core experience of this book will be familiar to Gen Z from massively multiplayer online games. The absurd number of hours invested, the frequent, often identical failures, the urge to reach the next level, the sense of operating just beyond the limit of skill, the hope of success, the need to be part of something larger than yourself – today they run university degrees in designing such kicks, and long words exist to explain the pleasures.

Back then I just went for a drive.

I found myself exploring things I knew little about: Islam, deserts, machinery. I was also exploring writing styles, the present tense, reported speech, what might today be called a head-cam attitude, to find a less filtered narrative, bringing the reader closer to the experience, without quite turning them off.

Food and water are also important in this tale. Some descriptions are best read hungry or thirsty.

One forgets how mysterious and opaque life was thirty years ago. We thought we knew what we were doing, but we lived in a vacuum. There were no smartphone assistants in our pockets, no GPS locators, no satellite views of every corner of the earth. In 1988 a whole tract of Eastern Europe was closed – it even had a hermit kingdom, Albania. Public phone boxes could be godsends – and when the other party answered, the system peeped worse than a nest of raptor chicks, to be fed, in some countries, with unfamiliar *jetons*. The alternative was an acoustically insulated booth in a post office or an hotel. These cabins were allotted by bespectacled switchboard technicians who metered your call and charged you afterwards, with or without their mark-up.

By publishing my story now, I hope to recapture the spirit of that time for the generation which follows. What child of the West today would believe that Islam was so peaceable, so relaxed, with a Christian? That I was accorded the assistance due to a lone traveller, as the banker in Adana put it? Yet mutual respect came naturally. Even my Libyan interrogator was happy to be distracted from the threat I posed to national security to debate sharia law. Nobody was out to kill me. The spirit of peaceful enquiry, the generosity of people at the bottom of society across all races and creeds, shines out from these pages.

May our shared faith in humanity, which we so took for granted, strike a chord in these days of nationalism, prejudice and hate.

I would add for my children, do it whenever you can. Epic adventure is out there. The biggest horizons, the baddest geology, the boldest cultures, they all await. Get on with it. As the coronavirus pandemic of 2020–2021 reminded us, borders are not always open. But don't quit the day job.

My journey seems self-indulgent to the modern eye. It disregarded principles of the Highway Code pertaining to velocity, stopping distances and rest periods. Such rules have since been tightened by the spread of speed traps, dash-cams and on-board computers. Even without its carbon footprint, a phrase that had yet to be coined, driving as a sport on public roads today ranks close to duelling and fox hunting for political incorrectness.

Apart from not judging me by the manners of today, readers may be more inclined to forgive if they understand two other things: my budget; and the tax regime at home in the United Kingdom during the 1980s.

First, my budget. In the early days I usually slept in the car, or with it on a boat or train. By skipping the hotels, I could enjoy an occasional get-out-of-jail, five-star night or unscheduled air ticket. Admittedly, the many small savings never quite outweighed the few extravagances. But I had little else in my life. I was not feeding a young family at home, as I would have preferred. And I earned what I spent.

The other point was the UK tax code. Tax was why I had a company car in 1988. Tax was at the root of the adventure, which in turn started the travelogue habit.

During my childhood, successive British governments had racked up income tax. In 1966, when I was eight, The Beatles released their *Revolver* album, including 'Taxman', about a tax inspector who sings:

One for you, Nineteen for me…
Should five per cent appear too small,
Be thankful I don't take it all.

For all my formative years the highest income tax rate was at least ninety per cent. Papa was no pop star, but in 1968, the year Shirley Bassey fled to Italy, his marginal tax on investment income was 104 per cent. This became 114 per cent, he told me, because we had a cleaning lady, who triggered Selective Employment Tax (SET) of 10 per cent. To my childish mind that just wasn't fair. Nor did I know the worst of it. The top rate at the margin for the rich that year was apparently 136 per cent, plus 10 per cent SET.

The Rolling Stones departed to the south of France in 1971 and went on working. Dad channelled his energies into charities and local politics. A quarter of a century later, he was amazed to receive an OBE for Services to the Disabled. Mick Jagger's knighthood for Services to Popular Music took five years more.

In response to such eye-watering income tax, employers launched a range of tax-free 'company perks' to attract and reward good staff. Luncheon Vouchers – remember those?

The biggest perk of all was the company car. By the mid-1970s almost any British middle manager doing a reasonable job was loaned a car by their firm, whether or not the role required it; or indeed if they really wanted one. The taxman paid the company to depreciate or lease it, the employee saw little or no addition to their pay slip, and the employer's social security and pension contributions were unaffected.

Successive Thatcher governments reduced income tax. The highest rate dropped in 1979 from ninety per cent to sixty per cent. However, the company car perk survived largely unscathed. Then, in April 1988, top-rate income tax was cut to forty per cent while the tax on company cars doubled. However, for thrifty businesses, older company cars were assumed to be fully depreciated, and so were taxed less. That sloppy definition of 'depreciated' as 'old' landed me with a classic Bentley I did not need in London, and in a colour which should frankly have been parked outside a church.

*

The world of those days is still recognisable to us now. Cars aged three years and more underwent annual safety tests, MOTs. Special Forces needed stubby sub-machine guns. Embassies were prickly about security.

And yet. Can it be that, in our own lifetime, a UK MOT was issued in Turkey? That water pistols were sold which looked identical to 25-shot Uzi SMGs? Or that a private Bentley was treated to a suspension rebuild in the British Embassy in Cairo, on the back of a polite letter of request?

Can it be that, if you took it into your head to drive around the Mediterranean, you actually could?

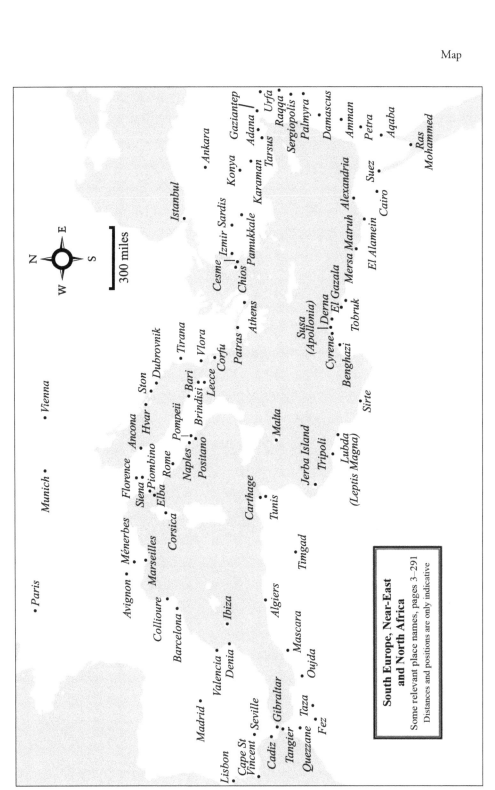

South Europe, Near-East
and North Africa

Some relevant place names, pages 3–291
Distances and positions are only indicative

300 miles

Chapter One: False Dawn

Italy, Greece, Turkey
Saturday 24th September to Tuesday 29th December 1988

Day 1

The track up the volcano runs out just short of the summit.

I park and scramble higher, on hands and feet through the fog, zig-zagging to lessen the slope. Dewy rock shavings cling to my palms and shoes.

I am early to the top. The sky grows bright, but the sunrise bides its time.

I pull this pen, which was under the dashboard, from the inner pocket of my jacket; and then the pad. The pen was a gift from the petrol station back home in Kensington, the first time I filled up the Bentley, three months ago.

'So you swapped the Bombshell for that old tub?' the cashier asked, nodding towards the white 1957 S1 on his forecourt. My previous transport, a two-year-old silver Cosworth Mercedes 190E, had been known as the Blonde Bombshell.

'Well, yes.'

'It got a name yet?'

'I think maybe she doesn't have a name,' I said.

'Another She?' Then he frowned, doubting his readout. 'Twenty-two gallons!'

'And still not full.'

'The Lady with No Name,' he said, with a shrug.

He reached under the till and brought out a presentation box of ten shiny black and red ballpoints, spaced in the moulded white plastic like guardsmen on parade.

'Pick one, they're all the same.'

This was that pen.

'And keep coming back,' he joked as I left the shop.

The crêpe soles of my boots were starting to melt on a slick of gasoline. I slithered and grabbed the Bentley's wing. Petrol was everywhere. In the mirror as I drove off, I saw a wet trail follow us into the road. The filler neck had perished and gallons of fuel had flowed down inside the rear wheel arch.

The car was a rolling Molotov cocktail.

I parked over a sump in the mews to let The Lady dry out. The pen lay forgotten in the deep cubbyhole to the right of the steering wheel.

This pad has a story too. It was for painting in the Highlands of Scotland. The page here is sage-green where watercolour has seeped through from the sheet above. Turning the block in my hand, the backboard is dotted brown with dried blood. It was on the Atholl estate, six weeks ago. I had walked above Bruar Water with my paints and my 16-bore, unsure which would be needed. In the event a brace of blackgame started up, going away, a left-and-right, a rarity indeed. When I picked them, their gizzards were heavy with wild seed under the feathery sleeves, shifting and grainy like the light on the loch below.

Landscape painting was forgotten that day, but the pad still bears the traces.

The only active volcano in mainland Europe is wreathed in cloud. Fog pours over the brim into the caldera from the south, to meet the sulphurous exhalations from the maw. Petrol, sage, blood – colours now encamped across the crater to the east, while twists of night cling in the lava field below me to the west.

Then the vapours part. The far rim is revealed, jagged and brittle as tombstones.

I could climb into the yawning grave, down, scrape my soul on the bottom of the bowl, pumice away the anger. But dawn lifts many moods – daybreak can be hyssop, balm to the heart.

The first dazzling ray of sun blazes across the pit, dead centre, splitting the parapet symmetrically.

In the visitors' car park, mist still blows through. A bus tiptoes out of the shroud. Its only passenger, an old watchman, perhaps the ticket seller, steps down and passes me towards the slope I just descended. His cough is muffled by the fog. Pearl swirls back in, hiding all but the disc of crumble underfoot. Then, in the time it takes to write, the morning sun reaches down, wringing with cream. In front of me through the haze, My Lady's long bonnet catches the light.

Running a Bentley has been a boyhood dream. Aged six, sent on foot with a letter to catch the afternoon post, a similar car turned in by the pillar box, from Gregories Road to Cambridge Road, in front of me, its combined fog and indicator lamp winking, and I was smitten.

The dream became reality this spring when the Chancellor of the Exchequer, Nigel Lawson, doubled company car tax in the budget. The Bombshell had to go. However, I had spotted a loophole. Vehicles more than thirteen years old, worth less than £13,000, stayed largely exempt.

So, aged thirty, I hooked up with this thirty-one-year-old. She cost £6,300 in 1957, a king's ransom then, and £11,000 now, well below the Chancellor's ceiling and within my grasp. The tax I will save should more than pay for her extra fuel – now that the filler neck is fixed. And the company covers insurance and basic maintenance.

My Lady's engine design was inherited from W.O.Bentley when Rolls-Royce took over his firm in 1931. It was the last hurrah of the side-valve, pre-WWII straight-sixes, before the American fashion for V8s prevailed at Rolls-Royce/ Bentley Motors. This power plant appeared in many mid-century British workhorses, including the Ferret armoured car, the Dennis fire engine and the Humber one-ton truck. It is famously robust, with Ministry of Defence cash having ironed out any last wrinkles.

Originally gunmetal, My Lady was resprayed for weddings a decade ago, in the seventies. The deeply uncool white put her just inside my allowance from work. Being an ex-wedding car, she might look cheap in the UK, but she would exude style on the Côte d'Azur. The Promenade des Anglais in Nice was made for her. This I knew from our first drive. More than any present-day British machine, her mind was in the Med.

The fog falls away completely. The huge blue view crashes in. Pines stretch from the treeline to the Bay of Naples below. That first motorbus, parked teetering on a hairpin, starts up and chugs on down.

We must follow, before the way is clogged with weekend trippers.

*

When I was leaving England last week to fetch the car, my neighbour in the mews, Sir Alford, said, 'Watch out for Marseilles. The Rolls was graffitied with a red hammer and sickle there.' On a black Silver Shadow, that was modern art, I thought. But I kept it to myself – Alford is not a man to entertain such views.

After I collected the Bentley from the Luberon, she indeed spent a night in Marseilles. My four-year-old goddaughter, Fleur, and her Parisian parents, Hattie and Remi put us up. They moved to France's second-largest city recently for his job. My Lady slept safely outside on the street. Was Alford just unlucky? The born Marseillaises might have been cantankerous, but to me they were not vandals.

However, Hattie made dark warnings about Naples. She said, with her head cocked forward, only part in jest, 'You know, they send body parts to the relatives with the ransom notes?'

At three o'clock this morning, My Lady crept into the City of 500 Domes on full alert. For a town of such ill-repute Naples seemed to wear the night demurely, shutters pulled down to the rubbish-strewn setts.

Yet even at the quietest hour, the capital of Campania was strewn with traps. The cobbled canyon floors were laced with savage potholes. Boulevards divided into carriageways, which nevertheless reached the same place. Other streets were one-way in name only. Anticlockwise roundabouts might be taken clockwise. Traffic lights could show green in all directions. Then a power cut sprang on us like a giant weed, leaving even the dustcart groping its way.

And that was at night. Naples by day must be an order of magnitude more frightening. Pretty looks and proud pedigrees will serve for nothing. What matters will be skill. Rome was the same – I saw a humble Fiat Panda weave through the jam to overtake a police car with siren wailing.

And the Bentley's boot does not lock.

No, I will head south, away from all that.

*

Today, Pompeii cannot see the dormant peak which slew it two millennia ago. A haze masks the view of Vesuvius to the northeast. The Monte Faito range provides the drama in the other direction.

I look up from my corner of the ancient streets. Where would the volcano be, how far, how tall, if the air cleared? Surely it could not fill the whole sky? Yet it must be close, to have wiped this orderly conurbation not just from the map, but from local memory, for a millennium.

Inside Pompeii's walls whole streets and squares remain unexcavated, under yards-deep ash and acres of sweet tomatoes. I clamber up a twenty-foot bank of pyroclastic topsoil, and pluck one of the bright red baubles. It tastes so akin to concentrated *pomodoro* paste that no process of reduction is required.

Pompeii was originally excavated in the mid-eighteenth century by the Bourbon King of Naples, the future Charles III of Spain. Ten years earlier, a farmer had found Herculaneum while digging a well. That town, though rich, was smaller and buried under sixty feet of tough lava. But its discovery had the experts combing the Roman texts, and curiosity in the whereabouts of Pompeii grew. Once found, covered by a much shallower deposit of softer pumice, King Charles switched horses and began an industrial-scale search for artefacts here, to boost his prestige and line his pockets.

The real treasures, the suburban villas and farms, must still lie interred beyond the walls.

*

As the day passes, a nodding acquaintance with life in AD 79 settles in my head. The Pompeiians were like us in their love of fast food, cosmetics, hot and cold running water, graffiti, artistic perspective and gridiron street plans. All of that is astonishing.

But other sights jar: the shoe-box dimensions of their homes, the doll-sized whorehouse, even the slits below ground in the amphitheatre for shelving dead gladiators, seem small-minded in a way that contradicts the vastness of the Roman Empire.

Like all empires, from the Egyptian to the Chinese to the British, it relied on a mindset – part force, part bureaucracy, part myth. The Romans left us their roads, their calendar and their sense of citizenship. *Civis Romanus Sum.* I know a few lawyers who still think of themselves like that. The Roman emperors were called gods from time to time, but did their people believe it? So Pompeii raises questions about society and power. Roman might was military. How many of Pompeii's sons were away serving in the legions in AD 79? How many of the dead were slaves, and how many of those were enslaved by legionnaires? Rome's success remains an enigma.

*

Leaving the car park, I give a road mender a lift to the next village, Pioppanio. His viewpoint is that of anyone living beside a national monument. Pompeii is foreign to its locals.

*

My pale prancer is parked on a spur. Around her, the Amalfi coast plunges like a rock garden down sheer cliffs into an ornamental sea. Here man must choose between the vertical and horizontal. A coast road has been chiselled into the rock face like the body-shelves at Pompeii. When two buses meet it takes time for them to pass. Happily, the Bentley proves narrower than she looks, and slips several attempts to hold her, as smoothly as a bar of soap.

When the road swings round a headland, it is possible to halt and stretch my legs. Halfway down the giddy cliff is an hotel, the San Pietro di Positano. Its terrace is a hand-painted fruit plate, hanging in the air, a dais between the sea and the sky, ready to send a hundred souls to heaven. Behind soars the escarpment, cliffs terraced naturally upon cliffs, standing stacks and lofty pinnacles, each with a legend attached. Ahead, linked by a low wall, are elegant yellow and blue tiled love seats, spaced by shapely terracotta urns and umbrella pines. The distant horizon bisects the urns at their thin point, halfway up.

Lace-winged butterflies joust amorously among the stately silk floss trees. Far below, across the ionised titanium skin, a yacht motors silently, no hope of a breeze, an arrowhead to its wake.

A gold-buttoned waiter approaches. The budget will stretch to a gin and tonic.

The day gives way to gloaming.

Several fishing smacks hold out from Positano for a catch. They are black against the dying light, like horizontal slits cut by a fingernail through bright foil. Dotted at prow and stern, one man steers, one colludes.

The Italians invented Romance – but this place is so hugely, so palpably romantic that nobody should face it alone.

Day 2

Sleeping in the car saves time. I can drive further, without mapping a route, without researching hotels. When exhaustion finally prevails, I just dive onto the ample red leather sofa that serves as a back seat.

Late last night, after 200 miles caressing the lower leg of Italy, I found this farm gateway and turned in.

Over the walnut ledge of the back passenger side window is a garden from Arcadia. By moving my head I can see orderly olive groves, fruiting figs, and vines weighed down with grapes ripe for collection. It being harvest-tide, the field hands arrive early for work. Sunday or no, they come on foot and bicycle and tractor. The bliss of repose is replaced by the shame of idleness. I clamber over the slab-like backrests onto the front bench. As The Lady fires up and rejoins the road east, gangs of pickers are already lined along the verges to gather in the vintage.

The sun rises head-on.

Some mosquitoes were in the car last night when I stopped. I catch them now, one by one, covering the last twenty miles into Brindisi, Italy's southerly Adriatic port. Each is full with blood, though where they bit me is not yet clear. My car rug gave protection, as a christening present should – it has seen sagging prep school beds and sinful student picnics. A godfather wrote a note with his gift, foreseeing all this, and adding that the rug would keep my knees warm in old age too. I pulled it over me last night. But the B roads from Amalfi had left me too tired to check for gaps. And the mosquitoes got through.

*

In Brindisi the clocks changed this morning. They did so across Continental Europe, but will not for another two weeks in London. The townsfolk ask each other which way time went. Anyone in the know took an extra hour's sleep, and some rather more than that. The public timepieces have yet to be adjusted, of course.

'When will the ferry sail to Greece?' I ask the old salt at the ticket desk.

'They may use the time on the clock tower,' he indicates. 'Or maybe the time on the radio. The real time is whatever the capitano says it is.'

However, no boats are planned until after sunset, so we have a while to discuss this.

*

The antidote for many miles' galloping east is a day by a fountain. On one side of this square is Brindisi's huge natural anchorage. On the other, in a flash of civic pride, is a monument to the Roman poet Virgil, who succumbed here, this week in 19 BC. Generations of schoolboys faced with his *Aeneid* may have imagined that Virgil died of boredom. In truth he was travelling back from Greece with Emperor Octavian (subsequently named Augustus) and caught a fever on board ship. When he realised he was dying, Virgil tried to have the only manuscript of his poem burnt. But the Emperor overruled his last wish. The near-10,000-line *Aeneid*, which narrates Rome's founding legend, went on to become the central text of Latin literature.

Between the statue and the sea, flanked by blue-daubed benches, are lines of lanky palms. Their shadows waltz the piazza as the day progresses, finding new, unexpected points of intersection, like a child's geometric drawing toy, or an astronomical clock. Inside this time machine, the hours advance slower than life itself. The old men on these seats might live forever.

One such veteran, Raffaele, sits with me. I am on his regular Sunday morning pew and he is kind enough to draw me into his circle. He is so affectionate, clasping my neck, squeezing my face and asking me to join him and his wife for lunch, that I think perhaps he is mad.

'Lunch would be special,' I indicate, 'But today I am far from that.' And I point out the engine oil under my nails, my stubbled chin and this grimy T-shirt.

7

It is the shirt I wore straightening the Bentley's front bumper two days ago. The forged and chromed steel fender was caught in a minor crash last month. My Lady ran out of road on a late-night charge up into Ibiza Castle. With me were my twenty-year-old cousin, Simon, his younger sister Jessica, and two of her girlfriends. We had been to the huge new open-air nightclub on the outskirts of town, Pacha. Our limo was a first for the bouncers, and we were received like royalty. I was claiming that the Bentley is not as big as she looks, that she would even fit up through the fortress' cobbled alleys to reach the dirt parade ground overlooking the port, like the old Fiesta could. The girls said not. We did make it up there; the clearance on the narrowest straight was millimetre true, but the last left-hander had been tighter than I thought.

Afterwards we went to Amnesia, but I don't remember much about that.

The result of our brush with the castle wall was a new curve to the bumper on the driver's side, a rippled front wheel arch and a bent bracket. My hosts in Chianti, Ross and Annabel, let me put the bracket in their barbecue. When it glowed red, I hammered it flat with a brick and cooled it with a hiss in the garden cistern.

I had hoped my girlfriend in London would come out to the Balearics. Plan B was for her to join me on this second break at Florence's Peretola airport for the drive to Turkey. I was full of ideas and dying to see her. We would have the time of our lives. With the bracket straightened, I rang her to confirm her landing time in Tuscany. She pulled out. I had no Plan C. I just wanted to storm off. But the heavy bumper still had to be reassembled. I struggled in the dust under the Bentley's front wing to bolt it back to the chassis. Reflected wide-angle in the chrome overrider was my bulbous nose and receding face; and behind me the village idiot, relieving himself against a crud-encrusted concrete mixer.

I'm afraid I barely said goodbye to Ross and Annabel, and didn't change clothes.

So this is no fit state in which to be Raffaele's guest for lunch.

'*Tutto bene*,' he says, accepting that I might visit him when I am next in Brindisi – '*La prossima volta*.' And we exchange addresses.

At fifteen minutes past noon (or is that one or eleven?), after much talk of pasta and many consultations of his watch, Raffaele stands up, refolds the white kerchief which he spread on the bench to sit upon two hours before and bids me '*Ciao!*' He indicates that he will be back. In other circumstances I might have slipped away, but today's quality is in staying put; not exploring the harbour for turreted vantage points for sale; not looking for the post office to send cards home;

not crossing the piazza to the *gelato* stand for a bottle of water; not even escaping kindly old men. Today is for meditation before long ferry crossings.

How better than with these elders, awaiting the final ferryman?

*

The sun has dropped behind the Banca d'Italia. Only the leafy tops of the palms still catch the light. Small finches make shrill argument, the first sustained birdsong I have heard in the whole land. In Chianti we were visited beside the swimming pool by men with guns and dogs, walking purposefully past the prone sunbathers, like denizens of a different dimension. Even when the daily hunt was over, a distant bird-scarer would crack every ten minutes or so. Its sound cannoned up the valley, bouncing back to us off the village on the opposite ridge. After a while the echoes became comfortable, even countrified, and punctuated the silence they wrought.

Anticipation stirs in this little square of mine. Buses arrive and boat people heft their backpacks.

The Bentley, parked all day in a place so conspicuous that no one will dare try the boot, fades into the Sunday evening promenade. Two young boys, each with a goldfish swimming in a plastic bag, walk past with their mother. Older girls stroll across the piazza in threes. Some town lads in polished black cowboy boots approach a pair of more sophisticated women. The patriarchs return, now four to a bench. They say little – what could have happened since this morning? – but watch the human chess-game acted out before them.

The Italian *Tricolore* flags on the boats alongside the square flap with new life – green, white and red in the evening breeze.

Raffaele reappears. We shake hands and exchange slow, contented smiles. He knows the man on the bench beside me so, with a suitable pause, I write on. Raffaele's hair is immaculate after his siesta, but a dot of his wife's tomato sauce has spotted his starched blue collar. Only spaghetti can flick food that high up your shirt.

A group of five men at the bottom of the square, one of them in sailor's whites, wanders to the top, by the monument to Virgil's muse. They try to engage three attractive female backpackers in conversation. The girls persist in their own talk. The five men, quickly joined by other lads, appear to turn away. Then the girls cast a glance across and soon the original leader and the biggest newcomer are crouching with them.

It is half past five on Raffaele's watch (so, six or four?) when the peal of the Duomo summons us from behind. There is a general shifting and the townspeople, first the newlyweds, then the families, begin to disappear down the side street towards the bells; now the unattached girls, still arm in arm in groups of three; and lo, the gang of youths around the monument departs in that direction. The square is left to the grandfathers – and we few who are in transit. The sea is now as grey as the sky. Raffaele consults the time again.

A lunatic enters the piazza, singing and shouting to each bench in turn. We look on, except of course when he comes to us, for who knows what might happen should he catch your eye?

The parked cars now stretch right along the quay. Night is falling. The ice-cream stand electrifies the lights in the name board around its roof. The birdsong has stopped and the sound of the fountain is supreme. The bells make one last appeal. Scooters toot. Raffaele starts a conversation with an old man in a light-brown suit. '*Mio medico*,' he tells me, and only leaves when the bells have finally stopped. Another easy '*Ciao! Scrivimi*' – write to me – and he is gone.

*

The delirium of the crossing time begins, rendered more light-headed by the lack of food. A long-nosed West German backpacker sits with me on the dock. He seems depressed.

'I am trying to meet some friends in Turkey,' I say in German, to lighten the mood.

'Your car is a provocation,' he warns. 'A symbol of the elite. In Turkey it will be stoned.'

He says he has heard of Turks threatening a coach full of his countrymen by smearing the windows with goat's blood.

I have been reading Tolstoy's *War and Peace* in paperback. I try to return to my book. But Long-nose does not leave me alone. He dismisses my book, saying that literature for him can shed no light on affairs of the heart, because his girlfriend was recently killed.

I change the conversation back to cars. Like most German men, the subject comes easily. He tells me he heard on his radio that Alain Prost won the Portuguese Formula One Grand Prix today. Ayrton Senna was only sixth (it can't have been raining). Now Senna must win one of the last three races of the season, to be sure of taking the Championship.

*

My sultry thirty-one-year-old Lady, broad-sculpted, elegant and eager, is stopped at the loading ramp. The Greek deckhands of Hellenic Mediterranean Lines lean against her and pat her flanks. The mood is more of mutual respect than bristling machismo. I tell myself it will be the same in Turkey. Bloodlust does not rise without the scent of fear. Be unafraid. Strength respects tranquillity. For now I am tranquil. Long may it last.

*

I am in the top bunk, washed and shaved. The HML *Egnatia* shakes herself and slips quietly out into the Adriatic dark. The miniature bottle of Air France Bordeaux rouge, kept from the flight to Marseilles for just such a moment, tips me quickly into sleep.

*

A fat, decaying American in the bunk below has to be prodded several times to stop his snores. Telling old men to pipe down comes easier in the middle of the night.

Day 3

With a rousing shout and a bang on the door, the cabin attendant announces the approach of Corfu. In 1864, this island was the first example of British voluntary decolonisation. My Lady and I will continue to Patras, so we are in no hurry. Only when the ship has docked do I climb on deck. Broadside to us, a Greek MTB (motor torpedo boat) patrol craft makes its brutal toilette. Its crew hose down the deck artillery, torpedo tubes and skyward anti-aircraft barrels. It chills the onlooker like a bull found while crossing a wildflower meadow.

Beyond, just five miles away, is an even more hostile sight, Albania. Their Maoist dictator, Enver Hoxha, is dead, but his siege mentality lives on. Europe's very own hermit kingdom is hard to look at. The mind casts a black hole, from which light itself cannot escape; like the approaching totality of a solar eclipse, dolloping night across the horizon. Remember when the movie projector jammed and the film burnt through white, from the middle of the image outwards? Albania is the inverse, a negative of that.

Breakfast is bought with my remaining lira, a croissant – my first bite in thirty-six hours. Back in the cabin, now alone, I sleep and write dazedly. The space could be a prison cell. I imagine being kidnapped, ransomed, minor body parts removed for posting to relatives, spending years in this solitary confinement, no windows or room to move. Would they feed me pen and paper?

*

The afternoon is for Tolstoy, sun and more sleep on the top deck. Kutuzov is at Borodino, while the Greek Air Force streaks beside us over the flat silver sea.

The gentle motion of the ship and the steady breeze over the deck are as soporific as ever. The azure horizon shifts lazily up through the railing, with a contemplative pause at the top, and then, so gently, back down below it. Those few fellow passengers who are on their feet have long ago adopted the seafarer's open-kneed walk. It is easier to read than to write. Brainpower is diverted to rationalise the rocking of the boat. Logic tries to tell the senses, no you have not been poisoned. In the end, it is easiest just to lie back and be lulled to sleep.

*

Disembarking in Patras, on the western Peloponnese, the Bentley itches for the open road. She must wait while I clear her through customs. She has been segregated into the lorry park, away from mere cars. Ettore Bugatti would have approved; he once called Bentleys '*les camions les plus rapides du monde*' – the fastest lorries in the world.

Darkness has fallen by the time we roll out. A full moon rises, so brilliant that for a while before the Corinth Canal I drive without lights, just to prove we can.

*

Public transport for Athenians is improbably grand. This train has varnished wooden window frames and floral-pattern ceiling ventilators. Leather-hinged handholds dangle between crystal bowl lanterns, with all the crafted personality of a bygone age. But tonight the prize for personality still goes to my Queen B. With consummate thoughtfulness she has broken down on the dockside in Piraeus, stern-on to a dozen transport ships. Night watchmen on the boats have said they will keep an eye on her until morning. The boot obligingly locked itself, the first time I have known it; the train terminus was directly across the road; and Athens, complete, one supposes, with an agent for Rolls-Royce and Bentley Motors (brands of the same company, of course), is only a short trip away.

Her Ladyship's message seems to be, 'Here is the perfect spot to remind you who I am. And the way you've been carrying on, you deserve it.'

A similar incident occurred in Ibiza. Cousin Simon and I had driven the 1,200 miles from London over the Pyrenees, and caught the morning ferry from Denia direct to San Antonio Abad, on the west coast, where the sunset villas are. Bumping merrily off the ramp onto Fisherman's Wharf, we headed to Uncle Robert's and Aunt Jane's. At the top of the last crest, within sight of our destination, I stopped at the Es Cuckoo Tienda to buy a thank you present. But when we came out of the store, the Bendix drive on the starter motor had sheared. The Bentley simply couldn't start. Her meaning then was the same: 'You know who I am. So shape up.' Letting off the handbrake, we rolled down the slope in neutral, to the finishing line, and said nothing until I had organised a tow to the garage the next day.

15 XKN also mistrusts men, and me in particular. She is a misandrist, the counterpart to a misogynist. I could give many examples, but one will do. Ten days before we left England I was driving home from a Hampstead Heath picnic with Helene, a brilliant, beautiful and possibly even willing acquaintance, whom I met at Ross' and Annabel's wedding. Barely had she placed her athletic and mini-skirted thighs on the front bench seat beside me than the Bentley lost all electrical function. Frank Dale & Stepson in Hammersmith later diagnosed 'a battery short to the chassis'.

The misandrist can act selectively against women too. In her view, sisters should not let the sisterhood down. Before the new starter assembly arrived in Ibiza from England, a misguided female wandered into the workshop and saw the white wedding car. According to the reports, she cooed closely over the gleaming radiator, fell into the inspection pit and broke both her legs.

Day 4

It must be after midnight. Athens is asleep. The train drops me at Omonia, city central. I walk five minutes south to Constitution Square. Opposite the parliament building is the Hotel Grande Bretagne. A decade ago, the aphid-green Ford Fiesta came down to Greece for a blind date. Here is the fateful doorstep where I met the lovely Laidlaw twins. And inside, at 1 a.m., the head porter is still sufficiently discerning to find a room for a near tramp. A key, a marbled tub, a fierce encounter with a scrubbing brush, and at last I stretch out between linen sheets.

*

Panic kicks me awake. Before my head hit the pillow, the hotel switchboard said there was no Rolls-Royce agent in Athens. Or in Greece. Her Ladyship is immobilised, thousands of miles from home, and I can see no way to have her fixed. Game over. My scheme is doomed. They always are. She will have to be unceremoniously dumped. I reach for *War and Peace*, but the image springs back, a lump of iron alone amid the alien quays. My colleague Saker's dad pushed his Bentley R-type off the dock in Haifa when they emigrated, rather than let the Israelis have it.

Tolstoy's evergreen characters assert themselves, and calm returns.

*

Morning peeks between tall curtains. I telephone from bed to the Automobile and Touring Association of Greece, passing slowly up the hierarchy, then to another number and a man called Harris with a steady voice who chuckles when I say she's an S1... I like him already. We agree to look her over together when she arrives by trailer at his workshop around lunchtime.

Relieved, I dress up as a gentleman of leisure and walk through the gilt and alabaster public rooms of this Byronic pile to find an English breakfast. Then it is downstairs to the equally palatial barber's shop in the basement. Surrounded by mirrors and marble basins, cloaked in white, I ask for a shave and cut. The shipping magnate in the armchair next to me lolls extravagantly while he receives his morning ministrations. He is razored quite separately by both barbers in turn, before his face is wrapped in hot towels and left to steam.

Turning to me, the hairdresser says, 'Your skin is not good enough for an open blade.' Maybe the mosquitoes found my face. Or perhaps I need some tonnage.

'Then just a haircut,' I say.

Back in my room, unshaven but trimmed, I telephone Bruce, head of the workshop at Frank Dales. He has taken the Bentley under his wing, mainly at my employer's expense, when she is at home. We discuss what might have made her automatic gearbox disappear. The engine still revs, but there is no forward or backward engagement at all. Bruce sounds doubtful about the chances of a Greek mechanic replacing a disintegrated viscous coupling. But if it is just the vacuum seal, he could send out the part.

I retrace my steps to Omonia station. The streets are peopled by more beggars and lottery ticket sellers in grimy peaked caps than I have seen in any other European capital, many more than London in the Thatcher recession. One front page stares from every news stand, a celebrity being manhandled in a nightclub. Her eyes roll like a mare in oestrus. Again it feels anarchic, certainly more than the UK's Press Council would allow.

*

From Piraeus, I telephone the automobile club rescue service. They want the name of the road between the passenger terminus and the dockside where the Bentley is stranded. Then I hurry along the crowded waterfront to a ferry agent.

Today's boat to Samos has sailed. The one tonight would drop me off too late to make my rendezvous tomorrow evening. The only connection now to mainland Turkey would leave me with a 200-mile cross-country dash in four hours. Even if Harris can fix the gearbox, the rendezvous is impossible. My allotted holiday is almost over. The future holds nothing but garage bills and frowning faces in the personnel department back in London.

I sit dejectedly in my broken toy. Home is a withering 2,000 miles away. Idly I start her up. Gearlever down from neutral to reverse and lo, the 'box engages. Backwards and forwards I rock in my parking slot, drawing a flurry of attention from cars seeking a free space – and growing more and more dejected. There is nothing wrong. For nothing have I missed the party. If I had spent the night in the car, I would have tried this out earlier and caught the boat. Now there is little point pressing on to dread, hostile Turkey, only to sail back to lay up the Bentley inside Europe.

After several wrong numbers, dialled from among the deep-fried *loukoumades* – honey dumplings – at a harbourfront bar, I cancel the car rescue service. Then, on an impulse, I check for other islands leading to other parts of the Turkish coast. Oh my God, one option fits. To make it, just, perhaps, to the caravanserai at Kusadasi, I can sail overnight to Chios, the Greek island to the north of Samos. A landing craft bumbles across each morning from there into the Turkish fishing village of Cesme on the mainland.

For this The Lady booted out her admirer: to make him shape up, grab a night's sleep and lay the foundations of a rescue should anything go wrong on the next stage of our travels. We still have half a day in hand. Harris is telephoned with apologies. Bruce's call must come later.

Back on the wood-panelled train, I find myself next to a priest in a tall black hat. We are confronted by a blind man selling lottery tickets. It is Brindisi all over again. We stare steadfastly ahead, grimly hoping he cannot tell we are there. At the next stop the blind man suddenly becomes sighted, hops out and sprints for the adjoining carriage before the creaking automatic doors slam shut.

The priest and I exchange not a glance.

The Hotel Grande Bretagne is cordoned off by police cars. Other tall-hatted, bearded, massively-crucifixed priests robed in black, are meeting behind drawn curtains in the saloon where I had breakfast. Everyone in the marbled hall stands up – me included. One pace from the desk where I was writing, a small man in heavier robes stops. Priests come and kiss the hem of his long smock, or bow for him to extend his hand.

I hold my breath. The tableau freezes. The seconds pass.

Now the patriarch of all the Greeks moves on, and the foyer begins to settle. But we have been moved, and in my case torn – I was just polishing up that paragraph about equine lust.

*

The phone lines to England are jammed. To save something of the morning, I walk through the National Gardens in a long semicircle to find the Acropolis. Eleven years ago, I ran to the top step of the cliff but turned back, out of time.

Today the planets are aligned.

In the midday sun, the Parthenon is indeed perfection.

*

The hawsers of the *Nissos Chios* snake free of their bollards. Deck hands haul them aboard with two enormous peppermill winches at her stern, and coil them down. Then the ferry churns out of Piraeus to yet another radiant sunset.

My Lady, for her part, has not missed a beat all afternoon. I took her into town, tanked her up and watched, amazed as ever, while two men with buckets, sponges and a long-handled broom to reach the middle of the roof released a dazzling white butterfly from its cocoon of road dirt. Was that gratitude on my part for the gearbox mending itself? Appeasement? Atonement? Absolution? Or just shameless pride?

Deep in the boat's car deck, she sashayed down a corridor of gritty, island-bound lorries, and they positively purred. One diesel-stained driver asked in seafarer's patois, 'No Rolls-Royce?' justifiably confused.

'No Parthenon,' I agreed, making an angle with my hands and then indicating the curve of the radiator. He chuckled like Harris did this morning.

*

A dogfight of seagulls zooms and dives at the wake immediately behind our boat. The boiling water and the air rising off the superstructure excites them, but they catch nothing.

We humans are the same, wheeling and jockeying in a turbulence of misplaced hope.

Now the sea takes on the colour of dusk. The gulls, by pairs and threes, rise in ever-increasing circles up and away, back to the luminous landmass. The ferry has few passengers – just the girl backpackers, the lorry drivers and an islander or two, happy to escape the squalor of the city. After a ship's supper, I roll out my rugs on the deck to sleep. My jacket is off to one side. With luck any fleas on it will jump onto whoever stops to feel it for my wallet.

Day 5

A mosque. My first. The dome is cyan and flat, like the helmet of a WWI Tommy time-warped into a 1980s UN peacekeeping mission. I hear running water, and the shouts of children. A young man removes his shoes at the tall alcove by the door and prepares to enter, but the way is still barred. I lean back against a pillar in the porch. The shadow of the pen is fading.

It is twenty to six in the evening on 28th September.

The moment is almost upon us for which My Lady left her barn in France, crossed Italy and Greece and travelled back in time and technology. Today she reached Turkish soil. A whitewashed landing craft ran us the last mile of water from Chios to Cesme. We were the only vehicle aboard. The drop-front ramp clattered down, and the S-Type hit Asia Minor with the enthusiasm of a Sherman tank snorting onto a D-Day beach.

Our papers were franked in the little customs house, under the watchful gaze of a portrait of Kamal Ataturk, modern Turkey's founder. Then we raced fifty miles through the coastal range to Izmir, ancient Smyrna, to research our exit.

In Izmir an English Miss Fixit called McGrath, leggy, elegant and adored by her minions, warned me that flights home at this time of year are as over-booked as the last choppers out of Saigon. She also explained the new rubber stamps in my passport. If I am to leave Turkey without the Bentley, or my scuba-diving cylinder, I must turn them over to the authorities.

Informed but also abashed, I pressed south, to the caravanserai, the ancient camel-train terminus, in the coastal town of Kusadasi.

The young man waits patiently for the mosque to open. He is on the team selling Turkish carpets from the house behind me. He is charming, a great salesman. He says he will do his military service once he has finished his engineering studies. Although I will not buy anything, he likes practising his English.

We talk about Turkey's army and her dangerous neighbours. 'Worst are the Greeks. They took Cyprus, Rhodes and all our islands at the end of World War I.' I refrain from mentioning that Turkey had been on the losing side of that war, and moreover, Ataturk had been the commander who humbled the British Empire at Gallipoli.

'Second worst are the Syrians. Their fighters attack our villages inside the border. That's where medals are won today,' he continues. 'Then Bulgaria, Iraq, Iran and Russia. That makes six. We have no problems with Russia,' he adds.

Six neighbours. Small wonder the Turkish Army is half a million strong.

But the carpet seller is happier talking about women. He tries to teach me the outward marks of different nationalities of female tourist. The Italians will have some fabric tied on to a bag or a waistline, the Germans wear structurally sensible sandals. British girls have awful hats. His trick is to hail the approaching victim in her own language, first time off.

Carpet selling is evidently the peak of many a Turkish boy's ambitions; and the idea of a magic carpet simply the pinnacle of sales chat.

He offers me a job.

The entrance to the little mosque is being unlocked. I too remove my shoes and we tiptoe in. The floor is covered with dozens of Turkish rugs, nothing special, and modernity has been welcomed – microphones stand on the two pulpits which face the open room. In one corner an industrial-grade vacuum cleaner awaits. A string of prayer beads lies forgotten on the floor, lost in the patterns of the carpets.

I have a date at six. It is the wrong moment to do this, let alone think about jobs. I make my excuses and set off through the bazaar.

On the stroke of the hour I am at the rendezvous, using my new carpet-selling skills to identify two English speakers to share a drink with. They are girls from Belfast, relaxed, but they doubt my story.

The minutes tick by. Up the road where I parked, I can see My Lady drawing a small crowd. If the Hills and the Blackwells had arrived early they would have seen her too, and known to wait. But no. They have probably heard that Kusadasi is a dump and voted not to put into port. Christopher Hill would have taken the risk. But it would have been three to one saying I could not have driven an old car like that from Marseilles.

As the Irish girls talk, I feel the same aimlessness which came over me yesterday morning when the gearbox fixed itself. Perhaps my friends hit mechanical problems too, or were blown onto a jagged leeward shore. Are they now cast away, or worse, still at sea, clutching a broken mast?

Près du mât rompu,
prions à genoux!

Disaster, the reverse of triumph, whispers: 'So, Fergus, only you made it? Ha!' Kipling warned his son about these imposters.

Try not to think of the hassles to come. Must I now impound the car with customs in Izmir and camp out at the airport? Rather, immediately catch a boat back to Greece! But I can't stop the anger. How dare these friends, too, let me down? Or am I concealing even from myself the truth that no one was meant to come on this holiday – that all are blameless for not joining me? That this trip was chosen because I would be better off alone?

Be practical. Where shall I spend the night? Where are foreign cars safe in Turkey? I saw a place as we came down into the bay, back on the right…

Out of the western sun, like giants standing over our table, appear Christopher Hill and Philip Blackwell and their sailing companions from London, tanned and wild-eyed and in the height of holiday mood. Life leaps in my hand. With a surge of pleasure we embrace. The dream of meeting for a drink on the other side of Europe, plucked from the air above a Fulham dinner table, hooked from a stream of consciousness in a moment of folly, is landed. We have it still thrashing at our feet.

Compared with us, the world is very small.

Day 6

An unknown hour before first light. More panic. Should I take the car back to England? I cannot leave it here. I am wasting valuable time.

I stumble to my hotel window and look down at the Bentley in the dark street. Why did I park nose-on to the beach? Sea breezes are onshore during the night. Salt will have gone straight in through the radiator, and the engine will be a corroded lump. I pace about, calculating that a dash back to England is still possible if I start right now. The gang wouldn't mind if I just left them a note. I could reach Italy, France even. Better than condemning an innocent to die, and earning another black mark on my personnel file – 'Abandoned his company car in Anatolia'.

If I leave My Lady here, how would that work? It must be possible; doubtless tourist cars are at this moment sitting with customs. But she will rust. I must buy a cover for her. Some of the old cars in Izmir had them, the 1960s Yank-tank hand-me-downs. Even so, she would never start after three months of such neglect. She would have roasted to death, the battery acid evaporated, the leather crumbled, the rubberised electric cables rotted away, the veneer lifted, the suspension sagged, and the tyres irredeemably flat-spotted.

In fact she will not even start when I get up this morning, let alone make the trip to Ephesus which we agreed last night.

*

At last, with the first teasing rays of day, reason returns. Light begins to creep on to the balcony. Panic recedes. I am weak but comfortable. The thinking has produced results – I must find out from Bruce how he would lay up such a beast; and also telephone the customs compound to investigate conditions there. Easy enough. I call through to the others, to wake them up.

Days 6 & 7

Friends concertina observation, and douse reflection. Their presence is intoxicating. Disciplines and habits which were second nature are bundled out, replaced by new pleasures and concerns. Left to oneself, it is easy to sleep in the car, and difficult to be bothered with hotels. Among friends it would be a major adventure all to sleep in cars. Alone it is fun to eat in a backstreet bazaar. With friends it is easiest to patronise the best restaurant on the front. Alone, I am unlikely to swim in the sea. With friends the sea becomes irresistible. Alone I will walk the ruins of Pompeii all day. With friends I drop halfway round Ephesus. On my own, the loneliness wears off. With friends I want to be loved.

So, of course, I do not phone Bruce. There is no sensible checking of the situation with customs. We go and play. I remember the pair of black replica Uzi SMG (sub-machine gun) water pistols in the boot, accurate and powerful, transferred from the Blonde Bombshell. We run around like eight-year-olds, squirting each other. We wonder at a dancing bear; hold long discussions with onyx carvers; and haggle over fake Rolexes, knock-off Lacoste shirts and dubious

Roman antiquities. Each individual is discussed behind his or her back, as is each relationship. Where is it all heading?

We carry our world around with us, and the other world does not intrude.

And on the evening of the Seventh Day they sailed away.

Day 8

As Ms McGrath explained, my passport has the Bentley and my scuba tank entered on it. I cannot leave them unless they are correctly impounded. But yesterday morning, Saturday, the customs precinct down at the docks was already closed for the weekend. Tomorrow, Monday, I'm due back at work.

I spend some hours up at the airport, an endless cycle of pretty check-in girls and exquisite fellow tourists in search of the Holy Grail – a ticket home. To have one's fate decided among such players is a pleasure indeed. They respond to subtlety, they return charm. The check-in girls have the power to send one man to Heaven and keep another for weeks in Purgatory.

Persuasion is all; yet honour rules among the stranded. Old hands teach newcomers the ropes. The killer fact is this: check-in closes for any outbound flight when the inbound plane touches down. Spot an inbound flight that lands seriously early and you know that its outbound passengers are going to be in trouble. This is the moment to slip through on standby, just as the check-in is closing. If you miss that chance, the departure hall will immediately be rammed with legitimate travellers who arrived on time but still too late. They decimate your near-term chances of finding a seat.

There are people here who had tickets, with relatives dying in England; others have discharged themselves from Turkish hospitals to come – but are still grey with illness; others have run out of money and want to go home early. Among the old hands, the code is that couples are not to be split; only when all couples are placed can singles be catered for. I, who never had a ticket, and must anyway wait until tomorrow, am merely on reconnaissance.

However, I am proud to be part of it.

I offer one young English pair a refuge in my hotel room back in town. The girl could have stepped out of a Hermès advert in *Vogue*, which is why I got chatting. The man is too correct for her, or she too incorrect for him, but they show no sign of realising it. They are as in love as in need of sleep.

While they bathe and rest, the Bentley has a cover made. Her garment is sewn by a canvas-stitching street gang. The dressmakers measure her height and curves, and run up the voluminous sailcloth on the spot, while she parks out of harm's way beside the best hotel in Izmir, the Grand Ephesus (five stars, nice girls don't want trouble). The frock billows rather in the breeze; I must think how to prevent that pale complexion from being buffed to the bare metal by three months' flapping in the zephyr.

*

At the airport, I track down the customs director.

'Leave your Bentley in our staff car park,' he suggests.

'But won't my passport be refused?' I say.

'You can park for ten days without a problem.'

And ten days would be something. Yet a few hours later, when I have cornered an unclaimed ticket to Paris – close enough to London – he has gone home.

*

Later in the afternoon I tried to transfer the car and diver's air bottle to the passport of a girl who is staying the winter here. Then, after the *Vogue* dropouts had found a flight together and flown, I telephoned around Turkey to see if any customs pound opens at weekends. Not even Cesme, where the car originally decanted, would help, though I drove there to beg.

Dashing back in the evening, I overtook a police patrol car too aggressively and they stopped me for having one headlight out. It looked like a night in a Turkish jail for me, with its cocktail of disease and homosexual rape. But a colleague of Ms McGrath, whom I had let sit behind the steering wheel two days ago to try it for size, appeared from nowhere at the roadside. He told the police I would buy a headlight bulb in Izmir. Unaware how hard these headlight bulbs are to find, even in England, they sent me on my way with a caution.

Sometimes you wonder about guardian angels.

Day 9

The customs house on the dockside of old Smyrna port is deserted. Dawn rakes low and long across the grey marble floor, casting shadows behind each screwed-up sheet of newspaper, takeaway carton and pressed-pulp cup. Even cigarette butts stand out in this light.

Yesterday lunchtime, before I waved off my Hermès refugees, the three of us came here to have a look around.

Where once, for a week in September 1922, this dockside was jammed by 100,000 Greek civilians fleeing Ataturk's army, yesterday were furlongs of shrink-wrapped household furniture, cartloads of rolled carpet, and human-height plastic plants by the hectare, in the most lurid reds, yellows and greens. All were being shifted to and fro, hither and thither, constantly, simultaneously and individually, by a tumult of migrant workers connected to a Libyan ocean liner.

That ship is still tied up to the quay beside me. But now the only life is the sleepy nightwatchman, preparing to hand over to the day shift. He shuffles past, carrying eight washed-up tea glasses on a tray. Turkish tea is served in a clear cup, a cross between a shot glass and an egg timer, if possible on a silvered salver.

Five flies crawl on this plastic bench, undecided whether to date or doze.

Yesterday's reconnaissance was because this morning must go smoothly. I was supposed to be working in London today.

The vast flank of the Libyan passenger ship begins to inch down the quay, seemingly endless, clotted cream, blocking out the light. Slowly, silently, the hull turns away. For a few heartbeats the gap between dock and liner expands exponentially. The superstructure and then the two baby-blue funnels become visible. The latter and the sky are a perfect match.

The vessel slips off towards the mouth of the harbour, and the sea lanes to Benghazi or Tripoli.

Baby-blue for Libya is cheeky. The country trains, arms and finances terrorists. It started when I was barely out of shorts, with a boatload of weapons for the IRA being intercepted off Co. Waterford. More recently the shooting of WPC Yvonne Fletcher from Libya's London embassy redoubled hostility. And relations have only grown worse. Libyan agents blew up a West Berlin bar the year before last. A US serviceman died. That triggered President Reagan's bombing of Tripoli and Benghazi with F-111s flying from his friend Margaret Thatcher's British air bases. Last year the French caught another Libyan ship headed for Ireland with 1,000 AK47s, fifty surface-to-air missiles and two tons of plastic explosive. Two tons.

They export the tools of death and import the trappings of peace.

In front of me, where the flat hull plates of the ship blocked the view, the bay of Izmir reaches out, mountain-rimmed. Alexander the Great picked this anchorage for its shelter and ease of defence. His harbour town was expanded to a metropolis by the Romans. Izmir's classical name, Smyrna, suggests myrrh, the rare and intoxicating gum brought overland from Yemen and East Africa. Myrrh was the speciality here in Roman times.

The mile-wide sound has the dark, menacing colour of downwind deep water. The two pilot boats which led out the Libyan vessel scoot back to breakfast. Gulls feed on the water where the liner was tethered, bobbing like bath toys, an absurd contrast in scale. A telephone rings in the empty office beside me, falls silent and rings again.

Another day begins.

The senior harbour official arrives for work. I introduce myself. His name is Junus. While he is present, policemen who have been lounging for the past half hour busy themselves; a typewriter taps into life in the office at the end of the hall; the dock-zone duty-free shop opens – but when he walks away, it closes again. The typist falls silent.

Five janitors pass through, screeching the benches across the marble floor, scooping rubbish into a couple of upended forty-gallon oil drums balanced on a rickety trolley. A gang of blue-jeaned youths sits down near me.

I tell myself, one last push, one more dance. What better holiday than light-footing through the labyrinth of officialdom which the Byzantines bequeathed to modern Turkey?

I will kiss my desk when I get back to it.

*

The battle hinges on a table marked *Triptik*. This apparently means 'triplication'. Three times officials demand to make identical inspections of my car. Three times I put down my glass of tea to sign in a book of pantomime proportions: first for myself; then for my employers, who own the car; and lastly for the list of items which I am leaving – the diving equipment (customs seal intact), a full tank of petrol, a box of compact discs and a remote-controlled CD player, a camp bed, a tennis racquet and some pillows and rugs. These last are on the back seat. I overlook the black Uzi water pistols hidden under sweaty trainers on the black carpet at the back of the boot.

To protect her suspension, the Bentley will need to be chocked up on blocks. The Turkish clerk says he can arrange it at the car pound, but he wants his palm crossed with silver before he will climb in beside me. Shifting around beyond the red leather front central armrests, he guides me by signs out of the dock.

We traverse the railway tracks, behind some containers and a stack of wrecked foreign cars, into a narrow corridor of wire mesh. We are entering the Underworld, creeping between demolished lorries and more shattered cars, into a compound heaped with written-off vehicles of every description.

For a moment we are both speechless. It is a spectacle of automotive damnation. In the middle stands a Portakabin.

I drive over, park and we walk into the hut to meet the Cerberus who would be My Lady's keeper.

Mr Topkara is a compact and jovial Turk, his gold wedding band and grey hair belying the brown moustache and twinkling eye. He assigns me to a sassy dock foreman. The foreman and I drive the Bentley right out of the port zone to a pantechnicon weighbridge, where the old girl strikes a dainty pose on the juggernaut-sized scales and is issued with a docket saying 2,190 kilograms.

Back into the dock zone we glide, along the waterfront, right to the end of the furthest quay, and the sense of daintiness re-echoes as the Bentley halts between two ore freighters. We trot up to a first-floor office; the foreman removes his oily cap and smoothes his hair before knocking. Inside, three wise men review our docket for 2,190 kilograms; another signature and we are driving back to the wreckers' yard again. The foreman is now more relaxed in the passenger seat.

'Just leave her beside this rusting bodyshell, here,' he indicates.

I look concerned.

'Hey, what are you worried about?' Pause. 'No, I was only joking. Look, follow the boss.'

From behind the steering wheel I see Mr Topkara walking towards a warehouse. At snail's pace I follow. We drive into the dark void. The silence is cool and lofty. A couple of middle-range Mercedes-Benzes stand secure, out of the heat and wind. A bigger Mercedes, safe in a corner, is moved aside for us.

'You want to do what?' signals the foreman. 'Protect the tyres from the hard concrete? Then park it on this sheet of cardboard! No? You want to catch the car when its suspension sags? Then park it over this wooden pallet! No? You want to chock it up? I see. Well, you can't use those pieces of wood. They are part of a consignment we are storing. They might get crushed. Follow this man on a bicycle.' All this is conveyed in sign language, not words.

I set off on foot. The cyclist leads me to another warehouse just across the yard (so why the bicycle?), where we borrow some pallets, temporarily we promise.

Then we set to work, like turning a doughty dowager on a hospital bed, chocking the Bentley up extra high on one side while we try slipping two pallets one on top of the other under her. Now we will lower the wedding car down onto her wooden mattress.

*

We are halfway through this operation when the boss returns, beckons me to a door at the end of the warehouse, and then another, and out into the open. I left my jacket with all my air ticket cash in it by the car. But he is only heading for the carpentry shop. We bring back four perfect beams of wood, very thick and square, enough to carry 2,190 kilos no trouble at all.

With ten Turks to help, we try various jacking combinations. I listen to each suggestion, until it is clear there is only one solution, mine, and then we attack it.

Now the stately carriage is some six inches higher than her normal level. Her wheels are still on the ground, but carry little more than their own weight. The job could not have been done better. I am grinning, and the stevedores tilt their heads from one side to the other in bewilderment at what we have achieved. I disconnect the battery. With a final flourish I produce the car cover. Delighted, my helpers shroud the elegant body – surely to be unveiled by them from time to time in the coming weeks, but that is no harm.

Emerging into the midday sun, my white trousers are brown with oil, my pink shirt soaked with sweat. Mr Topkara and the clerk ask by discreet signs if I could bring them cigarette lighters on my return. I obtain a telephone number. He asks for mine. I point on his calendar to the Friday in ten weeks' time when I plan to return, December 23rd.

I swallow and hand over the key.

The clerk and I walk beside the railway tracks all the way back to the customs office, me lugging my bags.

As a final precaution they send me on a long hike, out of the port zone, to photocopy my passport. Having sniffed round the adjacent neighbourhood I find a photocopier in a stationer's, and return with the smile of the infant Hercules having strangled the snake.

And so, with a passport page full of rubber stamps, signatures and crossings out for a receipt, I collect my bags and join the taxi driver who has been stalking my movements around the facility for the past three hours. Airport, I say, and he has his catch.

*

Designer wristwatches gleam against skin such as comes only with a life of asses' milk and sunscreen. The faces are clean shaven, the fingernails manicured. The hair is glossy, the shoes too. They are Germans waiting for a Lufthansa flight home. The men read crisp copies of the *Frankfurter Allgemeine Zeitung* newspaper. The girls cradle matt-black Walkmans.

And oh how delicious, fruity, thick, nay coarse, is the Lufthansa orange juice. The three-stop connecting flight to London costs a week's wages. But I will be at the office to earn them in the morning.

Thursday 15th December 1988

Day 10

This is the part I find hardest. The start. My City fingers drape over my suitcase like a dying man's might fall across a Bible. They hold an immigration form.

Before me were others, millions, confused by foreign guards, herded like cattle into wagons, taken to vile places, their identity compressed into just such scraps of paper issued in cynicism, imputing rational purpose to the oppressor, dulling the last true instinct, which was to overwhelm their guards, kick and punch their way to freedom, or die in the attempt.

The airside bus stops in the dark outside the Istanbul arrivals terminal. It jolts me awake.

How long before I see home again? Supposedly twelve days, but excluding weekends, Christmas Day and related bank holidays only four off work. The trip here in September from Menèrbes, through Marseilles and Chianti, via Naples, Brindisi and Athens, took twelve working days, sixteen in all.

But that was travelling between friends.

This leg promises only strangers along the way. And signposts in illegible alphabets. And floods and snow and withering heat. And guns and knives and jackboots.

I came straight from work, barely packed. I have no Turkish lira, and nowhere to sleep tonight. The worm of fear turns in my guts.

Passport control. Ugh. They will reject my overstamped papers. Then customs police. Almost as bad. They will confiscate the collection of harmless gifts in my suitcase. Will I even keep the precious bag of compact discs snatched for nostalgia value last night while passing Tower Records on Piccadilly Circus?

The guard puts a chalk X on each bag and I walk out a free man. I stand in my office suit dressed like a Christmas present to the local thieves. But I'm in luck. Although it is 9 p.m., the shabby government bank still exchanges money. The lira rate is vanishing down the plughole, a fall of one-third in three months. In the caked and sordid toilets I change into road-trip gear; I am disappearing too.

A line of battered taxis conceals my next bus. It limps me round the airport buildings before setting out for ancient Constantinople. The night is shiveringly cold. This is midwinter in Asia Minor, and it feels but a short hop to the Himalayas.

Day 11

An elegant woman in a fur jacket, with ankles tapering on to high heels, strolls through Istanbul Airport's security control. Her briefcase matches the fine brown leather of her footwear. Around us is the architecture and decor of the modern police state: grotty marble tiles, strip lighting, stained wood panelling scuffed at the edges, chipboard pulp beneath the cheap veneer. A feeling of power lurks off-stage, in the administrator's office, maybe, or the VIP lounge.

It is seven thirty in the morning, office cleaning hour the world over. Two sweepers work their way down the hall between the suited businessmen, walking backwards, casting their rag brooms across the floor like fly-fishermen, flick and, oh-so-slowly, flick.

In the airport, the closer you come to the planes, the less the fear, and the more affluent and self-confident the people. Dark-blue overcoats, belted mackintoshes, trimmed black moustaches, healthy complexions. Out on the apron are twenty big jets – it's a real gateway, Istanbul. One wide-bodied Boeing in white and forget-me-not blue has only two passenger windows along its whole sleek fuselage. Imposing letters say simply 'The United States of America'.

We are bussed to a similarly large plane, to Izmir, but the effect is spoilt by a ceremony at the bottom of the steps. Pick out your bag from the luggage lined up on the concrete. Afterwards one black holdall remains. Is it a bomb? Is its owner at this moment undergoing interrogation for some minor transgression? Or do the airlines think the baggage handlers are morons? I dawdle to be last on to the plane (it often lets you choose where you sit) and from my window seat the black bag looks small and alone on the acres of arid runway.

The plane levels off above the clouds, then banks towards Izmir. The engines become quieter. Was it another dream, the Sultan's Mosque at midnight, the freezing one-star bed, the taxi waiting in the dark while I sipped today's first glass of Turkish tea?

*

Like pressing rewind on the film, a Bentley is liberated from Izmir customs by retracing the steps that put it there. Back and forth across the customs hall I shuttle, fortified by more shot glasses of tea. All the familiar faces are present. Only the controller and assistant controller in their glazed-off cubicles have changed. Junus does not recognise me, but the clerk who helped with chocking up the car thinks I have forgotten his lighter and I kid him along for a minute.

With battle thus rejoined, I stride down the cold quay to the stacks of wrecked cars, a familiar, even welcome sight. Mr Topkara and his foreman are huddled over a stove, looking no older because, of course, only seventy-five days have passed since I saw them.

'*Merhaba*' – hello there. We greet each other with the customary salutation.

The manager accepts my small gift, mercifully enchanted. He licks a stamp and gums it to the back of my exit docket before franking it. 'Sign across the top with your full address please,' he indicates. I blink – this is new, the first discontinuity; an additional bureaucratic requirement, down from on high. The film stops rewinding and reels forward.

The boss is talking about a taxi. I do not believe him. Then I am sitting in a crumpled hitch-a-ride minicab which whisks across Izmir, with the foreman in the front, and me crammed up next to a local fellow with fat hands. Ah, well, if they have driven Her Ladyship elsewhere in Izmir, it is all for the best – keep her joints oiled and battery charged. But how did they start her? Reconnect the electrics? No, this is a Ministry of Defence building. Where is my Bentley? What does the Turkish Army want?

Inside, all is Islamic Berkshire prep school, gothic wood and white Moorish mouldings against aquamarine walls and ceiling. They want money. The bill is made out slowly and in stages, as if corruption is a plague afflicting even the lowest bureaucrats, controlled by the strictest of quarantines.

Every stage is double-checked by a more senior clerk, each with his hand-driven adding machine. Presumably a ferocious import duty holds back the flood of electronic calculators while Turkey hurries to build an assembly plant of its own; and in the meantime someone lines his pockets selling these clankers.

The basis of the maths is US dollars, but I have to go round the corner to change mine into Turkish lira before I can pay. As at customs, whomever I approach discovers a pile of paper which he/she has conveniently to hand and works steadily to the end of before looking up.

*

Topkara's foreman is worrying about the time – we have taken three hours to come this far.

I did not notice. It has been a fascinating initiation, a rite of passage, a prolonged overture before the curtain rises.

*

Back at the pound I refuse to sign. They want me to state my complete satisfaction without seeing the car… 'Follow me,' signals Topkara and I follow, at a walk. 'No run.' I run. What has gone wrong? Don't think about it. You can do nothing. Duck under the door into the warehouse. A dust-brown, shrouded hulk sulks in the corner. Awful pause. I watch as the cover is raised.

There. Just as I left it. But just, to the inch, the millimetre, the speck; complete, like a time warp back to the moment we last met. Her. She. I feel like a gymnast who lands square and solid from some marvellous, somersaulting, twisting vault. The urgency to complete the forms before the compound closes is forgotten.

Then a stevedore shouts from the doorway. Sprint back to the boss' hut. Sign. Across to a new warehouse. Shout up. Back round to another building. Up to the mezzanine level. Write my address again. Back to the manager's hut.

And now, with her key like an amulet in my hand and the mullahs calling midday across the rooftops, I approach the apparition.

Raised on her blocks she floats delicately above the warehouse floor. It takes an effort to lay a hand on her. I open the boot and connect her battery. The foreman jacks her clear of her chocks, kicks them away and lowers her gently. To prevent damaging the engine, I pour oil into the broad throat in the rocker cover. Naughty not to oil the cylinders through the plug sockets; but it just feels like I was away a day. I slide behind the slim steering wheel and the scent of her hide is in my nostrils. At the amulet's touch, dashboard dials twitch. Needles jump. Petrol pumps purr. The maid breathes. Twist further; the engine cranks slowly and fires once. I turn again and the six cylinders catch together, a smooth, even burst, the full orchestra, below a roar, more like the fell wind sucking around the shutters of a Cumbrian croft.

I hold the revs steady to let the crank bathe the big ends and splash lubricant up onto the cylinder walls. The red leather sighs, the walnut glows. My Lady is awake.

*

Smyrna, city of magic carpets, what a day we have then – snow chains are made to measure on a street corner; epoxy glue is bought from a wholesaler who insists on selling it to a retailer and buying it back so that I can pay the VAT; roadside repairs are aided by the motorcycle police (white PVC greatcoats, my dear) so that now both headlights work; safety pins are sourced from the post office. And always with a little glass of tea. 'In Izmir,' says a man in a Rothmans-branded anorak, 'nothing is impossible.'

*

The Bentley takes her leave at nightfall, and we press into the interior in driving rain and heavy traffic for five hours.

After 120 miles of spray and blinding headlights, her body is again encrusted with road dirt. I rub the raw, flaring pigment from behind my eyes, while she is given a gleeful free wash by a garage where we fill up. Another schnapps-glass of tea. The downpour abates.

Then, with Beethoven's Ninth whispering and thumping from the twin amplifiers, we roll the final forty miles to Pamukkale, close to exhaustion.

Here is the last surprise, a chance to swim by starlight in a vast, warm, effervescent, geothermal pool, strewn with fallen columns from the time when it was a Roman bath. The waters come hot from beneath the toppled marble. Submerged electric lamps increase the wonder. Around all this antiquity someone has built a hotel.

A local wedding reception is winding down now that midnight approaches. In a side room the night porter settles me with a raki and a chicken kebab. Then I change into swimming trunks and sink into the ancient aquarium. Microscopic bubbles cover my body with a fur of gas so thick that I am silvered like an air pocket.

Day 12

By morning the rain has overtaken us again. It is Essex coastal, a leaden sky worthy of childhood reflection in grey puddles on the Frinton promenade. I ought to be 'occupied indoors all day', as my mother would say. A large jigsaw puzzle, or better still a complicated scale model of, say, Brunel's SS *Great Britain*. Instead I shave, study the map and hanker after a policeman's PVC greatcoat.

Run for the car, drive 100 yards to the gleaming limestone terraces. Jump out.

These multi-metre calcium lily pads hover above the carbonate escarpment like gargantuan pastry flans, white on white. If it was a bright, dry day they would brim with blue mineral water. Just now they are filled with rain. Nevertheless, I can imagine it in the sun. The fragile moonscape of Pamukkale would make a spectacular alternative to the Villa d'Este or Monterey for a classic car photoshoot.

Then I beetle into the modern centre to telegram home: '*All is well, and Happy Christmas eight days early.*' Probably I will forget to call, or simply can't, on the day. Turkey's post offices are the nation's pride. Even more than the customs posts, they bear the print of long-dead Ottoman hands.

*

In the towns, the streets are like rivers. We climb through broad, rugged glens. The raindrops turn to sleet, and then to steady flakes of snow – sometimes building up until they jam the windscreen wipers.

Two hours of snow in the afternoon.

*

Lorry wheels bite through snow far better than normal motorcar tyres do. Our convoy of trucks passes several Turkish-built Renaults and Fiats abandoned in ditches earlier this afternoon. No other car but ours has reached as far as this.

Then, in the half-light of evening, we hit a section where the ice-white road is cambered for a left-hand bend. The convoy slows to a crawl. One after another the three lorries ahead of me slide sideways out of my beam down into the field. You can see their headlights lancing under the downy surface. The snow is that deep. One artic is on its side.

I manage to stop the Bentley on the level verge above the slope; then I grapple with the snow chains made this morning, fingers numb and clumsy in the slush. When my hands become useless I warm them on the chrome radiator top. Then I scrape away the ice crust thrown up onto our bows by the trucks ahead. The frozen mask stretches from one massive front wing across the lights to the other.

Lorries' headlamps tail back round the big curve behind me, stationary while each driver walks the treacherous terrain and weighs his chances.

After several attempts, like an eager matron in a Breugel skating scene, my adventuress has her new boots on. Then, crab fashion, keeping her bow pointed up the slope of the road to balance its tendency to slip round, she takes the corner with aplomb, passing the truck drivers cheering in the snowfield below, and continues alone.

*

We plough on through scenes more associated with Napoleon's retreat from Moscow – the unrelieved drudgery of foot-deep slush at muddy crossroads, vehicles abandoned where winter has entrapped them. On and on the white wedding car surfs, irresistibly, ever forwards, snow chains chinking like horses'

33

harnesses, big wheels and long travel springs breasting the ruts and drifts like the carriage running gear from which they are descended. On the level she can do twenty miles an hour before the steel links begin to lash inside her rear wheel arches and her nose starts to float off the road and steer itself.

But we take downhill sections at a crawl.

*

The CD plays a delicate piano sonata. A lone café presents itself. I pull over for a breather. Snow still feathers down through the Bentley's feeble iodine beams, but no longer adds depth where it falls. An occasional lorry plumes past. We should be over the summit now; it is hard to judge in the dark.

Time to change into dry clothes. The hut has sawdust on a tiled floor, and hot food and tea. After eating, I unshackle the snow chains and hang them from a bare branch. They must each be seven feet long. No wonder the tyres on this car do not seem to wear – there is so much circumference. I start to beat the chains with a shoe in the dark to knock the ice out of the links. The tree above trembles, dunking snow over me. Change clothes again.

*

Although it is still raining, and sometimes snowing, things go much faster now we are back on bare tyres. My thirsty companion has put away half her tank since the heavy weather, which must mean 100 miles. But the first garage only sells diesel.

Twenty miles on, the next one has a pump saying 90 octane. I have to shout to stop the attendant forcing open the remote-controlled filler flap, presumably a world first in 1957, while I consult the handbook about octane. I have been sticking to four-star Super up until now, 96 octane. Two-star is 92, I think. Here it is. Surprise, surprise. If I want to go below 80 octane – yes, it says 80 – then I have to adjust the timing. So we are OK.

Snug under my double layer of car rugs, I twitch the fuel flap release, the baffled pump attendant heaves a sigh and the small crowd that has gathered scoots for the shelter of the cashier's hut, with its central stove and tea pot.

On reflection, I run to join them. Tea, *chai*, for me too, thanks.

*

The white witch is gradually reminding me of her character. There was an incident yesterday leaving Izmir when I was rather too pushy in a traffic jam. Her water temperature gauge began rising and I switched off. When the queue

34

freed up, her starter motor had disappeared too. Blushes and horns blaring. The message was clear: 'If you insist on embarrassing me, find another friend.'

Today I was trying a quick three-point turn. I had taken the wrong road out of Dinar. With a bus approaching, the gearbox dropped all its cogs, as at Piraeus, for about ten seconds. The message was the same: death before dishonour.

*

The blue-tiled mosque at Konya passes in a trice, its dome supported in mid-air by floodlight beams, like a magical aquamarine water tower.

*

I drive until no amount of shifting in my seat, no vigorous scratching of the face and scalp, no hitchhiker, however weird, no fright with the verge can keep me awake. Seeing a side track I reverse down it, climb into the back seat, pulling the rugs with me, and sleep. Hail patters on the roof. I wake occasionally to check on the frost – the radiator is short of antifreeze, with all the topping up since it first threw a fit in the Camargue, among other white horses, eight-foot marsh reeds, pink flamingoes…

Day 13

A diamond light prises me out of my blanketed dreams. We are parked in the middle of a huge plain. Sky dominates the whole 360-degree panorama. The sun is still behind a low range of hills far ahead to the east. The snow-topped mountains in the distant west are the only hint of what we went through. Telegraph poles stretch to infinity, marking the road we have come down. The land is covered with dark-khaki heather, crisped by hoar frost, without a sign of agriculture. This is the open frontier of Cappadocia, and no place to walk for help.

Wrapped in the rugs, I climb laboriously over to the front seat and start the five-litre motor, which fires very neatly. Then I run around outside to wake up, changing the CD cartridge in the boot and organising my possessions into new piles, while the cylinders box unevenly on choke. To add cheer, with a new Verdi, the sun comes. The first sun since Heathrow.

On Friday evening we did 160 miles. Yesterday twice that. Today, surely we can crack 500. Across the broad mustard plain the Bentley carves off half an hour. We pass a flock of sheep, dawn glowing through their heavy grey fleeces; then a village of turf-roofed huts, where men stand in cones of heaviest felt underlay against the wind. After sixty minutes, we are thundering right into the sun. The marble-smooth high road ahead gleams like a river.

For mile after mile, the only darkness is the intermittent silhouette of oncoming lorries. Distance travelled takes its measure from the changes in the monochrome vista. Slowly, far-off mountains gather on either side and bottle into a gorge. The remains of an older road appear, hanging precariously above us. Our new road cuts a straighter path, but the river cuts the flattest line of all. Over thousands of millennia, it has earned its gentle bed.

*

Stopping to look at the map, the next big town ahead is Pozanti. I lift my eyes to the mountains to see if the ones behind are bigger than those ahead. There beside me is the 'town ending' sign for Pozanti. Some conurbation: stacked around the gorge are twenty chalets, like an alpine hamlet, with a mosque belfry instead of a church spire. A forest of pines runs back from the little community, up to the snow line, but holding short of the clouded peaks.

*

This deep all-weather gorge issues out to the Mediterranean at Tarsus. Steadily, within barely a league, the vegetation transforms from Andean desert to Scottish Highlands to south of France. Gone are the rugs over my legs. Out come the sunglasses. And lo, flies on the bonnet, a delicate rose blooms beside me as I write.

The high plains above Tarsus are its livelihood. It feeds them with the little luxuries of life, and they reciprocate with mutton, raw wool, and a steady carrion of tortured machinery from the descent to this intersection. After four miles climbing to the last ridge, and eight miles of gear-crunching, brake-smoking descents to the coast, some vehicles simply lie down to die. Tarsus is a scrap merchant's paradise. The last mile, through green farmland, is a long shopfront of used parts for diesel trucks. From the chrome fenderwork and neon signs, you could be entering Las Vegas.

My Iceni queen is heavily streaked from two days of winter rampage, and I am close to sleep. It must be noon. A man over there is washing out the boot of his car with a hose. He scrubs the underneath of the boot lid; why? It is all too much…

*

Slept, refreshed, and with the Bentley coachwork (but not the nether side of the boot lid) sluiced and beaming, I spot a ruined crusader castle dominating the approach to Tarsus from the east. I drive up to investigate. A young shepherd is there, with his flock, his dogs and his wispy beard. He wears the traditional over-roomy trousers that have been the costume since Konya.

I tell him my name, 'Fergus', and ask his.

'Gustavo.' Odd. Sounds Scandinavian. Gus for short, perhaps. Me too.

I gesture to the heavy storm clouds approaching from the west, and we both grimace. They are racing me for the next range of mountains, clearly visible in the east of this wide panorama. I must press on.

*

The Bentley takes an hour to pull clear of the weather. Then comes another toiling climb; three lanes for two directions of juggernauts, one hell of a chance to collide head-on with a mass bigger than me. I am using the stick shift on the steering column to drop down to second gear, and even first for overtaking. Beside such grinding giants, the old mare is once more a nimble filly.

I want to beat the storm over the top. And here comes dusk, all too quickly. Pull over to check the water level in the radiator, put on mountain boots, blankets back over legs, one last gaze at a green field, and go!

*

From the middle of this long narrow room a stove cures woodsmoke into six of us. Four are sturdy men. Another, bald and grizzled, is bent double on the floor in the corner, praying to the south. Beside me stands a fragile little boy, who took my hand when I entered, kissed the back and pressed it to his forehead. My mind is dizzy from the endless roulette with the *routiers* in the dark and sleet.

The welcome is as strong as the smoke. Grandfather is through with his praying and pulls on his woolly hat with a one-tooth grin. Father, lean and leathery, leads me into the other room in the hut and takes from an otherwise bare cupboard a dish of scraps, cubes of lamb and fat. Fried up, with the glass of tea and some bread, they are delicious.

I am quick to pay. But is this a home, not a restaurant? Did I eat these people's last morsels? Just now, between this first food of the day and the merciless wet and dark road outside, there is no contest. Accept what you are given and be grateful.

The fire doesn't make much heat. Being near it in one orientation for long enough, that side of you stops growing colder. The tea is good and hot, and the breath through my teeth fogs the damp air.

Mysteriously caped and silent men come in and sit with us around the stove. If I had not just been made so welcome and shown such generosity, I would think

37

to have fallen among thieves, perched on the edge of the world, in a bend in the mountain pass above Gaziantep.

I ask the time. It is only 5:30 p.m. How strange are the dynamics of long winter nights. Even at the equator the length of day must vary; and do they have seasons in the Congo? Shouldn't eastern Turkey really be on Moscow time? That would make it 6:30 p.m., GMT+3.

Gradually, the centre of attention moves from me and repose settles. Food and rest were what courage needed to flare again.

With handshakes and salutes I go back to the car. The first lorry that passes I pull out behind, and if a faster one overtakes I latch on to him instead. In this way the Bentley is dragged by tail lights through the gloom. Each hour clings on with the tenacity of a tooth. When the fastest tow I catch turns off, I too stop for petrol and listen to the engine, which suddenly sounds rough. Then I catch a new pair of lights and follow them through the spray for another two hours, until they become devil's eyes, gazing out of Hades.

By 10 p.m. I am at Urfa, 370 miles from the cold plain where I awoke. After walking the main street looking for a guest house recommended at Izmir airport in the summer, I give up and check in to the local Grand. At least they have hot water and understand English. My Lady is parked in the compound behind. The nightwatchman was sleeping, dead to my greetings – drunk or deaf – but the porter locked the gates once she was in.

Day 14

Zooming feelings in the dark; despair and confidence. I had forgotten how this business whips up panic. Tonight the dreams were garbled French and German, until wrenched apart by the pre-dawn call to prayers.

Turning to *War and Peace*, the story takes up with Pierre duelling his wife's suspected lover. Against all the odds, Pierre hits his man. I am filled with optimism and sleep at last.

Up much refreshed at 8:30 a.m., I stomp round the muddy streets.

Beggars crouch in blankets and steaming nags pull high-axled carts. Fewer baggy trousers and more desert headdresses here. In the catacomb bazaar, the cloth is Arafat-style patterns, chequered blues and reds, which you never spy on the street, where dark browns and greens are interspersed with black. I see one bulldog-like old Turk, bow-legged, with knee-crotched trousers of a lighter hue. He wears a more delicate, woven cosy on his head, and under his plain jacket a yellow tweed waistcoat and silver watch chain. With a fine wooden staff in his right hand, he is the one glint of elegance in town.

Boys of four or five years old offer to polish boots that have forgotten the meaning of the word.

Holy Urfa, Sanilurfa, by Judaic and Muslim tradition, was the birthplace of Abraham, Ibrahim, father of Isaac, patriarch of the Israelites; and of Ishmael, progenitor of the Arabs. Others say that the biblical Ur was at the city of the same name in southern Mesopotamia. But the shrines are here.

Beyond the bazaar, I come across a temple complex. It has notably large pools, a moat even. This must be the Balikli Göl, the Pool of Abraham I heard about at the hotel, where God saved Abraham by a miracle, after Nimrod threw him into a fire. Fire became water, and the burning logs turned into fish. Balikli Göl's great fish basins are choked with rubbish now, but by some second miracle their stock of sacred fish, big as pike, lives on. They seem to be fed and oxygenated by warm underwater springs which make the pools steam in the cold air. But looking down from the bank, many of the fish are diseased and mutant – I feel sick as I walk back to my room. The nightwatchman completes my discomfort by indicating that he is indeed deaf in one ear. He demonstrates how he was scratching with a sharp object, and pushed it in too far.

Between the potholes, my intrepid explorer picks a course by backstreets to the edge of town. Here the road to the Syrian frontier begins. I am now convinced that the Syrians will not allow me across. I don't have the visa; I don't have the bribes; I have only deutschmarks and they will want US dollars.

*

Out in the countryside, a boy is trudging along the left-hand verge in the same direction as me. I stop, lean across and wind down the passenger window. 'Akakale?' I ask. He nods. Akakale is my border post. He crosses the road and hops straight in the front, unfazed by the missing steering wheel on his side.

*

The border between Turkey and Syria has a railway running along the Turkish side. The train from the east runs west as far as Akakale. Then the passengers climb down, walk along the line and pull themselves up into the train that comes along the same tracks from the west.

To reach the checkpoint, the Bentley weaves her way down Akakale's main street, avoiding the horse-drawn carts. She is an eggshell among whisking water beetles on a sea of mud. The road leads to the right, into the goods yard where the train changing happens. It turns in front of the warehouse buildings, over the track (big wheels essential) and up to a barbed wire compound where the platform would normally be, on the far side. Turkish soldiers look menacing with field radios and semi-automatic rifles, bayonets fixed. No sudden moves. 'Yes, of course I'll put the car back over the tracks. No, of course the compound is a military zone. I wouldn't dream of looking at it.'

The captain is called Robert, charming, though he will wash his hands after shaking mine. He speaks good German.

'Most of us have been at this post for ten months,' he says. 'Before that, three months on the Iraqi border; that leaves five months of military service to go.'

Robert, like a tenth of Turkish men between the ages of twenty and forty, has worked at some stage in West Germany. German businessmen would have a big opportunity to manufacture cheaply in Turkey – a whole class of managers is available – yet the Fatherland is currently the most vocal opponent of Turkey entering the European Economic Community.

From the look of the border, it may be permanently closed. The other side appears to be a ploughed field. No guards, no barbed wire. Just a ticket booth. Some low garden gates are held together with a lightweight chain. They sag inward from lonely gateposts, rusting on doubtful hinges. But Robert tells me these gates will open at two o'clock and stay open until five. It is noon now.

Leaving the car in the goods yard, I walk back into the village to look for the post office. I probably deserve the gentle jeering from the vendors and bystanders on mud alley. Mammout, the boy who accepted the lift with me for the last five miles, is by the mailbox, and delighted to meet again so soon.

In sign language I ask the postmaster to telephone Paris, to check with the Syrian embassy there whether my visa has come through. He laughs at me. Telephone Urfa, yes. Ankara, maybe, given time. Paris? Your stupidity might be embarrassing if it was not so comical.

I gesture to Mammout that I will buy him lunch if he shows me the right restaurant.

We sit and eat in relaxed silence, lamb and tomato kebab, rolled up in great sheets of unleavened bread. Occasionally we break into a hit-and-miss concoction of signs and speech. Mammout is not looking forward to his military service. He produces from his pocket four suggestive postcards of Turkish beauties. He prefers the blond with the half-unbuttoned shirt. This absence of women from the public gaze does nothing to change what the men are thinking.

We sit and converse, higgledy-piggledy, while food and tea come and go, cats fight around our ankles and the aroma of wheaten broadsheets drifts across us from the barbeque bakery behind, running its lunchtime production line.

*

Back at the frontier it is two o'clock and the place is astir. Turkish officialdom turns up for its daily stint. The customs officers, all men of course, make a show of dressing as capitalists, in grey city overcoats that are just too long in the sleeve for them.

After a few pleasant exchanges we walk over to the gates and shake hands through the bars with the Syrians, who make a show of dressing as Communists in green turtle-neck jackets.

Behind the clothes, the faces bear no malice, and in fact I think I prefer the Syrians – three soldiers and three more subtle secret police types in relaxed fatigues.

'Get yourself a visa in Ankara or Istanbul, and we would love to let you through, welcome it. Otherwise it is just an invasion.'

'But I have been trying to obtain a visa from Paris for four months, and in the end they told me I should try at the border.'

'We cannot issue a visa at the border because we do not have the rubber stamps.'

I turn the conversation to currency, cash, dollars. Not a glimmer of interest. I show my Egyptian and Jordanian visas. Interest, but get a visa in Ankara. So it goes. Gently I sally, gently I am repulsed. And in the end, gently I leave.

I had thought things might be possible at an out-of-the-way spot like this.

Wrong.

*

Will that be the end of the dream that dare not be spoken – to circumnavigate the Med by land? Was it ever there? What quality distinguishes mere notion from intent?

To my surprise, my mind is wriggling to find a way out. I need to know more about Ankara, and specifically the Syrian consul's powers compared with those of his colleague in Paris, his opening hours and turnaround speed – because the visa must be obtained instantly. If the practice of London embassies, to take your passport and only give it back later that day, also pervades in the capital of Turkey, no hope.

If quicker, maybe. And maybe is enough.

*

Urfa airport has one flight a week, and it left yesterday. We drive hard for Gaziantep, 100 miles back west.

Dusk falls while I am still near the Syrian border. Watchtowers silhouetted against the night sky, two high wire fences, a narrow ploughed strip suggesting a minefield, dogs, searchlights, low dark shapes that might be machine-gun nests.

I have accidentally veered south.

A sentry flags me down.

I smile and jump out, convince him and his comrades that it was a mistake and am slinking away – led by a foot soldier cradling a belt-fed machine gun under his camouflage cape in the beam of the headlights – when a siren wails and we are called back.

They want to see my passport. They want to search the car.

Slowly the cluster of friendly faces turns from excited delight to caution, then gravity. When they tell me to drive My Lady deeper into the compound, under the arc lights, I consider making a run for it.

But frankly, we are thirty miles from the nearest phone, and these weapons are heavy calibre, the sort that would rip the leg off an ox. Surely I can save myself by playing the happy tourist from a friendly NATO country?

As the fact that a snooper has been detained by the sentries filters up the camp hierarchy, it becomes less and less easy for the simple soldiers to let me go.

'*Es tut mir Leid*' – I'm sorry – their German-speaking corporal keeps repeating, but with overtones of the sadistic Molesworthian headmaster's 'This Hurts Me More Than It Hurts You.'

Meanwhile I test out explanations in my head. I was looking for the frontier, although without a visa and in the middle of the night. I was carrying two toys, harmless water pistols, although they are replica sub-machine guns, and Israeli ones at that, in a military zone where terrorism is a reality, sponsored by the dictatorship on the other side of that fence.

A violent shouting comes from deep inside the compound. I imagine the commanding officer, an embittered, passed-over schizophrenic, wintering with his dull subordinates in this remote farmhouse, woken in the middle of the night by some fool with more money than sense, a spy with a blatant, provocative, hiding-in-plain-sight cover. Building himself up into a flailing rage, beyond rational suggestion, he will at the least have me beaten up in front of him and thrown into the cells until springtime.

*

In the end, Her Ladyship saves us.

The soldiers feel stupid searching her, and fail to find the Uzis. The more senior the officer who comes down to look, the more obvious it is to him that spies do not drive around in white thirty-one-year-old limousines. Certainly not to come and look at this God-forsaken spot.

A major, whose warm handshake speaks instantly of the comfort of his bed, says *Grüss Gott* to me like a Bavarian. He has a torch. My heart sinks. Now they must find the Uzi water pistols.

But instead he explains to everyone what must have happened. Before my flight to Ankara to obtain a visa, I wanted to find out if the main border crossing, at the town of Kilis, was open all day. I received bad directions, there was no sign saying military zone, so I pressed on. Ah well, no problem; an easy mistake for a foreigner.

He shows me where I am on the map – before Kobane – how to reach Kilis from here, another hundred miles – and waves me away.

As I back the Bentley out of the compound I see in the headlights his bedtime woollen hose under his jacket, white with black rings down each leg.

*

After twenty miles we are under cover of woods, on the side of a ravine. In a mad hurry, I rummage deep in the boot, find the Uzis, cross the road and prepare to climb down and bury them. Suddenly two vehicles are coming, one from each direction, their headlights threading through the trees in the distance. I cannot leave My Lady apparently abandoned in the middle of nowhere. They are bound to stop. With the weakness of a cripple I toss the guns out into the darkness, leap back to the car and am moving by the time the two saloons reach me.

They pass without slowing.

*

I dine in an isolated bar, with plenty of raki, and sleep on the Bentley's club sofa, reversed down a track near Gaziantep airport. Two dogs bark in the dark for a while, but I am warm and happy under my christening present.

43

Day 15

Gaziantep is as big a city as Izmir. This is boom town; within five minutes I have a parking ticket. The police here wear green riot helmets and carry automatic weapons.

Bureaucracy is the dish of the day. Half an hour is lost in the regional headquarters of the Central Bank just changing US dollar travellers' cheques into US dollar notes – the only serious money around here, and probably only obtainable from this one branch, for an area the size of Ireland.

Then I am off to Turkish Airlines for a domestic flight timetable. After that, another half-hour vanishes in the post office while my call to the Syrian embassy in Paris connects. A young mullah is also waiting to phone. He is dressed like you or me and appears to have all day. He says that life in this part of Turkey, the central south, is expensive compared with home, the capital, Ankara; or with Istanbul. He himself is short of money. 'Tell me about Paris,' he says. 'I hear the girls are wonderful.'

If Iran under the Shah was anything like modern Turkey in Gaziantep, one can understand the Iranian backlash against capitalism. Rapid economic revolution unleashes greed and envy. The contrast between one area of town where no one wears spectacles, and another where people can afford them; between men who load their skinny mules with fuel wood, passed by others who fill their new BMWs with Super; between girls who have no existence outside their home, and their dreams of becoming a stewardess for Turkish Airlines; or a mullah who wants just one night in Paris; these are tensions which are lost on north Europeans.

For all the vertical distance between our young, upwardly mobile professionals, with their various other pejorative nicknames – Yuppies, *BCBG* in France, *Schickimicki* in Germany – and our hardcore unemployed, our societies are flat compared with here.

*

My call to France leaves me depressed. After four months they still have no news from Damascus about my visa application. I prefer not to be refused a visa down the telephone and hang up. I must go to Ankara.

So, back to the Turkish Airlines ticket office I hurry, for a seat on the 15:30 flight with an open return. But they too do not take travellers' cheques, or even a Eurocheque, and I want to keep my dollars for Syria. The Central Bank has closed, and another hunt begins. Surely someone must recognise such substitute money. I am directed from bank to bank until I walk past a new innovation, a cash machine in Turkey, and yes, behind it is a money house in the twentieth century. They want the cheque in sterling, no dollars, and they charge a fee in Swiss francs, before giving me Turkish lira. God speed a world currency, or the return of gold sovereigns.

On the way back to the airline office I meet the two men who earlier cadged a lift with me into town. We look in vain for a bookshop selling maps of Syria. All we find is a school atlas with Turkey in the centre of the globe, which doesn't do the job.

Then, with the flights in my hand, I retrieve the old matron from the excavations for a tower block, where she is hiding from traffic wardens. She storms up the side of the chasm at an angle which would flip most cars over backwards. Her crushing dismissal of this latest obstacle again wins cheers all round.

A warmth binds me to this strange machine – the way her huge wheels make fun of potholes; the stiffness of the chassis when you put half the car off the road at fifty miles an hour to miss some closing juggernaut – most vehicles would buckle on the ruts, or at the least become unsteerable; I love the small windscreen wiper hinged directly in the driver's line of sight, giving an ergonomically ideal pie slice of vision through the rain; the distant bull-neck of the radiator, black against a headlit road; the low frequency harmonics of the starter motor, and the deeper note from the engine and road at cruising speed; the oil-damped action of the speedometer – no trembling at low speeds like the 16-valve Mercedes. As someone with latent backache, I particularly love the armchair driver's seat, requiring no more than a stretch to recover from fourteen hours at the wheel.

With a glow in my heart and dollars in my pocket, I drive back to Gaziantep airport. The Bentley will stay the night here while I am in Ankara. Anyone trying to steal her must contend with the armed sentries.

*

Gaziantep airport is a major operation compared with Urfa. One flight passes through every day of the year. In the director's office I introduce myself. He speaks to me in French, learnt by default during the routine crises of the past three years.

'When I came, the air traffic controller here was Italian. He also spoke French and English, but no Turkish,' he says. 'Look, I have a Turkish–French dictionary to prove it! It was his leaving present to me.'

The director's office has five sofas, most comfortable. Tea comes.

I say, 'My car will be in your car park overnight.'

He says, 'There will be a charge.'

The conversation is purely for show, about nothing in particular, to impress the head of airport security and his pretty colleague; sitting together on one of the other sofas, they look increasingly embarrassed about not speaking French themselves. I ask for a hose to wash my car. The director does not want to have his leg pulled, but he comes round to the idea.

And so My Lady is the first British vehicle to be washed by the fire brigade at Gaziantep airport. After dousing her, scrubbing her and beating out the front carpets against a fuel truck, the firemen suggest cleaning and tightening the spark plugs. This, of course, involves the aero-engine fitters.

By the time my flight comes in on the runway next to us, the Bentley is hosting a tea-drinking ceremony with most of the airside ground crew. The straight-six engine sounds transformed as I hurry her back to the car park. Further friendly words with the director, whose sofas are now loaded with the passing VIPs of southern Turkey, then through the security check and onto the plane.

Day 16

This is the ballroom of the Bulvar Palace Hotel, Ankara. It is the grandest room I have found so far in Turkey – nothing less than the main civic space of an English provincial city. The tables have been set out for breakfast – thick toast, jam, butter, black olives and feta cheese.

Dressed in my resurrected business clothes, I am bubbling with arguments for the Syrian embassy. I will leave my baggage here, the better to charm my way to a visa. It is 8:30 a.m. Plenty of time to spend a quiet hour with Tolstoy and yet be there at 10:00.

*

Between an organisation that does not know what it is doing and one that is deliberately obstructive, is all the difference in the world. Turkish Post & Telephone's directory of enquiries service falls into the first type; you can find what you desire but you have to show you want it. The Syrian embassy in Ankara is squarely in the second; just to arouse it from sleep you must wage open war – to win you must risk everything.

Prospects are bad. The hostile attitude begins outside the residence, standing in the cold sunshine, trees bare with winter, talking through the railings; and then, through a bulletproof window, men who look like they would rather kill you, as they have visitors before – well, it was hopeless. They argued that Paris originally submitted the application to Damascus, so only Paris could issue the visa. It was not their problem.

Now I am back in the ballroom with a landline extension to the hotel payphone and an hour to think.

One answer would be to call Damascus. The British Foreign & Commonwealth Office in London could give me the number, but is not yet out of bed. Even if it was, international long distance rarely connects from Turkish payphones.

What about asking the switchboard girl at the Syrian embassy here for the head office number in Damascus? It works; a gruff question in French extracts a timid straight answer. I dash down to the slovenly post office for more payphone tokens; long delays, angry queues, but now I have six (£5 worth), which was their entire stock.

Back on the internal balcony of the ballroom, with a chandelier hanging between me and a women's coffee morning, I am dialling and redialling Damascus. A queue forms behind me for the phone, which means that the various tones coming through can be discussed with others. For each discussion I let the next in line go in front. After establishing that the Turks themselves do not understand these different tones, I am through to a voice. I ask for visas. More voices. The head of the diplomatic corps (protocol section) is on the line in English, charming but regretful. There is only one place in the world for Syrians to obtain British visas – Jordan. There is consequently only one place in the world for British citizens to obtain Syrian visas – Paris. It is called Reciprocity.

This is worse than Piraeus.

I slump at a bare round table and stare at the white linen tablecloth. What, I wonder, is the price of a flight to Paris? Hell, I simply cannot face going back over those mountains to Tarsus to look for a boat to Cairo. I want to be walking the remote ruins of the Syrian Desert, Sergiopolis and Palmyra. I want to see Petra in Jordan. The women's coffee morning on the opposite balcony is singing quietly, a tremulous Arab dirge. Today is Wednesday. Say I drive for Tarsus, and by some fluke catch a boat on Thursday which drops me at Alexandria on Saturday, I would have two days in Egypt to find a place to abandon the car until the spring.

Whatever I do involves Ankara airport.

So get there!

Sharing a taxi out of town, the options become clearer:

1. Catch a ferry from Turkey to Egypt. Maybe, but I don't know enough about the ferry routes and timetables.
2. Drive back to England. Sensible, but it means defeat, retreat, tearing up the dream (sorry, what dream? Round the world?), but I have the papers to get me home, and six days for 3,000 miles is not unheard of.
3. Fly to Paris and bully them using my new contact in Damascus. Impossible. The Bentley has to be in a customs warehouse somewhere, probably Izmir, before I can leave the country.
4. Smuggle the Bentley into Syria, and out the other side to Jordan. Some hope after last night!
5. Effect a diplomatic reconciliation between Syria and Britain so that visas can be obtained from any embassy. Well, not with these telephones…

Let it be Option 1. A boat to Egypt.

*

The drive from Gaziantep was going so well. The airport director had charged the royal sum of 900 lira for the overnight car park – about 25p. The roads were dry, we had crossed the two mountain ranges before Tarsus. Then the red warning light for the dynamo came on, just after the second crest.

Perfect timing from Mme Comedienne; it is nine o'clock at night, at the top of one of the longest gradients in the world and the voltage meter has swung from gently positive to seriously negative. I coast for miles on sidelights, spinning out the remaining charge in the battery, saving all its juice for the spark plugs.

A village appears. In the square, one of the boys signals that his father owns a garage on the main strip. A cousin joins us and my ailing aristo staggers a further half mile, to the best *otoelektrik* around. Now about seven Turks are involved and, with a supreme effort, the dynamo has been removed and stripped. The problem is worn bushes. A pair from a lorry are being ground down to fit.

I sit in the adjoining shelter, crouched towards the brazier in the middle of the room. The crowd comes and goes. Three boys are in here with me; the one in the rudimentary cot has a crushed foot. He has wrapped it in newspaper and a rag. He will never walk straight again unless it is fixed immediately.

We are all disheartened. The electrician seemed to have traced the fault, but now the red warning light is back again after thirty seconds of running. Excitement has curdled into lassitude. I do not believe the *otoelektrik* is on the track of anything at the moment, just experimenting, puzzling, and that will cause more damage, blow fuses, I don't know.

I have only dollars to pay my new rescuers: the mechanic and the unemployed boy in the village square, Alp, who has not had work since he left the army.

And what about the child with the crushed foot?

Day 17

Wow! Blue sky in every direction.

It is first thing on Thursday morning. Squinting out from under the blankets on the back seat, I see a man with a broom sweeping the concrete forecourt of the petrol station. I risk a frozen hand to wave at him. He waves back.

Dawn slices through the view, strafing a stationary goods train, raking the distant indigo hills, and beyond them the pink, snowcapped mountains. It is a time for introspection, to rub bristled face against pillows, inspect grime-ingrained hands and catch up with the journal.

Heavy traffic roars along the main road from Tarsus to Mersin, twenty yards away.

Last night ended well. I gave the *otoelektrik* $20, and to one side $10 to Alp. I next settled a larger sum on the garage owner, a sincere man with reasonable English, to have the boy with the crushed foot dragged to hospital, to see that the foot was set and to have him tied to his bed until the cast was safe to walk on.

But I then realised it would take the garagist a whole day to do what I asked. If he did not, he would have to live with the sight of the lame boy for the rest of his life. But I would have it on my conscience too, suspecting what had happened. So I offered to drive the two of them to hospital. And they accepted, the boy and the garage owner. A message was sent to the boy's family and they came and bundled him onto the back seat, while the man sat up front.

The straight-six could run all night on dipped, but not on main beam. However, one of the dipped filaments had blown again, so that to show two headlights we had to pass all real and suspected police cars on full beam. The garage owner seemed worried about the police stopping us.

I dropped the two of them at the hospital, a gleaming new building, drove back for a while and found this garage.

Before I could sleep here the pump attendant checked me out.

'You hiding from police?' he asked.

'What is it with you guys and the police?' I said. 'I am too tired to be on the run from anything.' With that doubtful logic, he left me alone.

Maybe worrying about police in the night is what you do in curfew countries.

I am suspicious of my motives; I relished it all too much, the private, bossy chat, saying that the boy must understand the consequences if he did not have his foot fixed, and then the heroic midnight dash from rustic shack to health emporium.

Anyway, they should be home by now.

As for me being on the run. In my heart of course I bloody am.

*

Mersin is the main port for the coast west of Antioch. It was the springboard for Turkey's invasion of Cyprus in 1974.

A shipping agency. An upstairs back office. The walls are hung with maps of the World, of Turkey and of Iran.

We are waiting for an English-speaking friend of Ibrahim, the manager, to come and discuss transport. The radio wails Turkish music, and the room is full of tobacco smoke. Already I have talked to two other shipping agencies. All three say the harbour is very quiet just now. For example, Ibrahim has a load of iron going to Port Said, but only on December 29th. That is too late for me.

No ferry runs from Mersin to Alexandria.

Option 2, the proverbial retreat from Moscow, is beginning to look inevitable.

I have been measuring the distance on the shipping agent's world map. The mileages are not inconsequential. When we were in Akakale, we were halfway between London and Mumbai. It will be five days of manic driving back to the English Channel. And I did not bring the cross-Channel return ticket…

This should all be infuriating but I am too weak for rage. Only the Turks' natural hospitality prevents me bursting into tears. The endless glasses of tea are making me shake.

*

After several other agencies I track down Mr Salim, the best shipping brain in Mersin. His telex machines chatter without interruption and his staff treat him with awe.

Young, Western educated, credible, he tells me in plain words that there are no roll-on roll-off boats to Alexandria. He could crate the car there by the 29th, but I would have to fly ahead and receive it. He does not give much for the chance of a boat just happening to leave for Port Said in the next twenty-four hours. Yes, I could take the ro-ro to Turkish Cyprus, but the only way out from there is back to Mersin.

His words convince me that my one option is to drive back to London.

*

Within a mile, the dynamo warning light glares red again. I raise the driver's side bonnet and leaf through the handbook in a furious sulk. A small motorcyclist props up his moped nearby, strides forward, pushes me aside and peers over the wing down into the engine. Grudgingly I point to the voltage regulator. Dynamo charging wildly. Could it burn out the electrics? He nods excitedly, hops on his moped and waves to me to follow behind him.

We drive at a scorching pace through the local traffic, into the heart of breakdown city.

While a new wizard tinkers with the unit marked in the handbook as '*To be adjusted only by a trained Bentley mechanic*', the motorcyclist beckons again. Jumping on his bike, he indicates to mount up behind.

He takes me on the back of his machine to a workshop where, like a saucer from Mars, a Parthenon grill glints from the darkness. A 1974 Silver Shadow is about to be resprayed. Camouflaged in tape and Turkish newspaper; is it art or agriculture? But still, a wondrous silence pervades inside the machine, walnut dash, right-hand drive and all.

In the corner of the shop is a 1947 Norton motorbike in working order and, as my eyes adjust, I see various other scalps from Britain's industrial past standing among newer products of the Far East.

Upon returning to my own fragment of engineering tradition, the electrician has not only fixed the voltage regulator, but also the half-out headlight, and provided a spare bulb. I pay $10 and we are all very happy.

So, with matters almost back to normal, and some travellers' cheques cashed into lira, the Bentley and I gird ourselves for the bitter retreat home.

*

We are at the snow line again, but heading north. This is a different pass, up to the central plain, much easier, a dry road with virtually no traffic and a full moon, the stuff of fantasy, fast straights where a thoroughbred can have its head, swooping bends where two tons of steel can be set up within an ace of drifting, speeds squarely in the power band of top gear. Air resistance is the only brake required.

Supper was a spread of kidneys, liver, yoghurt, sweet rice, bread and salad. The restaurant owner was called Ali. He was nineteen when his father died and has six siblings. Now he is twenty-two, and his staff treat him like a Mussolini. By sign language and drawings we do a complete lesson of English, while the TV reports a horrible air disaster in Scotland – a Pan Am 747. Ali helps me put antifreeze in the Bentley's radiator in anticipation of a stop in the mountains.

Heading north lets me keep the options open. Perhaps in Izmir My Lady could have a service and go back into storage; a boat might even take us to Alexandria. Alternatively, I could forget that diversion and head for Istanbul and the fast run home. The news on the BBC these past few months has been of ethnic rioting in Yugoslavia, which frightens me. But the green Fiesta did the inland route via Belgrade in 1978, Athens to Bristol in forty-five hours with no radio, so it is not impossible. And the roads will have improved in the decade since.

Between the two choices is one small distinction, the difference between delay and defeat. Retrenchment and retreat. What use would it be to dally? If I had a Syrian visa by the spring, could I do the Izmir to Cairo dash then, and maybe even reach Tunisia? Such an achievement could save the round trip and bring the Bentley to England in time for her MOT next June.

The moon is up, the night is chill. For now, let's just roll the last 300 yards down this hill and fill up at the pumps there ahead.

Hey, fifty miles from anywhere, on the roof of Asia Minor, and it is a British Petroleum service station. Good omen? The boys are playing football under the arc lamps. Let the attendant come to me. I stay snug in my motorised igloo, under the blankets and rugs. Even at this late hour, in this cold, workmen are digging a trench for a new filling point. Three sheep carcasses, flayed of skin, hang by the roadside under an awning. The canvas flaps in the freezing wind, and the shadow which this casts across the arc light makes the meat flash bloodily, like a disco strobe in a slaughterhouse. Two articulated lorries, monsters of the road, are manoeuvring on the forecourt, boxing me in.

The pump man explains that he has almost no petrol left, only diesel. He gives me a gallon and indicates that there is another station, ten kilometres along the way. Let's hope I do not have to run the engine to stay warm in the meantime.

I am still quite shocked by that air crash report.

We climb on up. The full moon dazzles off the snowfields. I remember this time last year, skiing by moonlight in dark glasses in Arosa with cousin Simon and family. Likewise, when the S-Type landed at Patras under a beaming Greek moon, we bowled along with no lights, to prove it could be done.

We reach the summit, 1,610 metres says the sign. The road leaves the snowy mountainside and descends into a cutting. We are safely past the worst.

Coming down from the col, a pair of headlights can be seen gaining rapidly on us from behind. I think, here comes trouble. They'll hit this ice and skid. So strong is the sense of danger that I start to repeat, 'As the fast car came up behind, he had a profound sense of foreboding', rolling the phrase in my mind. In front, the moonlight shows a broken-down truck, and another near it in a side road. Distracted by the lights behind and the truck, I barely swerve in time to miss a great rock in the middle of the road. Instinct saves me. In the mirror I watch to see if the lights behind, which have already caught me up, will miss it too.

Crash.

My front driver's side wheel hits a second rock. The whole car rides up over the boulder and smashes sickeningly, bumper down onto the tarmac. 'Broken wheel' flashes through my mind, as I struggle the spark-grinding bodyshell to a halt on the verge away from the ravine. The chasing car sweeps past and disappears up the next hill. I can still hardly write I am so angry.

As is the local custom, the driver of the broken-down lorry has placed warning signs in the road, in both directions, to mark an obstruction ahead. Normally these are put out only in fog, and the warnings are small stones, well to one side. But this driver has hauled out boulders, and positioned them on the central white line. The moonlight is so monochrome, so shadowless, and the rocks so far out into the middle of the road, and the road so curved, that the boulders simply disappear until the headlights catch them at the last moment.

The Bentley's front wheel is rammed up under its wing, with the chassis resting on the ground. A river of hydraulic fluid, or is it engine oil, runs back down the slope behind.

After helping the culprit lorry driver secure a towing hawser from his own rescue lorry, I jog beside his truck and, abandoning the Bentley and my worldly possessions, climb up into the cab as he trundles along, trying to jump-start his engine on the downhill sections. With occasional shouted instructions, which I attempt to interpret into action, we are towed to the top of the last rise, released, left to freewheel down to the petrol station mentioned by the BP attendant, and stop.

Then begins a series of shuttle runs in a six-seater gravel bowser with eight excited Turks and me crammed in it. I restart my stranded dreadnought and back her, scraping flintily, until she is off the shoulder of the highway and gouging ice and mud up the side road. I rescue a few essentials, including a torch, and leave again in the gravel truck.

A plan is hatched for tomorrow for a farm tractor to half tow, half carry the wrecked machine into the next town, twenty-five kilometres away. Personally I doubt a tractor can raise one corner of the hulk without lifting its own front wheels at some stage and crashing too.

*

I am lying in the bottom bunk, nearest the fire, in a dormitory hut for road workers, about four miles beyond the cutting. It is almost midnight.

An old man, decades of navvying in his back, comes in and gestures to me to hide my money in my cot with me. Well, if they attack, clutching my purse won't help much. There are twelve of them. But I'm not too bothered. Twelve men cannot trust each other enough to hush up a murder. Still, it is good to feel the torch under my pillow.

My girlfriend was right. This was not the leg of the journey for her. I have to admit it. She made her seasonal excuses, 'An only child has duties', and… damn. If she would love me back, I would not be here at all.

I doze off, boiling hot, legs across my jacket, clutching the pocket torch, and sleep less fitfully than expected. For several nights I have been dreaming strongly about my grandparents' house, on my mother's side, and school.

Day 18

Awake with the sunrise, I wash under the cold tap in the corridor. One thought predominates: to tow the Bentley to the nearest town, Karaman, as soon as possible.

That was simultaneously the prettiest daybreak and the most repulsive soup I have known. Peeking over a treeless earthscape, the sunrise caught last night's full moon coolly bedding down among blushing mountains. By contrast, the soup is a searing, lardy bathwater. It leaves a scalded mouth empty but coated with grease. Anonymous strips float in suspension. Gazing at the staggering view is sufficient distraction to swallow. I show enough delight to be a good chap, but not so much as to be doled a second helping.

On the table beside the window, a television is tuned to a breakfast show. Twelve road workers sit glued, watching a Turkish PE instructress in a green leotard.

The old man, now sporting a woollen cap, warms thirteen glasses with a shot of boiled water passed from one to the next. The water is then cast in a curve across the dirty board floor. He half fills each glass with dark-brown fluid from one kettle and tops them up to the brim with boiling water from the other. He adds two sugar lumps each and passes the tray. Take a glass and a teaspoon. All stir together. Tinkle, tinkle, tinkle. Close your eyes and you are over for tea at the vicarage.

The TV news says the Pan Am flight fell on Lockerbie.

*

Once again the road menders' truck takes us to My Lady's crash site. She is still there, frosted like a corpse on an ice floe.

Achmed, a handyman, lives in the shack next to the road where she is lying. He speaks German from an earlier life building Leopard II tanks somewhere on the Rhine. With a pickaxe, he breaks out the iron soil under her doorsill to fit the jack. Once the lifting gear is in place we can lever the body off the ground to inspect the damage.

Things do not appear too bad. The break seems to be confined to two rugged connecting lugs. These could be removed, by unscrewing four bolts, and welded back together. We agree it needs a proper tow truck, not a farm vehicle. A passing lorry is flagged down, and Achmed and I hitch into Karaman. We are unable to stand down the other rescue attempt, which is no doubt already on the way with the tractor.

We walk through the streets of the frontier town in the white winter light. The high plains wind bowls tumbleweed at us. The air is clean, the people strong and tall. We are looking around us for an expert, a man equal to our task.

*

Achmed and I have found a tractor repair workshop. It is headed by two burly, bearded Turks, one in a brown leather jerkin who I think is the proprietor.

Together the four of us ride in an old yellow taxi with a bootful of tools to where the Bentley sits – we considered taking a tank-towing truck, but decided it would be expensive and damage her front chromework.

In my absence, Her Ladyship has gathered a small court around her, even here in the mountainous wastes. An old man gives me some apples. Another indicates that there is normally two feet of snow at this time of year.

The wheel is coarsely chained back on to its hinges. I climb inside to start her. Black smoke plumes out behind, accompanying a hacking wheeze from the engine. Yes, to add to our problems, it looks like the radiator needed much more antifreeze. If we have a cracked cylinder head then the next step must definitely be back towards England.

But at least the oil levels in engine and gearbox are stable. I remember how the green Fiesta hit a rock on Mount Olympus and a front driveshaft popped out of the transverse gearbox, all shiny silver and pouring oil on the dry earth. I leaned down into the dusty engine bay and touched it, more from thoughtfulness than experimentation, and it popped right back in.

No such miracle here.

*

The wounded snow lynx crawled down from the mountains to Karaman under her own power. The chain held, but for that hour and those fifteen miles to the workshop she left a continuous black skid mark from the toed-in right front wheel. The two mechanics led the way back in our taxi. They stopped off for midday prayers at a village mosque, but soon caught up.

It is lunch time. They are now stripping down the broken suspension. It isn't just those two little pieces. The top wheel mounting has sheared off. It looks big, the sort of thing that cannot be welded…

*

Karaman has the flexible, craft-based economy of a medieval market town. From the grimy lock-ups around us comes a steady cacophony of bangs and hisses. The same team of mechanics could have waved us on to any one of three forecourts, and the same team of welders could be doing the sub-assembly repairs in any of those three friendly workshops.

The sun is already past its zenith, but it warms me as I sit out on the high pavement in my boots and heavy socks, into which are still tucked the office suit trousers which I put on to visit the Syrian embassy a million years ago.

*

We are in a workshop at the other end of the street, with the sun slanting low over our shoulders. My two mechanics are enjoying a celebratory tea. A fair-bearded master welder, looking Scandinavian and evidently relishing this intricate repair, taps around the edges of his handiwork. On the bench are two wheel-mounting brackets. They were once in pieces and are now remade as before, like parts of some rare fossil reassembled. Next on his list is the lower wishbone, and last but not least is a hydraulic device, which might be a damper, but I fear is to do with the steering. Welding that back together would be a masterstroke indeed. The mechanics' young assistant did not realise it was hollow, and he accidentally split the end in the vice.

Watching these craftsmen I realise that England is no longer the best place to maintain a car of this age. As technology advances, the skills to keep old cars on the road accrete where the people would otherwise have no motor vehicles at all.

I sit and write and am warm with fresh, golden tea. Friendly faces from earlier in the day, earlier stages in the rescue, call by in the afternoon promenade and smile.

The world is in harmony.

Crikey, they've brought the coiled front spring to show me. In two parts. What exactly was *not* broken in that impact? It is a catalogue of horrors.

*

An hour passes. Two more teas. The master welder shows me his work. Bentley Motors would be impressed. He has built up steel where the stresses run. The parts should have been designed as strong as that to start with. In London such attention to detail would cost hundreds of pounds. The fact that the car is a Bentley would put the figure nearer a thousand.

In front of a blinding white sunset they turn off the oxyacetylene torch for the castings and switch to the arc welder for the coiled spring. Phitzz, phitzz goes the electric arc; bang, bang goes the hammer. Phitzzz, phitzzzzz, thud, thud. When the hammer hits red-hot metal the sound is dull. As the steel cools, it begins to ring again.

The split hydraulic casting is to be repaired by blowtorch. First the welder licks the flame across the whole pump (if that is what it is) to warm it. Then, with metal wick in one hand and torch in the other, he turns the flame to a scything blue and sets to work. It all falls on the floor because the boy was not holding the clamp properly. Raised eyebrows, but no harm done.

I am hypnotised as the welder works around the pump, dabbing mild steel onto mild steel. He moves with the deftness of a painter, brushstrokes which can flow so easily when hot, and lock so hard when cold. And to think I hoped to use epoxy glue on this noble mineral. Once again the workmanship incorporates a degree of strength not previously seen in the design. The bulk of the pump has increased visibly. Stress points have been spread back from the old break.

Street life continues: ten yards away a transporter rumbles through, hauling a large digger on its flatbed trailer; a husband and wife on a motorised tricycle pick-up return from the bazaar; a pockmarked man dangles a tray of tea glasses, like a flat scales; an old lorry stacked with silver birch trunks toots as it passes.

*

It is done. The sun has set. Smoke curls away from the workbench as the pump cools. The next job is someone else's. The master welder comes to me. He gestures downwards with his hand. He cannot be telling me to sit, as I already am. The gesture means follow me.

He walks steadily, silent, looking at his watch. Through a wicket gate, he approaches a wall with stools and taps over a trench. I wandered through such a place, much bigger, in sacred Urfa, and thought it was a public convenience. He wipes the seat and sits on it facing the wall, loosens his shoes and washes his hands, face, ears and the tongues of his shoes over the trench. I stand and wait politely.

The master welder takes me round to the side of the mosque. He removes his shoes in the porch; I remove my cross-laced boots. We enter the room on the right, duck-egg blue, quite small and empty of furniture but for prayer rugs laid over the floor.

The prayer service begins. I imitate my new benefactor in movements, kneeling and standing and bowing and touching my head to the ground as he and the thirty other men do.

*

Afterwards I return to my still dismembered transport, lock the doors and put her cover over the whole. I am then given a lift on the back of the welder's moped to an unfurnished room. He lights the stove and tells me to wait. The chamber is roughly a cube, spacious and painted green. It has a window high in one wall, a cupboard in one corner and a kitchen sink in another. The coal-fired stove is in the middle of the third wall. Two mattresses and a square tablecloth are on the floor in the centre. Above head height hang Turkish and Arabic quotations and pictures of Mecca.

The welder's home must be nearby, for after a short time he returns, his two children with him. He has brought a tray of food; warm meat balls in water, chick peas and rice also in water, tomatoes, cheese, halva, bread. We sit cross-legged on the mattresses, the sides of the tablecloth pulled up over our knees, and despite our lack of common language, the friendship between us is clear.

His son is exhorted to try out his English on me. He is twelve years old.

After supper, the little fair-haired daughter is ordered to bed, but she procrastinates as only a five-year-old can until the instruction is forgotten in the welder's preparations for evening prayer. Again he washes his hands and neck, and then both feet, hooking them up in turn into the kitchen sink. He pulls on a green garment and hat before reciting his devotions across the room.

Then he brings from the cupboard a loose white robe and tall white hat worn by members of the Dervish sect based around Konya, to which he apparently also belongs. He takes off the green robes, puts on the white ones and the tall hat and demonstrates a whirl for the three of us. His arms are held horizontally outwards, right palm cupped towards heaven, left palm facing down. He spins on his left foot like a dancer, continuing until his dizziness almost puts him under the spell. I imagine that when Dervishes are together they go the whole hog, becoming completely entranced, but fortunately he spares the kids and me tonight.

I am inspired to attempt a spin for myself, without the robes. I do not stay upright long. Then all four of us are trying it.

While I recover, the welder explains that I am to stay the night in this room, sleeping on the mattresses on the floor. He has brought a blanket. He will lock me in when he leaves, for my own safety. He exits with his children and the tray.

The room grows more frigid by the second. I move my mattresses closer to the coal-burning stove, lie them end-on to be longer, and cover myself. The room is already too cold to crawl out and see how the stove works.

And the Bentley. Will she ever be the same again? I doubt it.

What should I do? Tomorrow is Saturday. Four days to drive to England. Still not impossible. Could I leave the old girl in Izmir? I do not know. The cylinder head is one problem, though even if cracked it might survive. Just how much oil she uses in the next 200 miles will be the test. Should the steering pump, or whatever is being repaired, be polished inside before it is reassembled? Will they remember how everything goes back together? And how do we prevent an airlock in the brake hydraulics?

Behind these technicalities is a more fundamental question. How can a welding shop feel holy? For that is where the sense of Allah, or Zen or Godhead is strongest. All is done with neatness and economy, lathes oiled, drills cleaned, swarf swept up, in the humble praise of something higher than us.

Was it thus in a carpentry shop in Galilee, two thousand years ago?

Day 19

First light. I have stumbled from my blanket to fuel the stove. It flared up in the middle of the night, seemingly hours after I last threw on a load of coal, when I thought I might freeze to death. So I do not expect instant results; the kettle will boil by seven o'clock when my benefactor said he would return.

I sniff the scent that was rubbed onto the backs of my knuckles by the mullah in the mosque, before we began to pray – me a foot taller than anyone there, sticking out at the end of the front row. What level of religious tranquillity would one attain if one prostrated oneself thus before God three or five times every day over many years? Then again, if stirred to anger, what fanaticism could emanate from this regimented ritual? The sense of solidarity and righteousness, even invincibility, was overwhelming as we formed lines and then bowed as one.

But not all the service was so drill-like. Afterwards the praying became more individual, and the ranks were broken so that each worshipper could follow his own rhythms.

My teeth are chattering. No doubt the Bentley radiator has frozen for a second night. Who cares? What hope has she of getting back to England anyway?

I am too cold to think straight.

I must phone Cairo and tell the mechanic at the British embassy that our rendezvous is off.

We need hydraulic fluid.

The steering pump requires gaskets, or it will leak all the way to England.

Since the split end has not been repaired, the tracking of the front tyre will not be controlled. I will have to keep the spare inflated in the boot in case the skewed wheel shreds. The spare is currently flat. The Bentley's tyres are over-wide, and the spare only fits in its slot when deflated. But there is a chrome-plated hand air pump which you place vertically between your feet.

What do I do if I hit snow in central Europe? The rate of progress needs to be, let me see, forty miles an hour for twelve hours a day for five days.

A new idea, call it Option 6, begins to form in my mind. Could I reach Izmir, surrender the car and then fly home? I might drive her to England in the spring. Perhaps Mr Topkara at customs will not take her back. Would they have some rule about people who abuse their hospitality? We could drive on to Greece. Or she could join Topkara's scrapyard – but I know what my employers and their insurers would say about that…

Central Turkey, Day 12, 'steady flakes of snow – sometimes building up until they jam the windscreen wipers' (page 35)

Central Turkey, with a couple of the many 'Tehlikeli Madde' tankers which My Lady merrily tailgated, until I learned the translation (page 65)

Turkey, North of Mersin, Day 18, 'The wheel is coarsely chained back on to its hinges' (page 56)

Turkey, Karaman, Day 19. Early morning outside the workshop (page 63)

*

The luminous spot on the ceiling, which watched me with suspicion whenever I awoke, turns out to have been the reflection of the moonlit window in the naked lightbulb hanging over my head. The knitted shirt which I wore as a shawl to keep warm is now down round my neck. A dog is barking.

The day is still only approaching. Life consists of hoping the coal stove will miraculously catch light a third time.

I fall asleep and dream it, and it happens.

*

The welder gave me breakfast this morning before we left on his moped through the freezing sepia mist. He had brought fresh bread, jam, cheese and olives, and a cassette player, into which he put a tape of holy readings, accompanied by music. After eating we exchanged gifts. I gave him a piezo-crystal flintless cigarette lighter, brought for such occasions, and he gave me some prayer beads. The player snarled the cassette's tape while he was out of the room. The readings were a write-off.

Three young boys are sweeping out a workshop for the day. The welder, woolly cap pulled down over tousled head, has parked me here. He stokes the fire in his own workshop next door. He appears to be a diesel injector repair specialist. Diesel injectors mean gaskets. There is some hope for my steering pump.

These boys will never go to school. They pick up a job sweeping out when they are five or six, and graduate to stoking the fire and fetching tools for mechanics when they are aged nine or ten. When they reach puberty they take to crawling under vehicles to undo difficult bolts, or to holding the inspection torch. At fourteen they are fixing brakes and stripping small sub-assemblies, and at sixteen they can refit clutches and repair gearboxes. By the time the kids are adults, they can handle a complete engine rebuild. This is the craft apprentice system, respectful of experience and wasteful of manpower, ensuring a superb support team for every adult mechanic and dooming the economy to low productivity.

The senior boy's trousers are soaked above the knees. They steam when he stands close to the burner. I think he wet himself in the night rather than get up in the cold.

*

Now the steering pump is being reassembled. I ask them to keep the dirt out of it. To no avail, I fear. Here we are, wondering which bits go where and banging the poor thing with hammers. It will have to be replaced.

Well, fancy that, it is a curious shock absorber, not a steering pump at all. The senior boy uses a piece of paper, carefully cut to a ring, as a gasket. Now the great coiled spring is resisting being fitted, and now the proprietor himself is tapping straight the hubcap. It even looks as if the antifreeze may have held its own against the frost last night, but doubts remain about the night before.

The used car salesman whose German has come in useful from time to time approaches. He says his business has suffered because my mentor asked him to stay and interpret. I say there are plenty of German speakers around, so he should blame the garage owner, not me.

The head mechanic is worried, the brake pedal has gone floppy. I set off to the post office to try to phone Bruce in England on the question of airlocks in the hydraulics.

At the moment my two-tonner, though she might roll again, will have only her handbrake to stop her.

*

A round of celebratory glasses of tea for the entire street; photographs of my rescuers beside the car, oily woollen caps, bushy beards, breath fogging the cold air. I am straining to leave, but hooked to them by a code of dignity which has only just been taught to me. We stand in the muddy, sunlit street and honour their craft. Ten mechanics, one welder, two days, total bill $50.

*

We are 280 dry, hard-charging miles from Karaman. Below us, far away, through the clear night, lies a twinkling town; and from its centre two veins of headlights snake out into the hills beyond, marking the alternatives. One way to the north, and the other on to the west. At this junction the dice must be cast. The decision can be delayed no longer.

Do I take the car back to England or entrust her to Izmir customs once more?

Technically she could probably make it from here to London. Or to Cairo. But beyond Cairo would lie a further 3,000 miles of savage roads, to be crossed in the heat of summer. With a front wheel of uncertain geometry, a patched-up shock absorber, a cracked cylinder head and a dying gearbox, the odds are pretty long.

If she breaks down irredeemably before or after Cairo, I will have to pay for her to be carried home; the company's recovery insurance does not extend beyond Turkey. Also, I will have to pay the State third-party policy in Syria, Jordan, Egypt and so on, which could be exorbitant.

On the plus side, by leaving My Lady behind, I would not have to face the snows of central Europe. Moreover, I could fly to Cairo, check out the local conditions and carry on home with the Cairo–Heathrow air ticket I have for Wednesday morning. Also, driving to London, I might not make it by Wednesday. Just one hiccough on that infamous highway to hell in Yugoslavia would scupper everything. I know, I have seen it, and I was ten years younger and fitter then.

The advantage of dashing back to London is that it puts an end to the adventure before it becomes a super-costly crisis. The sorrow is that the saga never becomes an epic.

OK. It's decided. The madness goes on. To Izmir! To the place where we started this chapter. No stronger, no wiser, but fundamentally still here, still ourselves, and better luck next time.

But will the old girl start? Evidently not. Is this a protest? She does not seem to want to spin beyond a tickover, wherever I position the accelerator. Just tickover.

Switch off. Think. Could I, by some extraordinary slip, have been pushing the brake pedal? Try again. Vroom, everything in working order. We will never know. The Bentley guards her secret still.

*

We enter one patch of freezing fog more than I can be bothered with tonight. I spot an isolated petrol station and hide round the back of it, away from the floodlights. Beside me is a tanker trailer carrying a large skull and crossbones above the words *Tehlikeli Madde*. For a week of this leg I only knew these trucks as the demons who overtook on blind bends, sped up in poor visibility and swerved out murderously if you dared try to overtake. The skull and crossbones was forever roaring past and cutting into the line just ahead of me, as a motorcycle might expect to do in the rush hour, except these were twenty-five foot, multi-axle artics. At worst, you followed them overtaking a long tailback, and they would dive into the last available gap and brake, leaving you staring into the furiously flashing lights of an oncoming monster. But they were skilful at speeding up slow convoys, and their *Tehlikeli Madde* name made them even comic.

Technically mad, of course, but lovable.

Then, yesterday, I established what it means: Highly Inflammable. They are the rolling pipeline which fuels Turkey's interior. Should one crash into you, the fireball would be seen for miles. I too now give them a wide berth. Nor do I latch onto them quite as I did.

With memories dancing in my head of real-life, cinematographically perfect, trailer-off-road slides, of fuel tankers driving on the very blade of a jack-knife, I curl up in the familiar ball on the back seat. My new Karaman woolly hat, seventy-five pence to you, is pulled down over my ears. Heat loss from the head is a high proportion of the body's total. Not for me tonight. I am for sleep.

Day 20

CHRISTMAS DAY 1988. Fog gives the bare walls, trees and parked lorries a surreal transparency. I hear a cockerel; and a foot breaking an icy puddle. A wheelbarrow trundles somewhere in the gloom behind me. The morning is so still I am afraid to move. My scalp tickles under my woollen bonnet.

*

A mighty, mighty temple once stood here, where today is a misty green valley with not a house in sight.

I don't know the name of the place. Mid-morning on the damp dark road, fifty miles short of Izmir, I wanted to stop to stretch my legs. The trucks were driving too fast for My Lady to park on the verge. At the next crossroads, I took a turning south into a lane, just yards. And stumbled on this.

This is not Ephesus, though we must be near, maybe sixty miles away. The Temple of Artemis at Ephesus was the third of the seven wonders of the ancient world, as listed by Philo of Byzantium in the third century BC. It has vanished, broken up for stone, or sunk into the soft ground. I know. It wasn't there in the summer with the Hills and Blackwells, the day after we met at Kusadasi.

But here, ruined, forgotten, are the stumps of a building which must have compared. It was clearly larger than the Parthenon, also seen this summer. Where the Parthenon's column bases are six feet in diameter, these are more like ten feet. Those which remain here are carved with fantastic artifice. They remind me of two huge round plinths I saw in the British Museum as a child. Then I thought, 'No one makes columns that big.' The detail here has not eroded in 2,500 years. So they must have been buried for most of that period. Which means archaeologists excavated, though not in tourist-minded times or the site would be signposted.

The temple looks longer than on the Acropolis, too. I count twenty columns to a side, as opposed to, I guess, seventeen in Athens. What wealth could have financed such a building? Were there gold or silver mines in western Turkey?

This find alone justifies Option 6, returning to customs in Izmir.

The highway runs straight past here, blindly, just the other side of the hill.

If you stop to look, the mounds and terracing suggest a lost city, but from the main road, even on foot, you might not notice. The villagers' huts all face the modern highway. Did their ancestors need a temple, two and a half thousand years ago? No, this edifice was first dreamt in a single person's mind. It was built for a king. He was a man of overriding wealth, vision and ambition.

What is it to enact one's dreams? Divine or futile? Do megalomaniacs build as carefully as craftsmen?

Today's inhabitants work in vineyards ranged out northwards beyond the road. They toil year-round in *côtes* that can be, as now, as bleak as war cemeteries. With their backs to the past they are like the locals at Pompeii. They never aspire to the feats of their ancestors, their Eden would be a garden, not a city fit for gods.

The king dreams as helplessly as the labourer. In the end it all vanishes. This superb, daunting temple trumpets the certainty of oblivion.

Back at the crossroads village, I drift into the tea house. I am still reeling from my find. It would be great to telephone England and wish my parents Happy Christmas. The crowded room gazes silently at me. I have seen friendlier looks from a herd of bullocks. It is their space, not mine.

What are we dreaming? Is mine a worthy dream or an escapist delusion?

The tea house has no *jetons* for the telephone.

Press on to Izmir, where I can change dollars and make phone calls on Christian holy days.

*

The road passes a marble factory. I was planning to tile out the bathroom at home. But marble in the UK is expensive. Maybe this is the answer. Chance discoveries like these are the seeds of trading empires.

Blocks of uncut rock, each the size of a domestic room, stand in lines down the outside of the hanger. I wander through the shop floor between the singing bandsaws to find the proprietor. He is a man of perhaps thirty, in a new leather bomber jacket. He takes me to his office. Over Turkish coffee he tells me in German about his bank loans, his margins and his workforce. To start with I think his prices cheap. They sell tiles in bulk for five per cent of the shop price in northern Europe. But of course I am not a bulk buyer. For me it would be twenty-five per cent of the London cost. On top of that would be shipping and import tax.

Italy's concerns about Turkey joining the European Economic Community are natural. The fact that the mill was working at full tilt on Christmas Day, which also happens to be a Sunday, and that the owner was there to show me round personally, shows the real grounds for their concern. But is the EEC a religious or an economic order? Here is a country where petrol can be bought for foreign currency, where city banks display interest rates of sixty-five per cent per annum but the economy is still growing in real terms faster than anywhere for 2,000 miles. How long before the EEC finds her southeastern neighbour acceptable? Ten years? Between the hostile, rich founders, like Germany, and the sympathetic arrivistes, like Britain, the balance will be held by France. Watch the Turkish ambassador in Paris for a future president of Turkey.

*

Izmir again. Sun warms the quayside I so recently quit with such high hopes. The noon ferry is boarding for Istanbul – a cross-Channel-sized ship with its bows tilted up high for loading.

I have been inspecting the Bentley's oil. The filler cap throat is white with a yoghurt of emulsified oil and water. The presence of water, since I did not put any in, means either a cracked cylinder head or a blown gasket. So far, the crack must be small: you can tell by looking for the reverse side of the leak, oil in the radiator. Only a slight film slicks the surface of the coolant and the level has not gone down. But even a minor break is a problem. Lubrication is all in a 90,000-mile engine like this. With watery oil, wear and tear, power loss and possible seizure will result.

What is involved in replacing a cracked cylinder head in Izmir? Money, tooling, perfectionism, contacts, time. The usual constraints. It is sad, sad, sad not to be sitting at the foot of the pyramids thinking these wise thoughts. I should have phoned Damascus months ago and bypassed the sleepy officialdom in Paris. Our mileage since Akakale could have brought us to Suez.

Smyrna is open for business. The burly phone box operator in the main post office welcomes me back. Turkish Airlines sell me a ticket to Cairo for half the price of one to London, so I will use my homeward flight after all. But the tone is wrong. The shop windows are full of extravagances, furs, leather handbags, shiny bathroom fittings, even gleaming German cars. I do not want them. I want the emptiness of the master welder's prayer room, no furniture, just neatly laid carpets and two old mattresses. I want to be offered a glass of tea, and to converse with people who are actually there, even though we do not know enough words to make one sentence in each other's language.

No one in Izmir wears, as I do, Karaman fashion, trousers tucked into socks to keep the street mud off. No one here will tell me that olives are the particular gift of Allah, which is why we eat them for breakfast. We will not say grace in the workshop, mechanics' boy, client and passer-by, heads bowed as one, before opening our lunch. Nor will lunch be bundles of spicy salad swaddled in sheets of bread and delivered steaming, in newspaper. Here one chooses a quayside bistro and asks for the menu.

The city, which seemed so crummy, is now so smart. Cousin Simon told me his family called in here a year ago, on a billionaire's floating palace, and were disappointed. Of course the sight of a Second World country aping the First World is dull, even when for a few square miles it achieves it. Transitional states are rarely dignified. But Simon should have left the waterfront, the choked urban sprawl, and touched the hinterland. That would have been an eye-opener.

What is happening in this restaurant? The food is taking forever.

Ah, at last.

As always, nourishment brings me round. Someone in the kitchen is stuffing the chillies before skewering them on the kebab – a glint of craft. The factory hand at the marble-polishing machine had a similar understanding. Does he add anything more than a robot could? Reading the stone, his boss said. But could a robot with x-ray vision imitate the judgement of the best marble grinder? He said not. My own view is that imitation may bring you closer to the truth, like a CD brings you closer to Beethoven. But you will still be a long way from the man, his dreams. The world divides between imitation and the real thing, creation. Talk to me of poetry and I will show you yourself.

Fish washed down with raki… it is creative, and not the conventional Christmas lunch.

*

The wind is from the north. The cargo ships out in the sound have swung on their anchors to face it. The sun is now in the west. Only I have not moved.

The ships become black freighters, like the lorries which bore down from the east in the sunrise after the night of the snow chains. The bay is their dance floor. The gulls swim on the choppy crests like blown litter after the ball.

The horizon is coming closer.

Waiter, please give me some more raki, and don't stand between me and that pretty girl at the window. The paterfamilias arrives to join the clan at her table, on crutches and wearing a sling. She takes his hand and kisses it, then presses it to her forehead. Her father is not old, forty or fifty; Turks age quickly. From him, from the pretty girl now in the bosom of her family, from the child gambolling between the tables comes the question of resourcefulness, to challenge my theme of creativity. Ah, to have a family, to stick together, to exploit the changes imposed by history and economics. But how?

The fat man across the restaurant from me is also sitting alone. He is me in ten years' time. The waiter is absorbed with the party by the window. The fat man and I are trying to be served. The telephone rings, the first phone bell in a lifetime. The head waiter is running with their salad. The girl is so pretty that he has forgotten himself as well as everybody else.

If I phone home now I will only interrupt the Queen's Speech.

Day 21

My transition is almost complete. The Grand Ephesus Hotel did the job. Scrubbed and shaved, in dry-cleaned cashmere and fresh whites, I am the gentleman tourist again. Nothing beats twelve hours' kip on pressed cotton sheets. Nevertheless, I eat my soft-boiled egg as the welder demonstrated silently two mornings ago: crack the shell and peel the top half off the unbroken white, salt the surface, place the end in your mouth and bite.

This conservatory overlooks the garden between the hotel and the seafront. Away across the green lawn, the morning traffic moves freely around Ataturk Plaza, and silently, thanks to the double glazing. The garden is in shade, but a cream and blue electric bus glints behind the trees. Beyond that basks the outstretched harbour. Time is a problem for other people. It does not enter this pampered womb. My second omelette and toast arrive. A night at the Ephesus costs the same as a complete Bentley suspension rebuild in Karaman, or about half the fine when you are clamped by parking sharks in London.

Now the problem of the cylinder head must be faced. Could I crate the patient up and ship her back to England? It would also be possible to change the oil, drain the radiator, put her back into customs and leave her for some future rescue mission. Ideally I should find out before I go whether the cracked cylinder head diagnosis is correct. Ask a Turkish garage? I can hardly ask an English one. Gosh, I'm hilarious this morning.

But what if only the head gasket, the seal, not the head itself, has gone, blown by the *otoelektrik* on the road from Gaziantep when he revved the engine so viciously? For that matter, what if it is indeed a cracked cylinder head? England is not the only place to make such repairs. The Bentley could be serviced in customs in the spring, perhaps by flying out an English mechanic for a Thursday and Friday, complete with an exchange cylinder head if necessary. Even better, since they weigh a ton, a new head could be shipped in advance from London to the bonded warehouse and await the skilled fitter.

*

On a tip-off from the head porter I find my way to the BMW dealership for Izmir.

They are real petrolheads here. The workshop has posters of recent Formula One champions around the walls, including the new reigning number one, Senna of course.

For an exorbitant £15 the Bentley's sump is drained of oil. The emerging fluid is then sniffed, rubbed between many a thumb and forefinger, stared at, discussed and ultimately pronounced to be free of water. Wonderful news, but how do they explain the white foam gathering around the filler cap?

'Have you been mixing different types of motor oil recently?' they ask in German.

Well yes, now that you mention it, there has been English, French, Spanish, French again, Italian, Greek and Turkish oil in there, normally the local economy variety. Was that a little thoughtless?

Refilled with a single brand of oil, and spilling over with contentment at the good news, My Lady drives round to Izmir's car-cleaning mecca. Ten vehicles at a time are scrubbed and tubbed here, to showroom splendour. Her engine is being steam-cleaned at the moment, and I suspect that half the paintwork is coming off too. Her whole front end was grey with the oily handprints of men and boys from the frozen uplands, and the steam hose goes to work on these too. Now the electrics are dried with compressed air, and I move her, like a wedding cake, to the vacuuming bay for the finishing touches.

Hanging above her to inspire the staff is a crude but unmistakable drawing of a Silver Ghost, greatest of all the Rolls-Royces. The communion is brief but happy.

*

The compressed air may have been a mistake.

I saw him, a stocky Turk, lean over the wing to reach into the engine. Maybe he opened the distributor to blow it dry and in the process he half sheared the rotor arm. Or maybe my Derby donkey is pulling a Piraeus strop. We had one or two massive backfires outside the car wash, and the old girl stopped completely three times on the freeway. When one of these cylinders decides to fire out of sync, it throws the whole block around like a loose board in surf. A shabby Izmir suburb was treated to the sight of an immaculate white limousine receiving instant roadside repairs from a man in impeccable white trousers, who tinkered deep in the engine bay without the slightest dirt attaching to him.

But behind the scene was a closing deadline. The customs officers' weekend was upon us.

*

The customs house was still open, with an hour to spare. But then nothing happened for thirty minutes. They were of course frightfully busy, stirring their tea.

After the break, the pendulum of luck at last swung our way. With a speed not seen since the snow chains were made, we cantered through the paperwork, cutting corners by referring questions of weight, engine number and so on to October's file, while I hurried out for the passport photocopies before they asked, knowing this to be their final trick; and in forty minutes we had done what last time took three hours.

I caught Mr Topkara and his foreman putting on their coats to leave. At first they insisted it would have to wait until Monday. But when they saw all the paperwork was done, the manager smiled and booked us in. He would see to the various dockets and stamps, and of course put her up on her chocks in the usual place. I explained that she was spluttering, that it was an electrical problem, and conveyed in sign language that I would be back with a fitter at Easter.

That, my friend, is what presents are for. Had there been no magic cigarette lighters at the car pound twelve days ago, if I had cheated then, as I was tempted to, there would have been no Izmir option. With a fantasy cylinder head fault I would now be driving like fury for England, and the story would be ending. Instead, reconnaissance complete, I am on standby tomorrow for Cairo with Turkish Airlines, for £150 less than a direct flight home.

*

The taxi is broad and long, the relic of some NATO officer's homesickness. It is now promoted to conveying foreigners from the customs house to their homes. The sun has set, and the rose sky and purple hills are reflected in the glassy blocks on the left and in the harbour on the right. The palm trees are ravishing. The taxi driver, a tidy man of sixty, sighs contentedly. I know his feeling entirely. It has been a long day, but home is in sight. I sneeze. He smiles and says '*Cok yasa*', which I take to be the Turkish for 'Bless you'.

Day 22

The Grand Ephesus Hotel woke me at five. The bus fuelled up with diesel in the dark on the way to the airport. My diving cylinders, for the backpack and the life vest, are returning to England with me. They caused a flurry at the security gate and check-in, the big one hissing away for about ten minutes to prove that it was real. I have left some air in it to be able to prove the same point to the Egyptians.

The flight has been called.

Chapter Two: Breakout

Turkey, Syria, Jordan, Egypt
Thursday 23rd March to Saturday 10th April 1989

Day 23

Brendan is a friend of Bruce's. He's been British for decades, and worked on Rolls-Royce cars for most of them, but he still 'gets 'assle' from immigration at Heathrow for his Indian skin. When security picks on his mechanic's tools, I play the toff to shame them, heaping embarrassment on itself. Istanbul is the opposite. Nothing beats the dismissive contempt with which Brendan tells suspicious customs men that a metal can is only an oil filter. He scowls at problems with his black moustache and pugnacious brown eyes and they evaporate.

So we travel, London to Istanbul, lugging the kit for a Bentley MOT. It is a slog of a day. But travelling multiracially makes it work.

Brendan sits across from me now, roughly where the woman in the fur coat sat in December. He sips his Coke and shuffles his lizard-skin slip-on shoes. We have cleared all the expected obstacles and now the Chinese water-torture starts. First drip: our tickets on to Izmir are made out for a non-existent connecting flight.

What of it? Istanbul airport is no longer the angular, strip-lit barracks I remember from Christmas. A restaurant has opened at the end of the hall, the public address system plays a love theme and Brendan's slipper wags. Two Italian tourists greet each other, stonewashed jeans and pastel cardigans tied where once were waists. '*Ciao!*' '*Va bene?*' The joys of prosperity. Even the Turkish businessmen now wear Burberry.

Where is the brooding Third World of Christmas time? It is only a question of focus. As soon as I put on my glasses, the faces become distinct, more awkward, closed. We are still in deference to a power somewhere off to one side.

At the last security gate, Brendan's array of wrenches and jump leads triggers the alarm. The bag of plugs and belts I am carrying is passed, but he has to check his war hammers and stiletto daggers into the hold.

I wait beside some Russians donning Walkmans they have just bought in Duty Free, shouting to be heard over each other's volume controls. They seem to be members of an athletics team. When Brendan is through, he points out a blockhouse of a girl, and says, 'I wouldn' like to get on the wrong side of 'er.'

*

The lights of Izmir spangle the hillsides like an earthbound Milky Way. The twinkling only stops where land meets sky. Our bus is swooping down the last dual carriageway, about 11 p.m. local time. The opportunities of the Orient reach out to me again, probing my stuffed-up London self, stirring juices under the City's agglomerated pith.

I love the fingerprints of personality change. They seem familiar, like the Smyrna street plan. Just here we will turn right into the avenue that leads to the sea. And here we will de-bus and look for our hotel.

However, I did not come to hang around in Izmir. I have a full diary of meetings back in London in just over two weeks' time. By then Her Ladyship must be in Cairo.

Day 24

Brendan has the wristwatch. He moans that it is six o'clock in the morning when I knock on his door. But everyone else seems to be up and about, so I suppose he's on London time, Izmir -2.

When we meet downstairs for breakfast the food is waiting for us.

'In Turkey, olives are the special gift of Allah,' I say.

Brendan eyes them suspiciously.

*

The customs house seems unfamiliar. The clerks have smarter furniture, laid out less helpfully than before; now it is even further to walk round the office. But the faces are the same. Junus arrives and shakes hands briskly with everyone, battling the languid tempo from centuries of bureaucracy. The *Triptik* desk was vacated at my approach, but I can wait. Brendan is already with the Bentley. He didn't like the look of the rebuilt front wheel at all – 'Needs a complete steering over'aul back in England,' he said.

Another old face. The man who signs the final papers has spotted me, and he orders a new recruit to attend. The sparring begins.

'But this is not your car.'

'It's this company's, as it says at the top of the page.'

75

'A letter of authority? But it is not in Turkish! You will have to find a lawyer and have it translated.'

My papers, however, do seem to match the photocopies on his file, and when I mention Junus' name the tide turns. Five more minutes and I am off on the circuit round the new, chrome-legged desks, with their chunkily castored pedestal chairs, some with the polythene covers still on them.

Neither the controller nor the assistant controller are in their glazed-off boxes, and a queue is building up. Lie back, sink into it, divide by ten. Time is only time; you could dash out with your precious papers signed and be knocked down by a bus. Requests are *Inshallah* – God willing.

*

I stand among the cacti in the carpeted office of the latest customs official and gaze at the immutable portrait of Ataturk. A feeling of anticlimax dogs each development. It happens again when the assistant controller in the red dress countersigns. Disappointment. Is it because, this time around, I am not alone? Is it because the Bentley is still in intensive care? Is it that these people have seen it all before? Or just the warm, heavy weather which spits gouts of rain down the windows?

Off to the Islamic Berkshire prep school to pay my dollars. No need for a guide. The lofty vault is still sculpted and beamed in white plaster, with that astonishing sky-blue background and gold filigree. The strip lights hang like Calder mobiles from noble ceiling roses on long, single chains of brass. In just three months the hand-cranked adding machines have been supplanted by sleek, seventies, mains-powered electronic calculators. The girl's fingers run over the buttons: 894,560 Turkish lira. My storage fee is about $400. Round to the bank again. How can the teller's English have improved so much in these thirteen weeks?

Counting out ninety 10,000-lira notes focuses the wandering mind wonderfully. The bank counts them, I count them, at the Ministry of Defence they count them too. Twice.

I hope Brendan is making good use of his chance to examine his patient.

*

Back at the warehouse I hand over my papers and presents, this time with the feeling of being scammed by both Topkara and the foreman. The boss does it with a fake phone call from the ministry saying that the bill I paid short-counted by 18,000 lira – as if that were possible. The warehouse foreman produces some cans of oil, for which he charges ridiculously over the odds. But My Lady is unharmed after three more months in a strange land, so who can complain?

Brendan has changed the sheared rotor arm, but says the starter is broken. I show him how to lift the gear lever to persuade the starter that the gearbox is in neutral, and he scolds me.

'Why didn' you say you 'ave a dicky microswitch?'

But he is also uncomfortable with the Turkish warehousemen smiling and standing around, and he thinks we are about to run out of petrol too. So we jolly the invalid off her cot, purring at kitten pace to save propellant, stopping only while Brendan runs back for the bag of tools he left behind in the excitement. At the gates of the customs zone we make our supplications. One more signature and a rubber stamp for me, one more crowd of mystified Turks for Brendan.

Beyond the barrier the Bentley immediately coughs with fuel starvation. She floats on fumes for half a mile to the Mobil forecourt.

*

The proprietor of the BMW dealership remembers me from our oil change at Christmas.

'Is the car still around?'

'Yes, it's just outside. Please could I use your inspection pit again to change the oil filter? I have the parts and a mechanic.'

'By all means. Ten years ago we had a V12 Lincoln Continental 1948 two-door coupe here. I sold it to the man who holds the Ford franchise for Turkey. He sent it back to America to be renovated…'

Underneath the company car, Brendan is at last in his element, complaining that the pit is too shallow. But he is scampering for joy. 'Where's that poxy spanner? Why's the flywheel so mucky?' He uses a mirror to look for the timing mark.

I keep out of his hair. Soon the 'six' is singing, and the Turkish lads are running short errands for him. A rhythm is established, which must not be interrupted. Hours spent now will be days, even lives, saved later.

Coffee time for Brendan. Turkish coffee – sugar, no milk – brought by a young mechanic. Brendan wipes his neck as he comes up from the pit. He's enjoying himself, right in the midst of it, working on the rear axle now.

This is the thickest Turkish coffee I have ever drunk, the sort that blocks sinks. The back of your mouth is floury after each sip. If it tastes good to me, who normally hates the stuff, it must boost a self-confessed caffeine addict like

Brendan. This could be a long day. From the way the BMW mechanics are joining in, we will have a trained mission control here in Izmir if the Bentley is forced to come this way a third time.

Now I am offered a warm, syrup-dribbling cake, baklava, which bites in your throat with its sweetness.

Brendan is taking a break to think about the MOT which My Lady needs for her insurance to hold good beyond June. He doesn't like the wear on the offside front tyre, and the camber of the nearside front wheel looks ghastly. Should I expect him to pass it? Well, if he doesn't want to, that must be accepted.

He tells me the handbrake was 'bloody miles out'. And he's balancing the brakes.

'She's got a carb problem, so she's firin' rough. The carbs need new diaphragms, but that won't give you no trouble unless you leave the ignition on and flood 'er. It could be fixed if I send you out some parts, but it's not serious. She'll run for ever, just not givin' as much power sometimes as she might've.'

Now the patient is jacked up to check the back axle. The rear dampers were nearly empty, but Brendan has filled them.

The Bentley hops down off the jack again, and she has a new confidence to her stance.

A young mechanic in clean BMW overalls (what would the Karaman apprentices think?) sprays a fine mist of water across the floor to damp down the dust and keep the place cool. Next door is a dump for soot – or is it low-grade coal, which blows in on the breeze? Whatever, it looks as good for your lungs as Turkish cigarettes.

Brendan has removed the fan belts. Both are in tatters.

'That was as close as you were going to get,' he says. 'You'd have been goin' up some 'ill and – wallop! You're lucky that radiator leak is on a low-pressure 'ose. It's a solderin' job really, not araldite,' he says with a shake of the head.

Turning to the tyres, I explain about the fifteen-mile skid through the mountains after the wheel was smashed in. The wear on them is not a result of the current alignment, I argue.

'£2,000 in London to 'ave that rebuilt,' says Brendan. 'But it's strong enough for another 10,000 miles.' So he will pass the MOT, I think.

Now the car is rolled back from the pit, and we whip off the Karaman wheel to reach the front damper. Normally a damper takes three or four squeezes of oil. This one takes the whole can.

Hit the quick-release jack; down comes the front wing like a portly bum into a club armchair. We are going to swap the worst worn tyre with the spare while we check the offside front damper for the same effect.

The man who gave us coffee brings a quart mug of automatic gearbox oil, which Brendan pours delightedly into its reservoir.

Then he feels the bottom hose of the radiator.

'A bit iffy,' he says and pulls away part of it in his hand.

I show him the hoses and parts which have been in the boot since England in July last year.

'All V8,' he says, 'Not a straight-six part among 'em. The guy who sold you these ought to be shot. Look, V8 'oses, points, distributor arm, belts. Take 'em back.' I refrain from saying it was friend Bruce's storeman.

In the BMW stores we find a likely looking Alfa Romeo radiator pipe and I say we should fit it. The old one splits as Brendan releases the jubilee clip around its neck.

'That was not an original 'ose anyway,' says he. Now we have the old pipe in our hands, we can go back and look for a better match. I am relieved to have detected the split hose, but furious that the new one from London is no good.

The carcinogenic dust storm blows down the street, but in the open workshop all is order and careful judgement. The mechanics are playful. The fat one pecks the one who brought the coffee on the cheek. Brendan has found a BMW bottom hose and declares it 'a pretty good fit'. It stands clear of the radiator fan and is only slightly too big in bore. We leave the London top hose well alone. After further tinkering, the engine jumps about on tickover, but revs 'sweet as a bird', as Brendan describes, that rising and falling roar of wind on the Cumbrian fells.

Brendan will have to leave it. He tightens the new fan belt one last time and turns to the gear lever microswitch.

'When I was workin' on the back axle,' he says, 'I opened up the fuel filter. It was so solid with muck, I 'ad to poke it with a screwdriver to break the seal.

'Don't worry about your wheel bearings,' he says. 'If they start 'umming, just repack 'em with grease.

'That's an old water pump making that noise, not tappets. Don't fret about your tappets, they're fine, fine. You needn't touch the new plugs for 12,000 miles now.'

The pigeons in the roof of our hanger are flapping around. My heart is fluttering too. I do not want this safe, comforting day to end. Brendan climbs behind the wheel and starts the motor without lifting the gear lever. The microswitch is fixed. Everything is complete. The car is as good as new, better than new. Already in my mind I am off and running. Then, to the mechanics' consternation, the radiator does its Camargue trick, several pints of water all over the workshop floor. Brendan decides to swap the thermostat, which will require infinite patience, gradually easing the screws on the cast aluminium housing. Ten minutes of restrained tapping and the lid comes free without a crack. Inside, the thermostat is fine after all, so we leave it. At least when the radiator plays up we know it is the radiator.

Brendan advances the ignition, re-earths the dark headlight, secures the loose connection on the horn and begins to pack up. I ask the garage for their bill. Another $50 poorer, we leave the BMW dealer and head out for a test drive. Round the corner in the road the engine misfires. Is she overheating, or worse?

Broken down over a stagnant waterway at Izmir's Spaghetti Junction, Brendan goes to work again.

'She was so sweet,' he says, 'and now she's sick as a parrot.' In five minutes we are still not going again. I wonder to myself how I could trust her across Syria.

But I say, 'She just needs to settle down.'

He seems too absorbed to talk.

*

My Lady ran very hot on our second test, flooding just as we parked at this café down town. Food and water bring Brendan back from the end of his tether. And talk of home revives us both. An hour later I bet Brendan that she starts first time and he almost drags me out to see if it is so. It is. Relieved, we check back into the Ephesus opposite. After a day of much labour, we deserve our treat. Brendan wants to remove the thermostat in the morning, to help the engine run colder. Then he will head for the airport, and I will set off overland for Cairo.

Last thing, I sneak out and re-park the old Road Warrior directly under my hotel window.

The room is smart, the bed is long, the sheets are again crisp and cool. Traffic toots in the street below, but I am falling, falling, falling…

Day 25

One hundred miles from Izmir, through a plain of sprouting vines and blossoming fruit trees, I pass the marble factory and the ruined city. The latter is ancient

Sardis. The temple was built by King Croesus – so it *was* local gold mines. Once world number one, the Temple of Sardis ended the classical era as the fourth largest. Its townsfolk were on the list of congregations to which St John addressed his Book of Revelations in the New Testament. And yes, the temple was excavated by American scholars in the early years of this century.

Forwards again along the path of retreat. My svelte sultana runs smooth as satin along this western spur of the Silk Road, cooler than before, because Brendan took out the thermostat this morning.

The earth is as red as the planet Mars, tilled by horse, without tractor marks, as easy-natured as raked gravel in a Japanese Zen garden. Later on, wind-borne sediment, the ochre loess, rises into soft cliffs, ten storeys high, swathed in grass and pricked with sprays of daisies and stubby buttercups.

Four new CDs are in the cartridge, the traffic is not heavy and daylight will be with us for hours. Contentment sprinkles down like falling confetti, the orderly, confident progress of the Grand Tour.

Bitter memories of our winter retreat are rolled back with every mile. Victory beckons. The struggle was great but the rewards greater. Gradually a rhythm mounts, like on a child's swing, faster and faster, up, up. We are rocketing past the other traffic. Judge the speed of the car in the distance, judge the oncoming truck, pour on the power. As the truck passes, hit the gap, balance the wheel as two tons crosses the crown of the road, stabilise. See the speedometer needle sweep round like the second hand of an old Swiss chronometer. The Bentley makes her pass. Recross the crown, glance in the dashboard-mounted mirror. As often as not the overtaken car is now clinging to its own kerb. Settle back, sight the next target.

The bull-neck bonnet and radiator become part of me once more, steering is subconscious, like a dream of flying; you only look and you are there.

Then a long, straight ascent breaks the spirit of my charging mare. She stumbles, misfires, backfires repeatedly. There is nowhere to pull over out of the path of the juggernauts grinding up the gradient behind us, closing in for their revenge. Perhaps there will be a lay-by, as sometimes waits at the end of such climbs – it would be lethal to break down on the slope itself. She struggles on towards the top. Come on, old girl, come on.

A petrol station, complete with restaurant, appears at the very last moment. As we pass the pumps, the suffragette protests with a tremendous backfire and her engine dies. We roll to a halt on the far side of the forecourt.

In the restaurant I look out at the gentle rain and wonder. Brendan is on his plane by now, so it is down to me.

If it is ignition timing then it should not have happened so suddenly. A part slipped or snapped. Anyway, I would not dare reset the points, trying to copy Brendan's trick with the mirror under the flywheel. But the condenser, well that's accessible enough. The only spare I have is for a V8, but then one of those already fitted is a V8's. Brendan was puzzled by that. I sit in the restaurant, leafing through the green leather handbook. It says:

In places where the engine misfires or fails to start, and this condition is obviously not due to petrol starvation, it is possible the condenser is at fault. The wire should be disconnected from the suspected condenser and reconnected to the spare. The faulty condenser should be renewed at the earliest opportunity.

Why can't I write like that?

*

A minibus waits at the hospital terminus right on the outskirts of Izmir. Its driver starts up, toots and moves forward a foot or two. The last passengers hop aboard. The bus lurches and sways. The road is too rutted for me to write.

*

Central Izmir yet again. The chef and owner of the kebab house in the street where Brendan and I ate last night are their usual generous selves. We work out the bill before he starts cooking. White Formica tables stand over sawdust on the blue-tiled floor. The ground is solid beneath my feet, and that is all. My beloved madam is on a forecourt 100 miles away, dead. And I am back at the coast. Tomorrow is Easter Sunday, so no help from England.

Size is of little consequence in the world of mechanisms. To lose a whole front wheel assembly, wishbones, coiled spring, damper and bearing-mount may look serious, but it has no worse effect than breaking the petal-thin flange on a distributor rotor – an inch-long sliver of foil curved over like a scorpion's tail. I spent this afternoon trying to replicate the conductivity, elasticity and smoothness of this small device. And failed.

First I thought it was the condenser. Well, I wanted it to be. I even found a third spare, a mysterious, well-worn lookalike of the original, which Brendan must have left behind for me. I tried all four alone, and paired in each possible combination, while the engine cooled and the distributor cap unstuck itself. When the experiments changed nothing, I put back the original two units, eased away the jammed distributor cap and looked inside. The foil contact, the scorpion's tail which should have pressed up to the central hub of the new cap, had snapped. A telltale dust of copper contact shavings lay around. How could it be worn out after so short a distance? I had pointed out to Brendan how strangely bent to one side the foil was when he fitted it, but he said that was the way it should look. Did he not see what I was pointing at? Or not understand what I was trying to say? But, he must have seen it. He spent long enough on the points. Was the problem the very number of times the distributor cap came off and on yesterday? No, the foil was bent from the start.

The remaining daylight was spent in the company of Salateen, a young man who drove me from the petrol station to the nearest village, and Shereef, the *otoelektrik* he took me to. We sat on a boulder in a sheep pen on the side of a hill overlooking the village school and the wet green valley beyond. Between glasses of tea we disputed the options in sign language. We made our rival replica scorpion tails from snipped-up cans and electrical flanges. We agreed on a Mark III version by him, gluing it into place on top of the original rotor arm.

For a hectic ten minutes while we were doing this, the village was ravished by long convoy of cars waving red flags with a white leaping horse motif.

'Democracy,' said Shereef with a look of despair.

Neither Shereef nor Salateen had seen the Bentley or had any idea about her. So they came along. We all enjoyed that moment when impossibility becomes belief as our Turkish chuff-chuff pulled up next to the Marble Marvel, upon whom we would test our backstreet handiwork. While they paced around admiring her and tried out the driving seat, I pondered again on her sense of timing, to have expired in this particular forty-foot fraction of forecourt on a road otherwise devoid of garages for forty miles.

We tried our DIY rotor, and the scorpion tail was too long. Snip, snip. And again too long. Snip, snip. The craft of an afternoon was chewed to nothing by rude pliers, while the battery ran down with our churning attempts to start her.

Rather than make My Lady a village spectacle outside Shereef's workshop, I paid off the unsuccessful crew, shut the CDs and my second suitcase in the car itself and hitched a fitful lift back to the suburbs of Izmir. Having picked up hitchhikers all the way from Marseilles, becoming one seemed reasonable enough.

Once on the two-hour ride, I woke to find my driver stopping on the gravel verge and walking back up the road in the dusk looking at the ground. I thought perhaps he had hit a chicken and wanted it for supper. In fact the windscreen wiper in front of me had come away while I slept. He did not find it, so there was not much to stay awake for after that.

Then came the unsprung minibus and a wet walk to Izmir main post office. Assisted at different stages by a shoeshine boy, a policeman, the man who sold phone *jetons* to me in the autumn and at Christmas, the international operator and several Turks with telephones with likely numbers living 100 miles due east of Izmir, I explained to the pump attendant at the garage where the Bentley lies stricken, whose phone number I had forgotten to take, that the car would be on his forecourt for at least three days because England was closed for Easter and the new part would not be flown out before Tuesday. A needle in a haystack takes hours. The correct Easter present for a Lady rather longer.

Day 26

EASTER DAY 1989. A cheaper hotel, the same old city. Yesterday, when the Bentley was running perfectly, there seemed nothing remarkable to life. Now that everything is in pieces, the story is equally plain.

After breakfast I go for a walk. A shady double avenue of palms presents a bench to sit upon and scheme. Pigeons coo overhead, like sonorous thoughts, as they did all my childhood outside my bedroom window. They hover as if to fan themselves free of dew. They settle in pairs on one branch, then take flight again for the sheer joy of existence. So it should be with my spirits. Whatever is happening to the car up in the hills cannot be stopped. It is pointless to worry, for example about the chilly breeze here meaning frost up there.

Someone turns on some music. But the pigeons coo louder. Their consoling tones are helped by the sound of tennis balls plopping in a garden behind me.

Intrusive panic is pushed back by the tide of morning calm.

*

The train station at the airport is as silent as a motorway church. Its passed-over peace is welcome after a morning spent scurrying between airline offices.

The airport ticket girls who understand the subtle migrations of European charter planes were as charming as ever. Was it their intelligent responses, their slim, pretty forms or their balanced, easy manner that made them so attractive? Their answers are what count: charter flights from London start on April 15th, nearly three weeks away. So my package of spare parts will have to come as cargo with Turkish Airlines. Hopefully it can make tomorrow evening's flight, leaving Heathrow at 6 p.m. There is not one tonight.

Or is there? I dash back up the platform, over the footbridge and into the departure lounge to ask (there isn't), miss my train (the last of the day) and retire grumpily to the groundside restaurant.

Looking down from the eatery window, vehicle spoor patterns the airport apron. Pools of clean concrete mark where jet engines have fanned back the marching loess that in time buries temples and even airports. Either side of the track which the service van takes towards the arriving plane, a gratin of soil has already accumulated. Each machine follows the trace of its predecessors, as if the level concrete beyond was somehow out of bounds.

On this field of infinite possibilities the sheep-like human mind is shown in all its mutton-headedness.

The top rim of the beer can blocks the distant black hills. They become waves rolling in from the east to the shingle beaches of family holidays. The North Sea rollers would build and build as they ran over the shallows where sea anemones slimed your feet if the tide was out. Relentless, muddied, always with that glassy, concave aspect, like furlong-wide ploughshares, raising the horizon, lifting short legs, they would advance on all without distinction, to be dived through or caught by the body-surfers. They were frightening in themselves and, like these hills, they were sure to tumble you and swill you in the gravel eventually.

*

With no more trains, an aircrew bus takes me back into the city. We drop the hostesses one by one at their apartments around Izmir. So elegant on board, they look gawky outside their natural habitat.

I am the last to be set down, some way from my hotel, and I walk through the closed bazaar, a mile of locked shops, finding instead a car boot sale of similar proportions. There are clothing lanes, bicycle parts streets, a cul-de-sac with battered baby-buggy wheels laid out in rows, and one with second-hand gas cookers. These are the fruits of serious scavenging, for a society which still repairs things, not for tourists. I get the hard sell only once in half an hour of prowling. Will the souks of Syria leave me in peace like this? I dump the car's documents in the hotel and return for more, now safe from pickpockets.

I have an idea these rotor arms may be sold in street markets, or at car boot sales.

*

After dark, down at the post office. What words to use when I call Brendan at home? Can I ask his help on his first evening back? Fear is lurking just out of sight. Sometimes it glints, like a jellyfish breaking the surface. At such moments I take to my bed. Then the stinging sack dives and I can walk the streets, but cautious even to cross a road, double-checking whatever might provoke bad fortune.

If Brendan can assemble the parts, someone could deliver them to the Turkish Airlines cargo desk at Heathrow. The items would catch the TK988 flight tomorrow evening, clear customs on Tuesday morning and by that night My Lady could be on the road. If the plan is set up tonight, there will still be time to search Izmir tomorrow morning for a rotor arm, even before England awakes, and call off the Red Cross parcel if what I need turns up. But really, now that the scorpion tails have shown their power, I must have two rotor arms, one spare, before it is safe to go on.

Brendan says there is no way he can help on a bank holiday Monday.

Think Tuesday. The direct flights are too early to be able to put a package on them. Think Wednesday. That means no delivery before Thursday morning, and a week wasted. Who knows what will have happened up in the hills by then? Think of friends who can help. Many will escape London for Easter. Most telephones are switched to answerphone. My girlfriend told me not to ring, it would be expensive and she might be out and would be disappointed to miss me.

I call her home in Halsey Street anyway. Her mother answers.

'Hello, can I speak to Miranda?'

'But, my dear, she has gone to Paris.'

Paris is where her old boyfriend is at business school.

*

My sister Celina is in. We discuss pick-ups and drop-offs down a crackly line and are cut dead in mid-plan. The international operator seems to be rattled. When I try to phone back, the same operator has a mental block and repeatedly dials an earlier number I asked for, where my older sister, Tessa, has now returned home, so that I seem to be going mad, or am the victim of extraordinary coincidence, misrouted again and again 2,000 miles to a completely different number, to a voice that is so nearly right but hasn't the first idea what is going on, and whom I hope to spare the bother of finding out because it's Easter and it's bad enough having to explain it once. We are all tied up in knots.

As I walk the dark waterfront, a saloon car screams past, horn blaring. Further up the harbour the road is closed by a crowd singing and dancing. In front of their headquarters, the people are celebrating a victory.

'What is this?' I ask.

He points me to the sign. *Sosyaldemokrat Halkçı Parti.* 'Social Democrat Popular Party,' he says.

The televisions in the seafront bars show the local election results coming in. The motif of the Social Democrats suggests a crown of spears. The leaping horse is not in evidence. The screens alternate between the poll coverage and a documentary/propaganda film of Turkey's economic transformation since the mid-1960s; how many electricity pylons have been built, the opening of the Bosphorus Bridge, children's playgrounds, waterfronts more bewitching than this one, smart boardrooms and groaning breakfast tables.

Turkey's democracy is young and fragile. The army seized power twice in the past twenty years. Political parties were banned until six years ago. Since the 1983 elections, a coalition centre-right government has been led by Prime Minister Turgut Özal. Özal started as a miners' union negotiator and was involved in a government liberalisation programme before the last military coup. His Motherland Party coalition was re-elected with a reduced majority two years ago and filed for Turkey to join the EEC.

Shortly afterwards, Özal's plane crashed in suspicious circumstances, but he walked away. He also narrowly missed an assassin's bullet during his party conference in June. His overtures to Turkey's minorities in the east have raised hackles. Apart from the Kurds' dream of self-rule (he is part-Kurdish himself), a question hangs over the country: was or wasn't there an Armenian genocide during World War I? Özal seems to be facing down the nationalists on such issues.

Today is also election day in Gorbachev's Russia. Here, as there, the riot police are sitting in their coaches in the side streets, with orders not to intervene. Free voting in Russia. Where will it all end?

Day 27

Monday morning, the day I should have been crossing into Syria, and I am still at the start line. The warren of shops in the motor mechanic district has yielded four correct headlamp bulbs, though they are like gold dust in England. Remember the night I told the police I would buy a bulb here, six months ago? Little did I know. But no rotor arm. Also, a new suspicion is forming. I have shown the distributor caps around on the off-chance – having brought both back from the interior – and Brendan's distributor cap looks different inside from the old one.

The new one has a smooth copper ring round the high-tension contact, but the old one has neat notches in its ring, making a separate contact for each of the six spark plug cables. That copper dust under the new cap when I removed it tells a tale: the ring must have been shaved down in its hundred-mile life. Even if the new rotor arm comes, it may not work for lack of properly phased contact. So, I need a new distributor cap too, although the original may get me through. How can I bother Brendan and my dear sister Celina in England with this latest deduction? It will take them longer to track down… and Cairo is as far away as ever.

*

Smyrna was a port before Paris had even been imagined. Its waterfront has long since forgotten that it was once untamed. Today the harbour remains deep enough for the biggest ships, and man still scratches at its fringes, scooping out foundations for ever taller buildings.

My Lady's delay means I can read up on this. The city was not just about myrrh. It formed the end of an overland artery from Arabia, Mesopotamia and India. The Royal Road of the Persians, perfected 500 years before Christ, ran from Susa, 1,500 miles away on the Euphrates, northwest to the granaries of Lydia and then to gold mines around Sardis, in the hills where my winged wonder lies abandoned. The Royal Road was a civil engineering feat completed under Darius the Great and matched nowhere outside China at that time. The Greek historian Herodotus records its relay runners' formidable reputation for speed of delivery, whatever the weather. His words are now the motto of the US Postal Service.

Smyrna rose in Sardis' shadow, rather as Piraeus to Athens, or Ostia to Rome. Around 500 BC Sardis razed it to the ground; but the offspring recovered, and in Alexander the Great's time surpassed its parent, as the gold ran out and the focus of power in the ancient world swung west.

Homer and Aristides paid tribute to the cool zephyr winds here which mitigate the Mediterranean heat, as they do this morning.

Two centuries before Christ, Smyrna had sensed the rise of Rome and sent ambassadors. The Romans in turn were captivated by the charms of this entrepôt culture. Like Sardis, Smyrna is a dedicatee of the Book of Revelations. But unlike

Sardis, Izmir has held its own through the ebb and flow of Greeks, Romans, Crusaders, Saracens, Ottomans, Greeks again and then, after the blood-soaked population swaps in the 1920s, Turks.

*

By train up to the airport, where a question at the air cargo office brings good news. As of this week a Tuesday night TK988 comes from London. So we will have the rotor arm at the car by Wednesday evening, latest.

*

The sun breaks through and the ships gleam in the sound. Time to celebrate with some seafood. Smyrna fishermen still catch big sea bass to be grilled and served at tables overlooking the panorama. Coffee is poured from brass pots into delicate blue and gold enamelled cups with matching saucers. The hubble-bubble in the corner makes me sneeze – its smoker's jaundiced complexion is no advertisement, but it sets off the orange of the tube mouthpiece. Watercraft chop into the wind across the harbour, sending up a spray from their bows which catches the light. Similar misty haloes hover along each ridge of the hills to the south.

In a different maze of shops, resorting to a compass when lost, I buy thin-nosed pliers, jump-start cables and a red metal oil can worked by a lever and lifting pump in the traditional style. Then I retreat to bed. Is all this sleep beneficial, harmful or irrelevant?

*

The P.O. boxes in the main post office are next to the phone booths. The postmaster has provided wooden steps to help the shorter customers reach the top row. There are 1,014 of these lockable cubbyholes. In all my time sitting beside them waiting for calls to connect, autumn, winter and spring, I have never seen one being used.

The latest call gets through. Dear Celina says that a package is landing for me tonight. Tonight. She's just brilliant! I can't believe it. An Easter miracle. We vaguely discuss sending a distributor cap to Amman in Jordan, rather than here. After she hangs up, I discover that the telex number I gave her for the Ephesus seems to be wrong; I ought to have used the telex number of this post office. But in England the family has now gone out to celebrate my parents' thirty-fifth wedding anniversary. Their home answerphone is switched off.

Tomorrow and tomorrow and tomorrow.

Oh, stop complaining! Grow up. Think how lucky you are.

*

In a narrow side street, under a starry sky, two restaurants stand opposite each other. Both have red doors, tables on the pavement, blue table cloths, bright lights under the awnings. Both are clean, both offer kebabs and mixed grills. The one with flowers on the table is more expensive. Neither has any customers. Are they in competition, at daggers drawn, or under the same ownership?

Out there at the airport my life is coming in to land.

Day 28

Tuesday morning, hot sunshine. Waiting for the bus to the airport. The telex link with my parents has been opened. Who would believe it, a telex machine in the house where I grew up? Trust Papa. He always was one for technology.

The latest plan is:

1. Collect the pack of parts from customs at the airport now;
2. Go out to the Bentley, start her;
3. Bring her back tonight and collect a second package of spares tomorrow at the same time – then I will have a replacement distributor cap.

*

Izmir airport cargo customs house, a whole new warren to run round and in.

Clutching several rubber stamps in each hand, officials in different corners of the warehouse hammer on the stack of duplicate forms that each package creates. At the start of the exercise I queried their documentation fee. What did it pay for? My question has been answered – a theatre ticket with audience participation. Like a paperchase, I run upstairs, downstairs, near and far. Thump! Another linocut hits my document. Go to the left-hand gate, says a woman. No, before you go, you must pay 1,500 lira warehouse fee, 50 pence, less than a dollar. You don't have a 200-lira (10 cents) Turkish postage stamp? Oh well, we'll sell you one. Now go over there and have this paper signed again. My, my! Is that the time? It's lunch already. Please wait an hour.

I laugh involuntarily as the bureaucrats toy with the mortal remains of my holiday. And tomorrow the novelty will be gone. When I fetch the distributor cap, I may burst into tears. Why would anyone take a holiday to such a hidebound hole? I look away, out of the office, out through the warehouse door to the horizon four ridges away. On the peak of the last mountain a ruined castle is silhouetted.

It reminds me of the distant Drachenfels in my schooldays. Was school so well conceived as life's sneak peek, that we grow sentimental for those ways?

*

Lunch hour is over. Tamely I am led to the next office for more bookkeeping and three further rubber stamps.

'Come, stand here.'

Two pieces of paper are offered and accepted. I wait.

The package from London appears, is handed to me and I am alone in the empty space.

*

Beyond the train window, a horse tills the earth, pulling a ploughshare on which a man stands wearing a turban. Each time the horse stops, the man topples against its rump.

The people lying on the railway embankment wave warmly as the train passes.

At the station a young man leaps from the platform on the other side of the tracks as the train chugs out, runs beside us and catches our last carriage. I have wanted to do that myself on occasion.

The images pass faster. The stream bed runs muddy but its banks are dyed blue. A brown nanny goat leads her two kids across.

A boy is flying a kite in the middle of his friends' football match.

The train stops at each station for maybe ten seconds. The guard of the train has a squeaky mouth whistle for 'All Aboard' that sounds like a canary. My ticket cost me about 3p, 5 cents. I can't work out exactly what it was from the change in Turkish lira.

The railway is an object of pride. Its stationmasters walk with a swagger. Its ticket inspectors are educated men.

People who live in the fork between two tracks seem to feel no resentment, rather a sense of drama. The men in the shanty towns are drab but the women wear yellows and reds. The tracks are green with grass and the trees are in bloom. Shepherd boys lead a flock down the railway line through the station.

The level crossing gates rise with the train still moving in front of the cars. The air stinks of raw sewage.

The platform guard snatches my ticket and tears it up.

We are back in Izmir.

And that girl is in Paris.

*

The second package of spare parts could not catch today's plane, and in a frantic exchange of telexes from the post office I ask my beloved family to send it to the other side of Turkey, to Adana airport, where I say I will be the day after tomorrow.

My job in London gives me thirty working days' paid leave a year, six weeks. The allowance was increased from twenty-five this spring. It sounds plenty, and if you add Christmas, Easter and weekends it is. But now I have wasted another six days dawdling in western Turkey, four of them working days. That is thirteen per cent of my year's quota. At this rate I will never reach Cairo.

As in the details, so in the broader picture: I must break out of this tail-chasing, or I will wake up with my life over.

*

A bus bearing a destination town name 1,200 miles away drops me at the isolated garage, back in the hills. I expect the worst. And yet, as if protected by her own improbability, My Lady stands untouched by the days and nights beside the Royal Road. I find that I even forgot to lock the doors. So much for coach windows bathed in goat's blood.

I plug in the new rotor arm, hook the jump leads up to a helpful car and spin the engine. The local populace stands around, one tractor driver being vastly hostile, and the motor just doesn't fire. The Turks are full of suggestions, the farmer hurls abuse; the only hope is to send them gently away and think.

I settle down to another infamously greasy soup. By alternating with spoonfuls of thick rice my throat is tricked into swallowing.

Brainwave.

Try the pre-Brendan distributor cap. After making the exchange, my temperamental Lady starts without jump leads. But one cylinder is still asleep. What are the odds of making it to Adana on five cylinders? If I practised whittling on Brendan's distributor cover, could I bring the cap that works into enough definition to get the sixth cylinder firing? Over a second supper, feeling almost heroic, even that seems possible. And if not, so be it. Adana is only 600 miles away from here; 600 mountainous miles on five cylinders is nothing.

*

One-hundred-and-seventy miles through the night, and we both deserve a rest. The temperature has been dropping steadily and the Bentley, without her thermostat or sixth cylinder, has been running very cold. Actually it is the fifth cylinder, not the sixth, which is proving problematic, as revealed by a little experiment with the engine running, pulling off individual spark plug leads.

To save the piston, I've kept our speed to between forty and fifty miles per hour, except on steep hills when around twenty is the norm. In any case, most lorries do thirty on the level and ten on hills, so overtaking is not too dangerous.

I got caught on the wrong side of a solid white line by traffic police on just such an ascent about 100 miles back and was spot-fined £9. With lorries doing five miles an hour, the police can fine every car that passes. Very lucrative. I was only managing ten miles an hour myself.

My Karaman woolly hat is on and I am looking forward to sleep. Nothing entices quite like warm, contour-stitched red leather.

Day 29

Cobalt sky, distant snowcapped mountains, cold; cold that drives you to the bottom of your blankets to suffocate rather than face the day. But buds and sprays of blossom on the trees peep through the windows, and the sun warms any skin that dares peep back.

Another workman pushes another metal-handled wheelbarrow. Without gloves. It doesn't bear contemplating.

Trucks around me in the fuel station car park are warming their engines. It is time to try starting mine.

*

The Royal Road crosses the upland plain north of Konya by a route different to my Christmas attempt from Pamukkale. For league after league, the pastureland rolls away on either side, dotted with an occasional tree. Spring is waiting in the wings. The bushes are dusted with the sheen of unburst buds. The land's musculature is enhanced by patches of green on its sunnier flanks and folds. On the distant hillside, sheep graze new grass high up the south-facing slope.

Flocks of small birds swoop about, now standing together on the road, now congregating in one shrub. A murder of magpies hops and flaps in ragged fashion, some pairing up briefly, then ignoring each other. A dozen of them fight a large harrier off a nest, one diving at great speed from above it.

The cows in the herd walk as if in calf.

*

The plain takes on new grandeur as we pick our way down to the holy city of Konya.

On one side of the road a thousand storks are feeding, scattered across two square miles. Others circle in the thermals, or patrol the perimeter airspace alone. They are on their way from Chinese-aligned East Africa to Soviet-controlled Eastern Europe via the NATO-favouring Bosphorus, oblivious to the affairs of men.

We have just passed a monumental old stone bridge, perhaps a royal one, stranded in a broad dry riverbed. The road that led to it on either side was long since swept away by the spate that comes down from the mountains in the thaw. Above it cruised three eagles, yellow as hills, their feathered wingtips splayed against the blue sky.

The countryside's immensity opens an ache, a glimpse of my lonely soul. I turn up the music. The requiem mass of Vittoria/Victoria, in crisp plainsong, steals into the cracks.

*

A hundred miles since I woke up. The day is warm. I have used this rest stop for a concerted attack on the fifth cylinder. There's a spark at the plug, but when I connect up the HT cable, it only slows down the engine, by reducing the charge to the other five cylinders. Perhaps the timing on the fifth cylinder is out individually (is that possible?) or perhaps it has a fuel problem (it shares a carburettor with four and six, so that's unlikely). Could that mean it's the distributor cap?

I am at a loss.

*

In Karaman they seem more oil-stained than in the depths of winter and even the bespectacled master welder has shrunk in height and grown fatter. Perhaps the approach of spring softens us. We have a little reunion, shaking hands, exchanging *Merhaba*s, acknowledging the durability of the front suspension, which passed the MOT, swapping gifts of fruit and drinking tea.

I mention my concern about the fifth cylinder. They tell me through the German-speaking car salesman that the fault is not electrical, but mechanical. An exhaust valve is stuck, they say. This means the other valves could go, roughly at any time from now on. They offer to do a valve change, having new ones and a new head gasket specially made in Konya.

Foxy, the car salesman, was determined I should open the engine comprehensively. The master welder melted away rather than be party to a rip-off, so we never said goodbye.

I declared that I would trust to luck and head on to the coast. The garage owner with the leather jerkin and eyes even more pugnacious than Brendan's signalled 'good', fingertips together, turned upwards like a bud.

The old Karaman is dying. They have bulldozed the ancient citadel. A gleaming red BMW is parked outside the local doctor's.

It felt comfortable to be leaving my friends.

*

Midday at the scene of the crash. The spot where the wheel broke must be one of the most barren in Turkey. The rock is too sterile to support vegetation. I stop tentatively. Dare I cut the ignition to soak up the memories of this unhappy acre? Could lightning possibly strike twice, and My Lady be immobilised here again?

I switch off and open the driver's door. The stillness and the morning sun stream in. At the bottom of the gorge which nearly claimed us, a brook is bubbling. A small bird bobs through the air in long swoops like a tail-heavy paper dart, twittering furiously as it flies. A breeze rustles the pines.

A *Tehlikeli Madde* fuel truck claxons at me from a long way off and takes the bridge over the gorge with more than a nudge of oversteer.

Peace returns. A ghost has been laid to rest.

*

The Gosku Pass is an exceptional descent, sweeping curves interspersing long, empty straights. Assisted by the steady gradient, the big tourer regains her verve. Ahead is a promised land of converging valleys and bluegrass horizons.

The elevation drains away. Gorge follows flood plain follows gorge. Depth, breadth, depth; each is announced by a fanfare of geological formations in penumbral purple. Clam shells clasped in rock thousands of feet up testify to a long stint on some antediluvian seabed. Platforms and cliffs drop from the snow line in textbook wave-cut tiers towards the fertile floor. First come pastures, then olive groves, joined by fruit orchards and finally fields of already half-grown wheat. Last Christmas' escape from winter, tumbling into Tarsus, is excelled by the Gosku in spring.

I drove up this road in the dark and saw nothing. Now is the opposite: perfection. The afternoon sun projects the colours of youth around me, scintillating mimosas, vital lilacs, all against the fertile verdure of new leaf. I stop for tea, a chance to try the soft nougat rolls bought in the freezing midnight, 300 miles back north.

*

At last the sea, and at last it is on the right-hand side, where in my dream it always has been. We still have five cylinders. I am short of words because the moment of truth is upon us. The valve check prescribed in Karaman is going to be bad news. But if I don't fix it, what chance does the car have in Syria?

*

The Tarsus crossroads, billiard-table-smooth dual carriageways after the gorge. Little traffic about.

The effect on the car is astonishing. The exhaust no longer rattles against the jacking point, and no hills demand to be climbed or lorry queues to be overtaken. The pleasures of travel are rediscovered. I have been expecting a tantrum, even a full refusal, after the liberties of the last twenty-four hours: 500 miles on little more than half an engine. Yet the woman in my wagon relents. It's as if she was insulted to be returned to her old lodgings in Smyrna, and this absurd dash through Asia Minor has restored her pride. What other explanation can there be? Denser air at sea level? Better petrol? Come off it.

Yet I cannot attempt Syria like this.

My head goes round and round the same hackneyed circle. It all started with some backfires. That means timing or valves, not the plugs or the HT cable, or even a holed piston. But now we have no backfiring. If it was an exhaust valve, I'd expect frequent explosions as unburnt fuel ignited down the exhaust pipe. Perhaps it's an inlet valve. We have a spark, we may even have combustion, but no power. What if a valve holed a piston? There would be no compression. A compression test would eliminate the timing question, but not the dilemma of whether the valve or piston was holed. If it was the valve, I believe you could tell by looking at the pushrods from the tappet end. Maybe it's the valve spring that's broken. That too might be replaceable without lifting the head – one of the benefits of a side-valve design, I think.

The problem with opening the top half of an engine is gaskets. You need a perfect seal when you bolt it back down to the block. On the other hand, Turkey is the country with the best intermediate technology. Could they not make a perfect one-off head gasket? Could they cut and grind a perfect exhaust valve? Would my long-suffering lass be permanently immobilised? Worse still, would their valve springs break up after a thousand miles, in Syria or Sinai? Is there a chemical trick for decarbonising valves? Where are the exhaust valves on this car anyway?

*

Adana. US super-base for NATO. The airport is closing for the night. In a cavernous hanger, dwarfed by empty voids, I receive instructions from Turkish Airlines cargo for the collection tomorrow.

Hurrying back to the town, the main post office is still open. A long-suffering postman agrees to send a last telex. It is, after all, 11 p.m. I fire their telex number off to England, to my equally long-suffering father, in hope of finding a message about the parts delivery on my return in the morning. Then I walk round to the restaurant. The heroine of the day stands there, far calmer than her driver.

When she swept up earlier to park on the reserved kerb, an oleaginous greeter opened what he expected to be the driver's door, bowing, quite beside himself at the size of tip he would so earn; and then had a fit when I walked off from the other side into the night to send the telex.

Now coming back to eat supper, I playfully creep behind him while he stares furiously up and down the street, and find a table without him seeing me. He scours the horizon right through my first course, only to have another fit when he looks round and finds the object of his fury sitting in the window right behind him, doing justice to the chef and my parking space. Childish, I know. I show my gratitude on the way out.

*

The white queen backs silently among her castles and pawns, the bins and washing lines between two tenement blocks. She is a wraith, a phantom, a ghost, a spirit stealing warily among sleepers. We reach the safest chess square, a small courtyard, out of sight from the street, and I cut the lights and motor. Without opening the doors I climb over the massive front recliners and into the back seat. For a time I loll across the sofa, listening as the bodywork settles and cools. A cat is walking on her roof, now lying on the warm bonnet. If one of those dogs I hear barking spots us we are both dead meat. But if not, we'll be warmer than either was last night.

The big-bore exhaust ticks gently as it cools.

Day 30

A blissful, fathomless sleep, comfortable and secure; and a slow awakening, with sunshine clipping the west wall of the courtyard. I am a deep sea diver decompressing slowly before the surface, stopping for leisurely pauses at every critical state between dream and reality. Three baker's boys in white coats look in at the dashboard and converse appreciatively for several minutes before they see me lying in the back. A cock begins to crow.

It takes me to Italy when I was seven and heard a cockerel for the first time and wondered what it was – sad suburbanite that I am. Italian cockerels don't go cock-a-doodle-do. This back seat shares the sounds of that farmhouse upper room.

A Turkish girl walks up, seven too perhaps, dressed in a parody of school uniform – blazer, skirt, straw boater, satchel and the trance of the just-woken. She trails her hand along the coachwork as she passes. After the constant sight of kids earning a crust on the streets or in the workshops, the idea of school and learning seems bizarre.

*

Morning tea with the director of the Central Bank branch in Adana.

I was changing some money in anticipation of garage bills, and he asked me into his comfortable office to join his daily ceremony.

In his dark suit, behind a high-tech black desk, he waves me to a black leather armchair. He is greying a little, but still lean. We are a long way from the road menders' hut in the mountains, but the solemnity of morning tea is the same. Glasses warmed. Water discarded. Outside, through the venetian blinds, the orange trees around the Bentley are being watered too. I guess he saw me park.

The banker talks about the elections I have witnessed; of sixty-seven Turkish cities, the government held only two. Although they still have a majority in the countryside, they have no mandate and will possibly have to relinquish power. The banker expects inflation to soar. But he seems relaxed about the wider future and his mind wanders to domestic affairs. He has two daughters and drives to Cesme of all places in August, to the bank's holiday apartments.

'The Mediterranean here is not blessed with zephyrs like the northwest. I would like to get out of Adana for the three months of summer, not just three weeks,' he says. 'But one must work.'

At the moment, springtime, we agree his home town is beautiful. Over a second glass of tea, I feel bold enough to ask about the importance of travel in Islam.

'You will find as a lone traveller that you are given respect. The Prophet (peace be upon him) was a traveller. Travel can bring us to know God.'

'Does the Koran say that?' I ask.

'Well, not in those words. But the lone traveller is mentioned many times. The traveller in difficulty is mentioned with the widow and orphan. And travel is encouraged. "Travel, go round the world!" This is in the Koran. Also "Explore the side roads". Then there is pilgrimage. The haj to Mecca. I have not done this myself, but I hope to. To go by land, not as a holiday, that is a real journey. Pilgrims are changed by it and afterwards will show this respect to other pilgrims. The journey gives humility.

'When we die we will be alone before our maker, and if we have travelled and seen his glorious creation, that should help. Islam has a saying, "In this world, be like a stranger or traveller along a path".'

'I believe that too,' I say.

'You will see, travelling is life in miniature.'

*

I walk up to the main post office and, yes, a telex has come in overnight. My father confirms that the second package should be at the airport already. Bless him.

Sons tend to find their fathers an embarrassment. It is a relationship doomed from the first time your dad swings you up impossibly high, kicks a ball impossibly far, untangles the impossible knot in your kite-string, or just sings you to sleep.

After that Superman start, fathers prove human, fallible, weak. They break promises, punish the innocent, ignore their paperwork, play mind games and increasingly run out of puff. Somewhere in your teens you are bigger and stronger and brighter than them. They become grouchy, critical, irrational and self-pitying, if not clinically depressed. They bear no comparison to other people's dads. They disrespect your mum. Half the time you wish them dead.

And yet, you doubt that you could do what they do, what they have done. If you were ever so lucky as to try, you would be a worse father than them. You would fail where they have failed. And where they succeeded. You could not afford the presents they could, let alone those they could not – remember that half-scale Lotus 49 Grand Prix car you lusted over, at the first Earls Court Motor Show your dad took you to?

What a spoilt brat you would have been, had he given you the chance.

You would be hard-pushed even to love as he has loved.

Hell, you even start to look like them. You fit their clothes. This tweed jacket with its two poacher's pockets? Yes, a hand-me-down from Papa.

Would I have the patience to source and send a classic car distributor head by courier to a son of mine? Would I follow up with a friendly note like this? Will my house, decades hence, be the only home in the neighbourhood with the equivalent of a telex machine, just so my thirty-year-old son can 'phone home'?

How much of the time will *he* wish *me* dead?

I hurry back to the bank to meet two mechanics whom the bank director has recommended.

*

Here is a garage in Adana I'd never have found on my own – something of an old-timer specialist. The approach is obscured by wrecked and rusting Americana, as the customs warehouse in Izmir was screened by crushed German metallica. I wait while a much-decalled Turkish Fiat has a wheel changed. Then my own problem child manoeuvres into the single bay. From deep in the front passenger footwell I release the left-side bonnet catch to demonstrate the spark plug mystery.

The foreman, short, round and again with that dictator scowl, shakes his balding head and shows his small audience that number three cylinder seems to be dead too.

*

Back to the airport by taxi, to the Turkish Airlines cargo building. The gloom reminds me of Izmir's Defence Ministry a year ago. A repair man is dusting graphite over the innards of a hand-cranked adding machine. With its cover plate off and basket weave of innards exposed, it looks even more like a dinosaur. But the technician is up to the moment, a skilled professional, as far as he is concerned.

An hour passes. Outside, the air over the roof of a black estate car is beginning to shimmer with heat, although the breeze is cool enough, when it blows. A giant ant runs across the concrete at my feet.

Eventually my queries meet a solid response. Turkish Airlines cargo cannot trace my package. Come back at two o'clock and we may have an answer. They've told the central computer (or maybe it's an adding machine) that the parcel is urgently awaited here. But it won't be coming in from Izmir. There are no direct Izmir flights. Knowing the capacity for creating paperwork at Izmir airport cargo, they might as well send the parts in a bottle round by sea.

Time for patience.

*

Her Ladyship is having her nails painted. A phial of pearlescent pink nail varnish has been bought from the chemist. The terminals on the distributor cap for cylinders five and three are being isolated using the nylon lacquer as insulation. An air hose is used to dry the lurid liquid. The distributor is then reassembled.

A small boy scrambles into the driver's seat, turns the centrally mounted key and My Lady catches like a Spitfire. For thirty seconds she runs smoothly and then the roughness returns. But to have heard those thirty seconds is sweet indeed. It means the problem is only electrical, not a valve or piston.

A burly mechanic in a green factory coat holds the varnish bottle up to the light with a discrimination normally reserved for sommeliers or the more expensive corners of wine emporia. The acetate solvent was not completely mixed. He shakes the bottle and begins brushing on more glaze. Nail varnish is a brilliant insulator, he signals to me. A dewy rose drop of the shellac falls on Bathsheba's front wing, perfectly complementing her white complexion. But the coating isn't yet doing what it should for the electrics.

I am happy to wait. A cure will be here some day from England. And nail varnish will never be the same again.

*

From where I sit on my nursery stool in the shade of the garage wall, I can see one black tail fin and the brown vinyl soft top of a 1959 Cadillac Eldorado Biarritz two-door convertible. Lanky and low, this treasure of Detroit's golden age is hidden up a blind alley between the paint shop and an exhaust shed, with a mere Mercedes backed up to its boot. I wouldn't want to be crossing deserts in one, but for arriving at a summer ball, or a beach party, nothing, not even a Bentley, could beat it. Just look at the absurd fins with double-torpedo red tail lights on each; the yards of quality chrome; the flawless, immensely long body lines; the ice-cream scoop of a tinted windscreen; the four-foot doors; the elegant power hood; the General's best V8, matched by a wildly ambitious speedometer; a boot you could manoeuvre a Mini in. Even the authentic cobwebs and dust swell my intoxication.

For the first time since England, I covet someone else's car.

The man says he is being paid about £3,000 to put it back on the road. The mechanics whistle at this vast sum. In its present condition, it must be worth much less than that to them. Done up in L.A. it would fetch five times, maybe

Above: Turkey, Izmir, Day 24. In the customs pound with (left to right) mechanic Brendan, the pound foreman and Mr. Topkara (page 75)

Below: Turkey, Adana, Day 30, 'A phial of pearlescent pink nail varnish has been bought from the chemist.' (page 101)

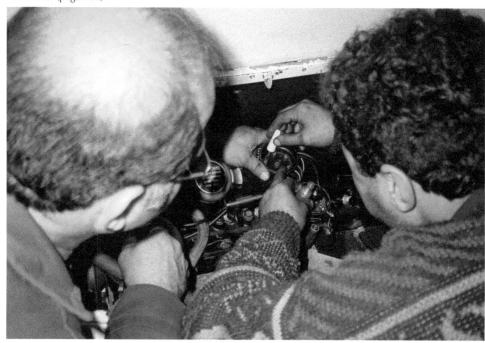

even ten times, more in the right colour. I dream that one day I'll fly out and place a bid. To drive it back to England would be enough.

*

The nail varnish has worked. The Bentley becomes a fluffed and boa-ed dame, a purring Persian White among the wrecked and riddled shells. The foreman turns his eyes to the crooked front wheel. What passed among the mountain men of Karaman is just not good enough down here in civilisation. Knowing how much it would cost at home, and the need to protect the tyre and hydraulics for many miles yet, I accept his offer to straighten the wheel up to vertical. It will give me a chance to check the coil spring too. Anyway, there is time while we wait for the package from London.

With a whole afternoon free, we could even talk to the paint shop. Anyone for a pearlescent pink Bentley to match the nail varnish? It's a colour they sell here off the shelf.

A boy I gave an apple to brings me some tea and a small tin dish of sugar. For the first time since the freezing forecourt north of Konya, I peel away the heavy woollen socks and jumper. I move my nursery stool into the sun and put the saucer of sugar on the ground near my bare feet. It distracts the fly that's battering itself against them.

Where is my sense of urgency? Am I numbed by the déjà vu? Or just falling for the oldest holiday mistake in the book. Losing track of the days. Relaxing.

Today is Friday. Or is it Thursday? Last Friday night was Izmir. Saturday up in the hills. Sunday, Monday Izmir. Tuesday north of Konya. Wednesday night Adana. So it's only Thursday. Good. We need all the days we can get.

After an hour stretched out in the sun warming my joints while the front suspension is stripped, I stroll the couple of miles back down to the airport to give the cargo department another poke.

*

A man is shouting down the telephone and I am deep in *War and Peace*. My panama hat is on his coffee table and the desk fan cools us in turn as it oscillates equitably back and forth. Through the net curtains, spring is turning into summer. The director of cargo services dials another number and yells again. They would hear him in Istanbul even if they hung up. He gives the packet number several times and repeats ADANA, ADANA. A long pause. Then more shouting. The marble floor was chosen with the dodgy telephone network in mind.

'SIR!' his voice is locked in a permanent shout from working his telephone. 'The packet will come from Istanbul tonight. Maybe. Come back at ten o'clock tomorrow morning.'

We shake hands and I leave.

*

We are rehanging the front wheel, running into the night to set up the geometry. The front left-hand wheel has a worn vertical pin. The tracking of the right-hand one is skew. We aim for the tolerances my father so kindly telexed from Jack Barclay, 1″ negative camber and $^1/_{16}$″ toe-in. It seems ambitious indeed. How the mechanic in the green overalls could expect to redrill the lower suspension with such accuracy, by eye and without taking any measurements, defeats me. But in the end we have them precisely.

Now we swap the two least worn tyres on to the front wheels to even out the wear rate among all five.

The starter Bendix drive has been oiled to prevent it jamming in the disengaged position; a hose from the engine to the demister has been changed; and a boy has tightened up the jacking point that knocks the exhaust pipe. I asked him to ease it off, but how much can one explain across a total language gap?

The foreman is quietly delighted with the present I give him, my remaining cigarette lighter with flintless ignition. The bill is £15. Everybody shakes hands.

*

The nail varnish lasts just long enough to glide the Bentley serenely to the airport. I put her behind the guarded security fence in the cargo compound for the night.

In the final moments, as the nylon begins to give out, a mysterious clunking comes from the right front wheel.

I catch a taxi back into town and send a last telex to thank Papa for the data for the wheel alignment.

Then I find myself a bath and bed.

Day 31

At the cargo pen this morning the Bentley has a flat rear tyre. It takes two men ten minutes to inflate using the stirrup pump. She is not short of volunteers. The problem is temporary, an unseated valve pin, not, thank heavens, a puncture.

When the tyre is solid, I fire her up. The nail varnish seems to have recovered some function in the night, and I drive round the airfield to the main customs warehouse.

The chatter of rubber stamps greets me like musket fire in an English Civil War battle re-enactment, with the occasional cannon, the big one they hit your passport with.

As in all serious war games, this one takes a morning. The package is apparently here, but work stops on the stroke of lunch hour, three rubber stamps before they have finished with me. The man at the last booth leaves to eat and pray. This whole customs industry is a disgusting drain on the taxpayers of Turkey.

*

Still varnish-powered, the Bentley thunders back round the runways to the cargo side for them to complete the import papers; and then the new cap doesn't fit.

Slightly too small.

Is this why the last one broke, because Brendan forced it on? A half-hour of whittling and filing with the Swiss Army knife brings it out to the correct dimensions.

And when My Lady starts she sings.

Off we fly to Syria. My face prickles with content. Our white whirlwind storms out of Adana, twin amps and six loudspeakers pumping, sea air pouring round the wings and though the windows.

Approaching the Crusader fort where Gus the shepherd sat three months ago, I turn off and up the steep track to stop and collect my thoughts. No sheep here today. I squirt a little oil around the back of the dynamo housing, trying to reach the bearing I saw when the *otoelektrik* stripped it down in the Gaziantep pass at Christmas. The radiator has also lost quite some water. And the front suspension is clunking over bumps. Misfires are becoming frequent, like the first stages of another distributor failure, but when I investigate, they clear up.

Far below the castle, a river meanders full and fresh, stretching ten miles to the sea. The fields bask in springtime. The Syrian visa in my pocket makes the view pregnant with hope.

*

At the corner where the Mediterranean coast turns south, we follow it. My Lady has no need for an obscure crossing like Akakale. Time is too short, much as I would like to see those particular Syrian border guards again, and not just for the looks on their faces. The road is as good as the coastal highway at Tarsus, with

105

signs to Antioch. Working from US Air Force maps of the Levant, I choose the route with as few steep climbs as possible, past Iskenderun, but even so, before the last mountain range, the Bentley starts to repeat her antics, misfiring, threatening no ignition at all.

A petrol station owner suggests a local *otoelektrik*, but no one comes to lead me there, so I pluck up courage and begin adjusting the points as I saw done in Adana.

I ease off the locking screw on each of the contacts and turn them slightly against the cam. The adjustments are sure to immobilise her permanently, and I will forget even how to set them back the way I found them. Nevertheless, by the time a small boy on a bicycle arrives to lead me to the garage, I have the misfire solved. Quite a boost for confidence. I stuff his bike in the boot and give him a lift back.

*

Long after nightfall, the Bentley slows at a hill village crossroads to ask directions.

We are five miles from Syria. I give a lift to an old bull of a local with one arm who suggests his nearest lakeside restaurant for my supper.

Waving him goodbye, I walk down into a tearoom. It is glazed and verandaed, a chalet from some north European resort out of season.

The waiter puts me at a table near three leather-jacketed farmhands. I ask if I can join them. One is a crop-spraying pilot who has strong political views and feels unable to voice them in such a public place. His face is mostly scar tissue from a plane crash. He has warm, modest eyes and a passionate interest in Nicaragua, El Salvador and everywhere else he considers to be under America's thumb.

'Turkey has been developed for the benefit of America,' he says. 'The country is in danger of losing its identity.' I ask him about Germany and Japan, both of which have come out on top from military occupations more blatant than here. And indeed he is optimistic for Turkey's future. 'Except for the capitalist exploitation.' He says crop sprayers are supposed to fly only four hours per day, but sometimes do eight. His face is convincing testament to the dangers.

Day 32

Up at an early hour, I spend some time at the lakeside with the bonnet raised, experimenting with the points. A tour bus of Turkish schoolgirls pulls up at the restaurant. I fear their box brownies may provoke an unladylike response from the car. However, when I move to leave she is remarkably composed.

It is a short drive across the plain to higher hills, where the Syrian border lies hidden.

At the frontier the Bentley loses two litres of water, delayed by Turkish emigration. She also springs a new trick. Turning the key produces either a savage grinding or just a whirr. In both cases the engine does not catch. I try poking through the oil hole in the Bendix drive with a screwdriver to loosen the cog. A push start would not work because the transmission is automatic. My Lady must be towed at thirty miles per hour before her gearbox turns the engine.

Nevertheless, I think I know her mind, and round up a gang of helpful juggernaut drivers to roll her a few yards forward in a show of attention. The propitiation is accepted. She starts, to another rousing cheer from the assembled hauliers.

No-man's land between Turkey and Syria. A single-file road winds up a narrow, grassy valley between hillocks, barely wide enough for oncoming traffic to pass. A queue of nose-to-tail HGVs appears, snaking out of sight. My Lady is the only car. After ten minutes of near-stasis, not one vehicle has come the other way. This unventilated uphill crawl will boil the Bentley's fuel lines. There is nowhere to pull over and cool off. My only option is to overtake. The place is almost too scary to squeeze off a photo as I crawl past, but the sight of all these lorries is irresistible. With one hand on the wheel I lift the camera through the driver's window, over the roof, and get my shot. If I am arrested at the top, I will ask which jurisdiction I was in.

*

The Assyrians had a bad press in Sunday School. The Old Testament books of Isaiah and Chronicles started it. Then Kings II records their invasion of Israel in 700 BC. Jerusalem lies apparently defenceless before the hordes. But their mighty leader, King Sennacherib, overreaches himself. He mocks Jehovah, at which an Angel of Death kills 185,000 Assyrian soldiers in a single night, and the king withdraws. An English poet, Lord Byron, wrote of the Destruction of Sennacherib with such imagery that for a long time I thought '*The Assyrian came down like a wolf on the fold*' was a Bible quote.

Sennacherib. Builder of Nineveh. Destroyer of Babylon. Worshipper of Baal. Heir to Sargon II. Murdered by his own son.

This was his lair.

*

Unshaven customs officers bulge through their khaki uniforms; epaulettes flap absurdly; chipped grey paint; diesel-stained concrete. I am not sure what is safe to write. Can I record 'Grimy, faded, listing portraits of President Assad'? Let us say simply that this strong man has survived several assassination attempts over the years, is quick to round up and execute suspected opponents and rules more by repression than consensus.

The border force has privy-like sheds with windows for insurance, customs stamps and foreign exchange. The insurance salesman foams like a mad dog. He shouts and waves his cigarette lighter and insists that my car is a lorry. Through a teenage interpreter called Ahmed I ask for his definition of a car. It carries four people. Ha! Gotcha! Come and have a look at the Bentley. The mad dog is whipped and I have my accident cover.

Led by this young friend, the rest of the sheds fall into a natural order. My book of customs carnets raises no surprises. Everybody has one. Its authentic art deco design, so incongruous when it arrived in the post back home, now looks run-of-the-mill. Each carnet is effectively a bond issued by the UK Automobile Association (AA) on the security of my worldly assets and, like all such securities, it needs to discourage the forger. The words and lettering are from the age of Empire. It promises that I will not import the Bentley permanently. This saves me paying import duty now only to reclaim it when I leave. But it does require the other half of the paperwork to be completed on exit. So, don't go losing it!

In the shed for passports, the henchmen want my mother's first name. Not her maiden name. I laugh because who ever asks this? The rabble of truck drivers laughs too – in Arabic, Zelda apparently means 'together', which she is.

Now my guardian angel interpreter has refilled the leaking radiator and I have three litres spare in water bottles for emergencies. We exchange glances when the engine stutters. She has been close to overheating in the queues, so it may just be fuel evaporation. But with newfound confidence about setting the points and timing, I am rather less concerned than him. No hanging about. I pay my assistant and make to head for the open road. But again the old girl needs a gentle push to earn the starter motor's engagement.

After a few miles the water temperature steadies at normal and the engine runs sweetly. Only the clunking front suspension remains of the nagging doubts brought with us from Adana.

*

Entering Syria, the dictator's den, all is calm, pastoral, sunny; the CD serves up the food of love, the armchair embraces me. A man in army fatigues flags us down and his friend flashes his Kalashnikov. We look into each other's eyes and see no fear between us. He asks my name, my nationality and waves me on. The sense of rolling on forever, the next sleeping place, the next border, the next country, unbroken.

*

Aleppo Castle stands on a mighty milk-jelly mound in the centre of a bare dining-table plain. Sloped, pudding flanks rise to meet sheer, gleaming walls. Is the mound an acropolis (natural rock) or a tell (man-made)? Surely both, for it to be so large and yet so oval. Below this Syrian Ayers Rock, low, whitewashed buildings spread away on all sides, as even as a linen cloth. The limousine glides through the outskirts like a cream jug passed from placemat to placemat. I am in two minds about whether to look for the Al-Medina souk, supposedly the finest in the world, or work on the car's electrics. Pedestrians and vendors in damask smocks assist with directions to the former at every corner.

As we reach a shady square, in sight of the four-spired Great Mosque, the misfiring begins again. So much for my tourist plans. Her Ladyship is starting to overheat. With her familiar sense of occasion, she stalls just as a parking space presents itself under the trees. I roll in forwards. Beside us, across the broad pavement, is a cool café with onyx tables and wicker chairs. It feels like lunchtime. A guitar is playing. An hour for us both to cool off.

Aleppo was the third city of the Ottoman Empire after Constantinople and Cairo. It has been a conurbation for five thousand years, possibly eight. Some say it is the oldest surviving metropolis on earth, it or Damascus. The UN recently named Aleppo a World Heritage Site. But its particular charm is that it has been in decline in the modern era. The opening of the Suez Canal undercut its trade route. Then the Ottomans picked the losing side in World War I and had their empire split up. Aleppo was parted from Gaziantep to the north, and Antioch to the west – the Turkish border runs round the city barely a dozen miles away. So it lost its economic hinterland. Aleppo became a capital without a country.

Consequently, the cityscape has largely avoided high-rise architecture. Only minarets punctuate the top-floor views of half a million homes; and, of course, the endearing, upside-down baby's bath with its flat bailey behind crenellated curtain walls.

The castle must have made for a perfect sanctuary, 3,000 years BC. Nothing else compared as a defensive compound between the Mediterranean and the now long-abandoned cities to the east, at the far end of the Fertile Crescent.

The café's bread is puffed up like empty crab shells. The hummus and the chicken kebabs are fresh and succulent. Soldiers on leave stroll by in twos and threes. They wear sand-coloured shirts and their trouser legs tucked into black boots. They are so young it might be a school uniform. A youth with one leg missing clunks by on crutches. He stops and speaks in my ear words I do not understand.

After lunch I change into my dirtiest clothes in the gents, then jack the car up. I lie in the street to pull out the starter motor clutch. My arms are black to the elbows by the time it is free. Stripping it down and trying to clean it, I squat on the kerb with the garden square urchins, who are riveted by the bullet-shaped mechanism.

I am looking for the cause of the dreadful grinding noise that has met the turn of the key increasingly today. Since it was fitted in Ibiza, this Bendix drive has worked perfectly. But now an ounce of metal shavings lie in the casting, also some gravel. Where did that come from? Under the car, at the base of the flywheel case, there is an inspection flap for seeing the marks for top dead centre. The cover has been left screwed down in the open position. Road dirt has been flicking up into the flywheel housing. Brendan remarked about it being mucky. Even after the Bendix drive is refitted, it does not engage first time. My heart sinks. I try again. OK, second time will have to do. I would rather not risk switching off again. So, no visit to the souk for me. Anyway, enough time has been lost.

*

The road signs point south, the highway to Hama, Homs and Damascus. This is the industrial spine of the country. Hama saw a Muslim Brotherhood uprising seven years ago. Perhaps 100 government soldiers, Ba'ath Party officials and civil servants were killed by angry locals. Assad reacted, besieging, shelling, bombing, gassing and bulldozing districts for nearly a month, and killing 20,000, possibly many more.

Mercifully I am not here for the modern Syria. I will be heading east, in search of an older way of life.

*

At forty miles an hour we trundle across the lone and level plain. The road is straight and smooth, steady enough to write while leaning on the steering wheel as we go. A mile-long plantation to the south; then a town of flat mud boxes to the north; three girls with aluminium pans balanced on their heads, wearing long, extravagantly floral frocks; two more on donkeys, side baskets stuffed with waving grasses; cotton dresses with large green, blue, red and yellow flowers against solid dark backgrounds. A two-mile-long concrete wall on my left.

The dimensions of the plain are breathtaking. The sun is setting behind me and I seem not to have moved at all.

*

We have parked at a busy crossroads on the edge of the desert. The western sky still glows after the sunset, colouring the evening commute. Men wearing red-and-white dog-tooth headscarves wait for their rides home. A trickle of transport picks them up: tricycle motor scooters, blue-striped buses crowned with tiaras of orange lights, and road-train lorries, by twos and threes, heading in all directions out into the dusk.

Night falls like a lid closing over us.

*

The Bentley sits in a sulk just beyond the petrol pumps. I have refuelled and now her starter won't even turn.

The night is warm and stale. The pump attendant watching television in the roadway cracks his knuckles one by one. The smoke of his fresh cigarette rises, light blue against the black velvet night.

I am stranded in a land where I know no one, speak not a word.

The knife-edge we are crawling along becomes sharper again. I must stop the motor when refuelling because to leave the car running while stationary means she overheats and stalls. But if I switch off she doesn't start again.

I find a table and open the pilots' map which I first perused on the floor of my sitting room in London. It shows the desert landmarks most noticeable from the air. The ones which stood out then were:

1. Mysterious mile-long ancient walls;
2. Mysterious mounds;
3. A mysterious ruined, fortified city.

Most of these features are many miles from any road, let alone conurbation, and some appear to be unknown to Western academia. Only the ruined city has a name, Sergiopolis. So I did my background research – at one time it was the easternmost outpost of the Roman Empire.

I imagined sleeping there one night under the stars. And now I have almost made it.

After half an hour with the map and a glass of tea I return to give the starter motor one more try and it works. My Lady just needed to cool down. Let's ignore the whole episode and head on towards the desert.

Running over the plain, the faster she goes, the happier she feels. The pleasure justifies all setbacks, washes the anger out of my heart with surprising ease. We will be waking up in Sergiopolis after all, with the dawn striking the pillars of the Forum gates.

Approaching the turning off the highway, a dirt track south, the dynamo warning light flickers. Torn between ambition and experience of this occasional wink, I drive on to the next big town. It is not far. In the outskirts, the dynamo charge drops, Gaziantep-style, and the light shines constant red.

Presumably spare parts are flown in to Aleppo, or would it be Antioch?

Let's hope it's just the bushes again.

I coast on sidelights beside the moonlit Euphrates, over a modern bridge into a crumb of civilisation's feast, a place I have never heard of, Raqqa.

Day 33

The night cools. Shortly before first light I pull my rug and then the blanket over me. Only when the sun strikes the top of the nearby wall and bounces into the car does any ascent to consciousness begin.

The walnut picnic table in the seat-back by my face stares at me, then the soft woollen headlining of the car smiles down, and finally the sky peers in discreetly through the window. I push myself up the pillow to look outside.

Six bicycles, each with a long shovel strapped to the crossbar and a ten-litre oil can tied behind the saddle, are standing on fold-down legs in front of the Bentley's bonnet. Two more arrive. A dozen Syrians in long smocks and red headcloths crouch on the corners of the street in twos and threes, deep in conversation. A tray of tea glasses arrives from the right and is passed around.

A lurid blue bus trundles through.

On three sides of this backstreet intersection stand sand-coloured, low-built houses, metal shutters rolled down in front of shop windows. The fourth side is a building plot and where we parked last night.

Contrast abounds.

A woman draped from top to toe in a black gown walks past, balancing on her head a pile of sheet-bread the size of a stack of Sunday papers. Another woman in khaki pullover and khaki pleated skirt, to a 'sensible' length below the knee, strides in the other direction.

A white American pick-up truck with ping-pong-bat-sized door-mounted wing mirrors pulls up among the grazing bicycles.

No one pays my limousine a blind bit of attention.

The sun is rising fast and strikes the burr veneer door ledge beside my pillow. The first shop's steel shutter is rolled up with a clatter. A tiny schoolboy with a beret and an orange neck-scarf walks past carrying a black plastic briefcase.

Why do the workmen arrive so early only to sit and talk at the crossroads?

I should get up now and start investigating.

With every drop of my strength and patience, I remove the faulty dynamo. It took two pairs of hands to do this at Gaziantep. Copious quantities of dung are lying around, and from time to time an Arab lifts his skirts and defecates nearby. Is this a public convenience?

But I am absorbed in a life-and-death struggle with an inaccessible bolt.

I have the device free and set off on foot, balancing its heavy mass on my shoulder. Every town has a metal-bashers' quarter. I just need to find Raqqa's.

*

Another warren of workshops. More oil-stained urchins standing over me. There is some message in all this circularity, a truth gnawing its way to the conscious realm. Yes, I am stupid. But it is more than just that. More than me.

Neither English, nor French, nor German words work here. The only connection is the physical: nuts and washers, worn bearings and ground-down armatures. A man in a striped Argentine football shirt, with hair smeared across his bald crown like a World Cup veteran, has disassembled the dynamo and shows me the problem. The copper seat of the end bearing has developed a frightful wobble. This in turn has skimmed the core rotor. The bearing seat can be replaced, adequately, but the shaved core is another matter.

For some reason the mechanic has to slip the drive wheel from the shaft, so he is chiselling the locking nut to a smaller size to fit one of his plug spanners. His patience holds. It's as if these British gauge parts were expected to be banged about by men with metric toolkits; their robustness under fire is remarkable.

*

The football veteran has re-sleeved the end bearing, using solder to widen the outside of the brass insert so that it sits tight in the worn socket. He repacks the front bearing with grease. The real question remains, what can be done to save the damaged core?

A boy is grinding a steel beam beside me. Showers of sparks fly past and the noise is deafening. In all this yard of hammers beating, welding torches hissing, red sparks flying, oil soaking into baked earth, old battery cases, crumpled tin stools and shapeless scraps of metal hanging from walls and ceilings, there is not a single blade of grass.

Missed it! I didn't see how he fixed the rotor! But upon reassembly the dynamo seems to charge powerfully. Ask as I might, I can't find out what he did. He washes his hands and face and blows his nose into the gutter. We sit down together to have some tea. In Syria you put the sugar into the pot with the tea leaves.

*

That isn't quite the end of the dynamo problem. After an hour back at the Bentley refitting it, during which it becomes more than clear I have parked in the main public toilet, I manage to tinker the distributor points into letting her start.

But the dynamo warning light still glows red.

So I take my courage in both hands and drive across town to Raqqa's wreckers' yard, the least lady-like place a wedding car has ever been.

They give us a rapturous welcome.

I show my electrician friend the problem, hand him the car keys and withdraw. I am too downhearted to watch.

In my bags is *The Economist* newspaper brought from London eleven days ago. The Russian Army is on manoeuvres behind Moscow. What does Gorbachev expect? Is he trying to intimidate the Muscovites? I am reminded of a nugget of research from my undergraduate history dissertation – about England's 'Glorious Revolution' of 1688. A riot broke out in London that November, after James II fled to France. Several pitched battles were fought in St James' Square in one day. Finally, as the inflamed mob, flushed with victory, was on the verge of torching the Palace of Westminster, by happy coincidence the royal artillery train, on the way from Windsor back to the Tower, marched straight through its middle. Stunned by this apparent show of force and mercy, the mob dispersed. Thus, a hundred years before the French Revolution, England escaped its Bastille Day.

Perhaps this is Mr Gorbachev's thought too: show them force, then mercy.

*

For another half an hour, with a multitude of friendly Arabs lending advice, football man works on the Bentley's wiring, down circuit from the dynamo, and all is solved. Two faults at the same time – very much My Lady's style.

It has taken the whole morning to sort her out.

But I have learnt a thing in this place where I am mute: about the universal and immutable language of physics, and electricity in particular; and also how just being there, just the presence of a man, how he holds himself, is more elemental, more important than what he says.

You can rely on physical presence as surely as crowd-diving off a stage.

I am tired of these mechanical mishaps, but I should be grateful for the lesson.

*

The Bentley has reached Sergiopolis, the eastern limit of early Christendom.

The city forms a square, approximately a third of a mile on each side. Its walls must be thirty feet high and fifteen feet thick.

The spot is not chosen to dominate the countryside. Nevertheless, from the top of the southwest corner tower, the view is miles across the sands in all directions. In that vista, say forty square miles of plain, I can see: some sheep grazing the thin desert grasses, and their three shepherds; three hamlets, each with a smattering of mud houses; and the dust raised by one vehicle.

This emptiness outside renders the gaunt acres of Sergiopolis' ruins all the more impressive. No living creature shows itself within the site. The sense of time having ceased is bewildering. The location has no signposts, no car park, no litter; just sparse long-eared grass, sprigs of yellow flowers, the dark exposed ends of cellars and foundations, and the alabaster glint of the perimeter walls.

The Roman Emperor Trajan cut his military teeth in the east, while his father was governor of Greater Syria. This was the senior Roman governorship, previously used by Vespasian as a springboard to the imperial throne, having crushed the revolt in Israel in AD 70 (after which he constructed the Colosseum). I mention Trajan now because, as a young centurion, he would have known of this place as Rhesapha, and probably visited. He was the extreme empire builder, the antithesis of the domesticity we saw at Pompeii. Later, as emperor, in two fighting seasons he took the Roman frontier from this outpost all the way to the Persian Gulf. In the process, he had his navy towed overland from the Euphrates to the Tigris.

Syria, al-Raqqa, Day 33

Above: the second attempt that day at fixing the dynamo (page 113)

Below: waking up in the town square (page 112)

Above: Syria, the ramparts of Sergiopolis (al-Resafa), Day 33. The Bentley is the speck on the earth bank in the top-right corner. Sergiopolis was an Assyrian fortified reservoir appropriated by the Romans and expanded by Emperor Justinian I c. 530 CE. The arched shadows in the left foreground open down into one of the cathedral-like cisterns (page 115)

Below: Syria, the al-Hayr (or Hir) al-Sharqi Palace, Day 34. My 'abandoned city of dreams'. The Lady is glimpsed outside the east gate of the main enclosure. The smaller palace is behind. Al-Hayr al-Sharqi was built in 728-729 CE by the Umayyads, the first Islamic hereditary dynasty (page 123)

A Syrian, Apollodorus of Damascus, was Trajan's architect. Apollodorus designed and constructed two marvels of ancient civil engineering, stunning in their technical innovation, still standing in Rome today, despite centuries of earthquakes: Trajan's Column, with its spiral staircase core and interlocking masonry blockwork; and the nearby Pantheon, with an astonishing unreinforced concrete dome, still the largest in the world after 2000 years.

Apollodorus thought big. His bridge over the lower Danube to allow Trajan's annexation of modern-day Romania was twenty-one spans of the Tiber Bridge, end on end. Probably that too would still be standing today, if a later Emperor hadn't knocked it down to keep the barbarians out.

Looking at Sergiopolis now that I'm finally here, the builders seem to have found a quarry with a high silicon content. These stone walls are almost translucent. Light penetrates an inch and makes the blocks glow. In patches, the surface is as clear as glass. Each of these four Lalique ramparts is braced from behind by 100 broad Romanesque arches, well, at least the side I bothered to count, and I assume it is symmetrical, so, 400 arches around me.

Taking a mouthful of water from my bottle, I walk over to one of the shallow pits. Water is the lifeline here. How could such a town survive the hot summer with no river nearby? I jump down into the shade.

The answer presents itself vertiginously. I have landed on the ledge of an empty, cathedral-like, underground storage tank. The yawning space below is lit from the far side by a row of upper windows like the one I jumped into. Powerful buttresses, columns as mighty as those at Sardis, soar up to carry the massive vaulted ceiling, which makes the street level of the fort.

I scramble back out, sick at how nearly I leapt into the darker patch of the hole. I walk from window to window, creeping into the gloom, clutching the sides, as I look down thirty feet to the floor and over perhaps fifty feet to the light.

Ah! Another tourist. We are so pleased to see each other that we rush across the empty ruins to shake hands. He is from Hungary, the other side of the Iron Curtain, on a Warsaw Pact visa. He has been driving up the Euphrates, starting in Iraq. He has seen ancient Ur, and Babylon, but did not have time to go up to Nineveh on the Tigris, now called Mosul. An Iraqi visa would be brilliant. But I just would not have the guts. Even writing in this notebook that Saddam Hussein runs a more terrifying personality cult than President Assad would be enough to get me shot.

I am seriously impressed. It seems so long since anyone spoke English that I tell him what I have never yet told anyone, and hardly dare admit even to myself.

'I am trying to drive around the Mediterranean,' I say.

'So you will be heading south? Just be careful crossing to Palmyra,' he replies.

*

Desert.

Night.

A breeze from the south.

Silence.

Only the ringing of my head from half a lifetime of blather.

A first night alone in the desert deserves some cheer. I pull the cork from a bottle of wine left over after the beach party near Kusadasi last summer. It comes out with not so much a pop as a choral toot, the loudest sound in the past hour and for the next eight or so, until I start the engine tomorrow.

The wine is Turkish white and smells rancid. Take a sip. Mmmm, rather good; images appear, in this noiseless, arid moonscape, of fertile river valleys, rich red soil, a bouquet of wild herbs; a dry, solid body of grape intact through to the warm, intoxicating finish. The label gives a telephone number – that's confidence. But the nearest telephone is leagues away, back in Raqqa.

The desert. Pretensions to be green in the spring.

In particular, a single purple crocus in front of the tent of a nomad family where I stopped for directions on their sea of roadless dirt. And indeed, I could not refuse the coffee or even the hand-rolled cigarette which was presented in response to my gift of a compass. Short wooden poles and long ropes held up the black coarse-weave fabric of the tent. The east side was open towards that solitary desert flower, and the spot, a respectful distance beyond, where the white Bentley had parked, her elegant lines belying her cross-country muscle.

The coffee was served by my host a thimbleful at a time, in the bottom of small beakers. It was so strong as to be essence rather than infusion.

Women could be heard, out of sight at the southern end of the tent.

A new, four-wheel drive Mercedes G-Wagen came steaming up from the south across the plain and stopped in disbelief, ten yards short of the Bentley, nose-on. The contrast was complete: the one festooned with jerry cans, spare off-road tyres, sand ladders, crash bars, roof-mounted searchlights, shovels, rolls of bedding and nets, winches and a flare mortar; the other with a panama hat on the back shelf.

After several minutes not moving, three lean north Europeans climbed out, one a girl. They walked over in their structurally sensible boots. As they neared I stood up and warned them in German about the crocus before which the encampment had so carefully been pitched. I had guessed the nationality right.

The Mercedes driver spoke passing Arabic. The girl wore a white veil thrown back from her face, and she sat at the edge of the carpets, looking stunning. The Bedouin were uncomfortable about her presence.

Then two big American 4x4 pick-ups swept in across the hard sand from the west, and there was a stir; the venerable head of the family, maybe even the tribe, and his eldest (forty-something) grandson had arrived.

I was sitting at the grandson's place in the square and he signalled me dismissively to move. Up until this point a mood of brotherly friendship had prevailed. Now we saw instead the pride of the nomad.

The West Germans stood up to leave. As they departed, the grandson refused to shake the girl's hand. I stood too, then walked with them to their exploration vehicle. Their leader checked the straps of the 4x4's roof rack. They looked worried and asked whether the terrain ahead was as bad as the crossing they had just made. I said it was pretty straightforward.

Later this same grandson tossed my present back to me, unimpressed. It was just a compass, and only my spare, but I was offended, veering towards outraged. We stared at each other at about one-quarter power until he looked away.

You are not worth a fight, he implied.

This is your territory, I implied back.

Later he asked me to stay for the night. But I was actually, in spite of myself, angry, and even if I had felt this was more than an obligatory invitation, I could not accept. Stupid, but only in retrospect.

The grandfather's eyes were the hardest to hold, when we were introduced. He seemed preoccupied. He looked into mine, but I could comprehend nothing in his. I was the wrong tool for his job, like his foot would be wrong for catching a fish. They were smeary, tired eyes, brown like the rock of the desert, spread wide in his small grizzled skull, shrink-wrapped by skin, a drying water pouch. His moustache and beard sprouted from his upper lip and chin like porcupine quills.

He accepted from 'uncle' the place of honour between the floor cushions, pulled his short legs up under him and lay on his left flank propped up against one colourful wool sack. His grandson did the same against the other.

With the Germans gone, the six senior Bedouin then ignored me for a while, and the plain resounded to the heated discussion for which the meeting had presumably been called. Small stones were tossed emphatically into the open sandy area inside the square of carpets.

Why did that arrogant Arab return my present? Because it was offered patronisingly? Should I have presented him with a more beautiful gift? My Swiss Army knife? My binoculars? My car? If I had given him my car, what would he have been obliged to give me? Might I have been the proud master of 500 square miles of Syrian sand?

His world and mine have no lasting meaning for each other, although I flattered myself that he would have been interested to converse. It was for him to choose and he knew it.

What if I had given the sweet baklava and nuts I am now finishing for supper? Food does not have the materialist connotations of a compass or a car. Refusing the gift dishonours the giver. Most gifts are symbolic. For the shepherd, it is enough to give a lamb. Not the whole flock, mark you. But an essential symbol of creation. Perhaps no true nomad responds to science.

When asked what my gift was, by the German, the grandson signalled to his watch. He thought I had given him a watch. Maybe he did not know about compasses, because he did not need them. His uncle knew about them, but then in that first friendliness he had already betrayed himself.

From the nomad tent I drove to a landmark on the horizon twenty miles south of Sergiopolis. The hill must serve as a point of reference for all shepherds coming down from the Euphrates to risk their herds in this desert in the spring. It stands out more than, say, an Iron Age ridge fort seen from the Thames basin. I was sure there would be ruins, just as prehistoric earthworks of more recent date would be found on such a brow in the British Isles.

The Bentley inched towards it across the wilderness, picking over rock beds one wheel at a time, tacking to the north side of the hill, climbing slowly until the angle was so steep I thought she might roll. Then I leapt out and ran to the top to beat the sunset. But no. The landmark lacked any sign of occupation.

The only traces were four neat little scree cairns, such as accumulate over the centuries on lonely peaks from the Himalayas to the Hebrides. My homespun archaeology must wait until tomorrow, when I hope to find the still unnamed ruined walls shown on my air force map about thirty miles further southwest.

Sitting there with the large-scale spy plane map, the mystery of the monumental cisterns at Sergiopolis was explained. A stream forms in the flash winter rains, running from these hills to the ruins of that ancient outpost. The Assyrians, and later the Romans, simply dammed its flow each winter until the tanks were full for another summer. Sergiopolis was a fortified reservoir.

That only leaves the question of food. The Fertile Crescent may seem nearby, but Sergiopolis was marginal for farming. It was no fortified granary. Sheep in the springtime is not the same as crops in the autumn. So we can imagine the town trading with the camel trains, water and overnight security, for food. If the trade route dried up, so did the food, and the need for protection from bandits.

Alternatively, the fortress town could have existed as a military base and lived off subsidies from a deep-pocketed empire, in return for protecting it from eastern hordes. But the mortal blow to Rome came from a different direction – the forests and steppes to its north. Later, the threat to Constantinople came up the coast, 100 miles to our west. The advance of Islam would follow the gentler road through Damascus, Lebanon and along the Orontese River.

In the end, it would have been the cost of transporting food, not lack of water, which did for Sergiopolis.

Day 34

The lonely night, the steady desert wind, and the threat to survival.

The vault of heaven displays the numberless stars of Abraham, which have moved halfway round in the sky while I slept.

For a long time I gaze up at them lying on my back on the rear seat, with my head hanging out of the door on one side and my shins out of the other. I do not need to lock up against thieves and murderers here.

But the prospect of sandstorms appals me. What would I do caught out in the open? The fine sand gets into everything and would surely kill the engine. The answer is, I don't know.

Then there is the matter of water – if the car doesn't start, when I try her in a couple of hours' time, I will need to purify the three litres I still have with me from the tap at the frontier and start walking. And the tyres – even if the wind abates and the Bentley fires up, it wasn't clever to drive over so much virgin desert yesterday.

I am afraid even to turn on the interior light to write, in case it doesn't work.

A shooting star streaks above me like a flashgun. The wind seems to slacken. My confidence returns. There's the Plough, Ursa Major, over to the north.

The tallest, slimmest, slip of a moon you ever saw rises in the east. Through the field glasses, the body of the sphere, the disc not lit by the sun, is blue.

*

Dawn from the top of the hill, working out compass bearings. I put a stone on a cairn like one does ptarmigan shooting.

Then to wake My Lady.

No joy.

The last few amateurish adjustments to the points seem to have made cold starts impossible. Will the battery give out on me?

Should I wait in case I have flooded the spark plugs?

The battery holds longer than the laws of electro-chemistry allow. I have lost track of what I am doing. This is now a race against the sun. Sit in the car and turn the key. Back round to the bonnet for some more random adjustments.

No, that is stupid.

Think. The screw that locks down one of the points seems to have lost its thread, so that the timing cannot even be fixed in the correct position once found.

I am at least a day's walk from civilisation. My best bet would be to retrace my way north and try to find the nomad tent.

But wait. The screws locking down the points are interchangeable. Perhaps if I swap them over…

Somehow, more by luck than judgement, the Bentley decides to start and, rather than fiddle any further, we'll drive to recharge the battery.

*

Fine dust coats everything in the car: the page, the leather armrest, the map. It comes in under the doors where the seals are shot. At no more than fifteen miles an hour we creep across the desert. A shepherd is seen, but too far off to give directions, although we wave to each other. The place is so isolated that you would not pass anyone without a formal salutation.

I follow the compass due south. Being a pilot's map, every contour of the country around me is marked. Were any buildings or power lines here, which they are not, they would be picked out individually. Such maps show few place names generally; pilots don't stop to ask. But in a desert, that is no loss.

Ahead on the right is a hill of unnatural proportions. You know immediately it is man-made. I see a terraced pyramid, with a flat, eroded top, massive as a town. It is a pure tell, unlike Aleppo; a mound of debris raised like an anthill by a thousand years of human habitation.

Yet no ancient cities are recorded for this part of the central Syrian plain. The earliest Mesopotamian civilisations to the east, Sumerians and Agadians, dating back 3,000 years before Christ, stopped short of here. The later empires, of Hammurabi and even Nebuchadnezzar, supposedly skirted round to the north. But there it is, an urban tell, as sure as those at Jericho and Troy, with several smaller ones now suggesting themselves in the distance.

All I can do is hurry on, for quite probably the desert is littered with civilisations waiting to be discovered – and the bones of gormless explorers with more enthusiasm than water. These are not today's objective.

*

My Lady has used twenty-five per cent of her fuel. The heat and dust are a real menace. Up ahead is Al Taggibah, the nearest village to the 'walls' I am looking for. They were noticed during those discussions on my sitting room floor with my supposed girlfriend. She did find this map in the first place. For that, if she ever reads this, I am grateful.

Picking a bearing depends on matching the peaks of topography with those on the chart. The compass shows My Lady to be due north of the settlement.

The Bentley has become a land ship. The tracks marked on the map exist no more than sea lanes exist on water. The reality is an erratic skeleton of paths. If you think you see a truer track for the direction you want, you set off across the raw landscape towards it, with stops to walk over patches of doubtful terrain before committing the Bentley's weight. In this way she has crossed a salt flat, waded her skirts through waist-high grass and even tackled what could only be described as a petrified ploughed field.

Scouting round the oasis village, she changes again and becomes the Tigress of Al Taggibah, a lone prowler, nosing behind ruined field walls, looking for the breach, finding the level gap between abandoned networks of trenches. I can see traces of axled vehicles on the far side of the baked earth hamlet.

The situation is safe enough for a quick detour. The settlement forms the flank of another man-made mound, less imposing but more accessible, and I follow the trail to the top.

Gingerly, I manoeuvre the Bentley so that she is facing back downhill, ready for instant departure. Then, leaving the engine ticking over, heating up by the second, I run to the dip in the crown of this new tell.

A shaft, a gaping circular throat, dives into the earth, its round sides clad with heavy, dressed stone blocks. The width of the well-neck must be twenty feet, and it plunges down twice that, even though it has partly collapsed or been filled in. A rusty pump, with broken pipes drilled into the sediment, shows that even in this century the ancient desert spring has been tapped for habitation.

But the well shaft harks back to a far more glorious past for Al Taggibah. Its parent was a city, when farmers irrigated land from here and merchant caravans stopped on the overland trek to Babylon and beyond, to Samarkand.

*

Navigating by compass southeast, searching for the ruins shown up by the military satellites which drew this map, you can only guess the distances in the shimmering heat. Every path peters into nothing, every ridge we crest reveals only another bare expanse of desert. We will have to abandon the search. It is hopeless. Half the petrol is gone.

A peak off the path to the left mocks me. See, it says, I have a flock of sheep. If they can be here, so can you. Come and burst your heart climbing me, it says. We drive to its footing, and I climb with field glasses, compass and map. Sitting with the shepherd boy, sharing the last of my nuts, I look down on to the next plain through the powerful lenses, due east. What is that hanging in the midday haze? Are those towers and high clay walls? Yes, the dancing yellow lines converge.

The abandoned city of dreams.

*

A princely palace, baking under a savage sun. A quarter the size of Sergiopolis, and definitely not Roman. Brown stone blocks with straight lintel entrances as well as arches. Birds of the desert, feeding on the springtime insect life, make an alarmed twitter as I walk over the evidence.

I see foundations of an early inner keep. Four later screen walls have been constructed, quite tightly to the original at the southeast corner, but embracing a larger ward with the other three.

A separate fortress stands across from the main gate. This is not the house of a citizen who wanted more space. Possibly the garrison was asked to keep themselves to themselves. More likely it was a palace for a disdainful autocrat.

Ha. To have picked out this lonely, nameless marking from an over-scaled Air Force map, spread out with the Sunday papers in Kensington; and to have found a palace on the ground. Who would have believed it?

But this is no place for self-congratulation. The sun flogs down from a platinum sky. Not even white paint can adequately reflect such radiation. And we are at the very limit of our fuel range.

Press on for Palmyra immediately.

*

Eight miles in forty-five minutes. Pause to wipe dust off glasses. A camp of Bedouin tents glitters surreally in the middle of a mirage, with scattered sheep nearby, killing time in the midday heat, apparently immersed in water.

*

Dry riverbed, and not the first. One wheel at a time, down the near bank, pick along the stream bottom, across, and with a rush, up the other side. Briefly the world disappears as the long bonnet points to the sky. Hope that the Karaman wheel is looking where it's going. Because, as sure as hell, I can't.

Out there, I know, is waiting one parapet too steep for the Bentley to climb. But she's crossed everything so far.

*

Cooling system misses a beat and the water temperature soars. I fling half of my drinking supply into the radiator. It is a tightrope: drive too slowly and the weak air flow through the radiator means the engine boils; but drive too fast and the doors suck in clouds of choking dust, while the Karaman/Adana suspension smashes jarringly on every rock.

Thank you, Brendan, for taking out that thermostat.

*

Two more miles, gauges look good at the moment. A distant sonic boom echoes across the plain.

*

Eight more miles, another wipe of my spectacles. A real flock of sheep. How does anything survive this far out?

Engine still running normally.

In this writhing landscape I've lost sight of my compass point, a tremendous cliff headland. It should rise like the Rock of Gibraltar, and was visible even from the ruined city, eighteen miles and half a lifetime back.

I risk switching off the Bentley.

I run to the lip of a ridge to find the landmark again. Instead a giddy drop confronts me, and a thirty-mile view. Somehow I have taken a path leading up the spine of my Gibraltar. I must retrace my tracks and find a way round to the foot of the escarpment.

*

Eight more miles, another wipe of the glasses. Difficult to find anything clean to wipe them with.

I am now driving on the far side of the Rock of Gibraltar headland. Way below it. Such decorative desert cliffs – white against the cream floor and ceramic sky. They stretch ahead, on our right flank, westwards for leagues. Their facade is eroded as if in china clay, like basketwork, or Meissen porcelain skirts. Or the fragile, dendritic ceiling of St George's Chapel, Windsor, laid on its side. A lace maker would lasciviate, a fan maker faint.

How can somewhere so fabulous be so dangerous?

*

Two miles and a wipe of the specs.

This is a terrible and desolate domain, no sheep, no living thing. A very serious place it would be to break down. An extreme test. I dare not stop to write, so we roll gently forward over the dust while I scratch this note. There is not enough water to save the Bentley if she boils again and still have any for me to walk out of here alive.

An old Russian once told me that deserts can make you see small creatures larger than they really are. A blackbird looks like a horse. Or something.

Concentrate and keep going, round that stone, don't hit that rock, smash goes the front wheel. This is nature's counter to the Piste Perdue, the ski run literally under the mountain at Val d'Isère. This is the pair to Chamonix's Vallée Blanche, up on the glacier. The fine mist inside the car recalls the first moments of a whiteout, when the cloud comes down on to the glassy ice. Then the skis beneath you are all you can see. The first sense of slope is when you go over the crevasse.

This is the will to live.

*

Sheep, coming towards me. A shepherd boy! We pass at walking speed, and again wave, almost close enough to touch; and indeed, two brows later the oasis village of Al Sakrah nestles in a dell among its scattered palms.

I stop at the ridge to enjoy the moment.

That was a ridiculous journey. From the map there looks to be three more like it before we reach tarmac again. Don't think. Drive.

Call that a village street? It was a torture chamber, absurdly rutted. I wouldn't dream of putting the car over fissures like that in the desert. This kind of countryside is why they invented tanks.

Bonnet up. Radiator cap off. Two boys help as I fill the radiator to the top. It takes all my survival reserve.

Now to find replenishments. The kids lead me across the village's central dirt-baked space, through a high iron door and into a courtyard. In the soothing shade, an aluminium pan of clear cool water sits on the flagstones. Two metal drinking scoops are floating in it. I drink a litre. I was not thirsty, but in the harshest conditions a body can evaporate its way through fifteen litres in a day.

Together we refill my four empty, one-and-a-half-litre bottles. At best one ration. It is a debt I cannot repay.

My water supply secure, I venture further down the raging surface of the street, to where some Arabs sit round a broken tractor. I pull over and ask for help jacking up the car on the driver's side and filling the shock absorber on the front wheel with hydraulic fluid. They are wholly bemused, but I find I can do it anyway myself; after which triumph all the hydraulic fluid drains straight out. The damper, so carefully welded in Karaman, is split from end to end.

To the spectators I pass round the box of soft Turkish nougat from north of Konya, then jack the limousine back down to the desert floor and head away.

The knowledge that the shock absorber has ruptured does not make the coming miles any easier to face. How long will the repaired spring and wishbones stand it? How many hours can I keep this up? When will Her Ladyship throw the almighty tantrum she has so richly earned?

Ah well, the only way out is forwards.

A tarmac highway presents itself, running across the dust bowl. Buses and road-trains pass occasionally. It's no mirage, just not on the map. The Queen of Sheba mounts it with delight.

After eighty-five miles' crawling through desert, the need for speed is irresistible.

The engine temperature climbs. Inside the car is pandemonium, dust everywhere, billowing around as I drive. We must look, to the outside world, like a demented meteor, trailing clouds of glory from the windows.

So I pull over for a general sort-out.

Scattered clothes, blankets, books, rubbish, CD boxes, spare parts, spanners, and now, suddenly foolish, binoculars, compass and defence department maps, are all soaked in cosmetic powder so fine as to be liquid. I dig out the water-purifying filter and organise my second proper drink of the day.

I feel panicky, hysterical. The chaos is over, but now it hits me. The symptoms present as part sunstroke, part post-exam blues. I am aghast that I expected, by rights, to be doing the same awful journey all over again. That was asking too much. I want a bath. Then I will come and swab out the car with a juicy wet mop.

The overheating seems to be a figment of the dashboard's imagination, so I press on. The desert sun is hard on the eyes. For company I pick up a hitchhiker, sporting yet another Arafat headdress, and we head west at a steady fifty.

I'm too tired even to talk. But when the music is on, the temperature gauge has a brief fling with reality and that gives me a lift.

*

Quite unexpectedly we are among more ruins. The tarmac has brought Palmyra closer than I supposed. Fabled Bride of the Desert, with an oasis spring that still spouts sweet water, Palmyra is an abandoned archaeological wonder conjoined to a twentieth-century township on its rim.

The buildings are like Sergiopolis, not-so-ancient Graeco-Roman, at least by Sumerian and Assyrian standards. Nevertheless, the remains beat anything in Greece or even Italy, except Rome, in terms of town plan. The central colonnaded street has echoes of Ephesus, but far more is standing here. If only Rome's Forum had been left like this. Its Pantheon and Colosseum, and the great bread-oven-like buildings in between, still take the laurels for structure; but Palmyra has the crown for majesty.

At the eastern end of the ruins is the Temple of Baal, synonymous in the Old Testament with idolatry and evil, but here revealed as a thick-set Roman edifice, foil to the matchless grace of Athens' Parthenon. Seen for itself, Baal's house is an equally ambitious construction, though pillaged and lacking an acropolis. Yet, as a travesty, a sinister mutant, it fulfils a basic expectation of Lucifer.

Palmyra's abiding mistake was to dare to challenge Rome. After conquering an empire that included Egypt, its warrior queen could not swallow her pride and return to cooperative ways. The Romans gave her a chance and offered a garrison, but she had it massacred. Rome's revenge proved terminal. The city shrank to the precincts of the temple, whose towering flanks became the urban walls. The population, which may have once reached 100,000, plunged to 500.

The temple purlieus enjoy the dubious distinction of having been stripped of smaller blocks and pillars for their own fortification. Either side of the main entrance, compact semicircular bastions have been built by stacking marble columns on their sides like wine bottles, necks inwards, held together with mortar.

I bang on the metal temple doors for several minutes. An old guide unlocks and lets me in. Among the postcards pinned up in his shabby office is an aerial shot of the ruins I reached this morning. I ask to look, and turn it over. They are, or it is, the Al Hir Palace.

*

Down in the oasis the menfolk are capping new stone walls. If they add one more tier I will miss the tops of the temple catching the sunset through the palms. The man at the kettle, surrounded by his rumbustious young sons, lifts the blackened pot off the burning palm twigs and shakes tea leaves and sugar into the boiling water. The water comes straight from the irrigation channel. Boiling is the natural way to sterilise it, and tea is the means to disguise the flavour.

This is an oasis, they indicate. Imbibe.

I look down the uneven grove of palm and olive trees which shades us as we sup. The randomness balances the absurdly regular axis of the site: several hundred metres of triumphal way, double colonnaded by Roman pillars.

The injustices of life have met their antidote. The petty slight about going to Paris behind my back is put into perspective.

Paris. As a Londoner it holds an ambivalent place in my heart, *A Tale of Two Cities*. Miranda and I even went there in the early days, for that glorious autumn weekend when the clocks change and give you an extra hour in bed.

Paris fashions, Paris food. Not just the wines and cheeses, but the alchemy. What a French pastry chef does with flour and butter and eggs and sugar; and what happens by adding alcohol, cream, herbs and fruit to his palette.

The mighty boulevards carved out by Hausmann, the Grands Magazins. The Left Bank intelligentsia, the colony in Montmartre. The rose windows of Notre Dame, the Hall of Mirrors at Versailles. The music of Fauré and Debussy. The Grandes Ecoles, the sweep of civilisation on display in the Louvre. We little Englanders feel chippy but we love it. We go there for romantic strolls along the Seine, and for cutting-edge maths symposia.

Yes, of course there is another side to France: from the death of Richard the Lionheart; through the loss of Calais and Louis XVI's cynical aid to the American Revolution; to Blenheim to Plassey to Quebec to Waterloo. From the persecution of the Huguenots to the racism of the Dreyfus Affair. From the Auld Alliance with the Scots to the French-made Exocet missiles fired from French-made Super Étandard warplanes which torched two British warships in the Falklands. From the savagery of the Reign of Terror to the menace of Napoleon's invasion barges and the repression of *Les Misérables*. From Marshal Petain's turn to fascism in 1940 to the ingratitude of de Gaulle in the 1960s.

However, I forgive that side. The France we helped liberate in 1944 was surely worth it, *banlieues* and all. British kids need to visit Paris young. If a seven-year-old can tuck those smells, that architecture, those sounds – of French being spoken, of mopeds tooting, of Métro doors closing – under his or her belt, they will be more open to what they see at home. They will return as inter-railers, as lovers, as businessmen and women, as teachers, as parents and grandparents. They will organise school exchanges, invite in French families, exalt their best differences and moderate their worst prejudices.

Here I should thank my mother, who took me at just that age to the top of the Eiffel Tower, under cover of one of my father's few business trips; Papa, who shocked me by spouting French when we got off the plane at Orly; and both of them for arranging a teenage exchange with a French family near Pouilly-sur-Loire in 1973, and then in Paris for New Year 1975.

At her apartment near La Muette, the magnificent, chain-smoking Mme Beslon put on an LP, clasped me to her ample bosom and taught me to waltz. How could such a large woman be so light on her feet? I can recall her musky Balenciaga scent immediately.

Forced to weigh France in the scales, we Brits will tend to be self-righteous, wary. Part of it, of course, is France's size, but this would be nothing without its fruitfulness. The land is such a superstore, so favoured by climate, water and fertility, that men and women have time for ambition and pleasure.

Meanness comes from plenty. Amorality is the offspring of abundance. The Eiffel Tower is awe-inspiring, but awful too.

The lesson of Turkey and Syria? Where the land is harsh, the people are generous.

From now on I will say I left my baggage in Palmyra.

*

From here to Homs is a long stretch. But after this morning, all tarmac seems like My Lady's Axminster carpet.

I pick up the tail lights of a fuel truck in the dusk and am towed once more through towards midnight. This is the road to Damascus, albeit not St Paul's. He came in from the other side.

Later, a Nissan saloon acts as pathfinder.

In this way the total mileage for the day pushes up steadily to 250 in seventeen hours.

I can do no more. Who cares about a pinch of talc on the back seat? I could sleep in a sandpit.

Day 35

The fine art of engine tuning is not learnt overnight. The Bentley's current set-up is hard to start when cold, as she takes pains to remind me. Good that we are hidden in the lee of a roadside restaurant where we took shelter from the dazzle of the damascene highway.

But once warm she packs an incredible punch. The torque between fifty and seventy is a match for anything on the road down to the Syrian capital. Firing up again after breakfast is a sound straight from my gap year in France, in the pit lane at the French Grand Prix at Dijon-Prenois, when the Ligier V16 passed us; or the night that June on the Mulsanne Straight, before the flat-twelve Ferrari faltered.

*

As I drive south down the Syrian–Lebanese border, 1,300 miles from Smyrna, three helicopter gunships swoop in. They take up formation alongside My Lady, to her right, the driver's side, so low I can see into the nearest cockpit.

Full desert 'crocodile' camouflage, retracted undercarriages – Russian Hind MI-24s, I think. Each has tank-busting rockets under its stubby wings and a heavy Gatling cannon angled below its nose-turret like a blood-needle.

The West was introduced to these airborne armouries when the Soviet Union invaded Afghanistan nine years ago – the troops finally left in November. It will be decades before the Russian bear looks for another fight.

The three army choppers can cruise twice as fast as me. Their yellow and ochre war paint stands out against the grey slope of the mountain behind.

The nearest pilot and I exchange salutes.

Then their exhausts plume as they turn away, down my line of sight. That spew would be a big signature for a heat-seeking missile.

*

Before driving into Damascus, I venture round to the west, trying to approach the Golan Heights. The Israelis seized these Syrian hills across the Jordan valley in the Six-Day War, when I was eight, and are still there. The occupation is not recognised by the international community.

I don't get far. Syria's militarised zone extends to the leafy but cramped outskirts of Damascus itself. The verges have been torn into canyons like the main street in Al Sakrah, this time by the wheels of military vehicles.

At the sight of my first tank transporter I head the Bentley's nose back east. I had my fill at Christmas of blundering into army bases.

*

Driving in a city comes as a shock. Have I forgotten how traffic works? Fortunately the west end of the Damascus Souk abuts a square, and I park directly outside. With so little time to reach Cairo, the best I can do is grab my jacket and dive straight in among the stalls and shops.

The market is like London's Burlington Arcade run riot. The width of a full street, dark because covered, barrel vaulted, but with as many upper-floor businesses as ground-floor ones. It must stretch a third of a mile towards the Great Mosque.

*

A fashion lesson. Arab headdress (*keffiyeh*) is styled by nationality:
- Both sides of the cloth forward over the shoulders – Syrian;
- Left side back over the shoulder – Jordanian;
- Both back over the shoulders – Kuwaiti;
- Piled up back over the ears – Palestinian.

This and other insights came from an hour spent in an attic with carpet repairers above the souk. I was not looking for a carpet, but big-ticket salesmen tend to be more relaxed, and also better educated. The types of carpet wear, their aberrations of colour, the small fantasies of the weaver; the dialects of Arabic in the regions which the carpets come from; the coarseness of Iran compared with the masculinity of Aleppo and the femininity of Damascus; all these we discussed as I grabbed my first sustained conversation since Turkey.

The prices dropped as the carpet repairer mellowed. The numbers became half those in the shop below, but I still found his wares very expensive. Anything over fifty years old, of tightly packed knots and more than three feet by five feet was going to be £400. Will I ever be close enough to the finishing post to drop cash like that? Perhaps a few decades from now I will be able to say, as Chagall did once in Paris, 'I'll take them all'. In fact, if I ever buy a carpet in Damascus, I will know I have arrived.

And so back to the Bentley it is, and the endless road.

*

Goodbye Syria, where small boys sell packets of cigarettes on street corners; where beautiful veiled mothers hitchhike on my red sofa with their equally beguiling daughters, grey eyes laughing from under their shawls; where peace is apparent in every beat of Damascus' heart, under the barrel of the Israeli outposts of the Golan Heights; where water is to spare for those coming out of the desert; where workmen invite you to join them at the roadside for tea; and the prison sentence for black-market currency dealing is fifteen years.

Goodbye Syria, I hope to return. Between the meteorological and economic drought that prevails, and the embarrassing military position, you do not seem the lion, the wolf for which you are known. However, neither could I, nor would I, stay. Enough of country towns with roadblocks on all routes in and out. Enough of being asked if I am Bulgarian. Enough of postage stamps to the Soviet Union being probably all right for the UK, enough of banks that give you half the natural rate, of men with guns in jeans flagging you down, of long man-smocks pulled up for a crouching piss in the street, of pedestrians with a death wish, of hotels just for Iranians, of signposts only in Arabic, of back roads torn to ribbons by tracked vehicles, of grey paint so greasy your blood would not stick to it, of faded, listing pictures of President Assad.

I feel with every breath that if one more customs man sent me back across the duty-free zone for a rubber stamp, or if one tiny niggle happened with the car, I would pack it in. Somehow I would just go home. I want it to be over.

*

And so it is. By comparison, Jordan is England. Cat's eyes mark out the smoking fifty-mile descent from the borderland to the capital, and a road surface good enough to allow you to throw out the rulebook for limousines in pursuit of some boy-racer tearaway in a hatchback – my former self no less.

Compared to Damascus, Amman is a raving confluence of hillsides, twinkling after dark. As the Bentley purrs down the steep, winding boulevard, I see the city's prime location, a prominence standing over us in the fork of two tumbling valleys. Any Western capital would put a fabulous old restaurant on top of such a hill, a Montmartre family concern with a Michelin rosette. I must check this out. A steep side-turning, a concealed driveway, suggests itself, and the Bentley bounds up like an excited gundog. Even when the road narrows to a cinder track we sprint onward, laughing at the tame surface after the dried-out wadis of yesterday. With thundering wheels we burst in on the Jordanian Army.

And there was I, trying to stay out of military strongpoints.

But the tea they serve is strong and slightly minty, and they show me the matchless view they have of the city lights; over there is the best hotel, and there the king's palace. Their oldest vehicle, a '67 Ferret scout car, shares our engine.

*

A swimming pool. I cannot resist. Here goes.

What is that, flaring behind my closed eyelids as the surface hits? Disbelief that so much water could be held together in one basin, and just for me to dive into? The old nomad's eyes? The thimbleful of coffee? Or the aluminium pan in the courtyard?

Spade loads of sand are lifting off me, washing out of my ears, from between my toes.

For a long time, two minutes perhaps, I lie face down in the middle of the pool spread out like a starfish, wriggling every part of me.

I am like a desiccated sponge, rehydrating. The pleasure quite swamps any pain from not breathing.

Back on the poolside couch, the hairspring which unlocked in Palmyra winds down to empty. I am jotting down rubbish to myself. 'Raw reality is so fickle.' Whatever.

I strike up a conversation with the muscle-bound pool attendant, to try to make sense. The water for this pool comes, I am told, by underground pipeline from massive desalination plants on the Dead Sea.

The country seems wealthy.

What is the basis of Jordan's economy? He doesn't know. Perhaps it just caters for the region's rich – doesn't threaten them, provides the pleasure dome, now that Beirut has shut up shop. The attendant confirms that the hotel runs a health club for non-guests. The number of rich members, the money-no-object homes being built and the price of houses generally are amazing.

*

Bed at last.

My brain is spinning.

How much wealth is based on trade, rather than production? Trade is selling for a profit what comes advantageously to you. The Iranians produce nuts, but the trick is to sell them to the Syrians. The Syrians make clothes, but the real money is in trading them to the Jordanians. The Jordanians sell lifestyle to the Saudis. The Saudis sell oil to the Japanese, the Japanese sell televisions to the Americans, the Americans sell pick-ups and software... well, no, currently not to the Iranians.

Is it trade or is it imperialism that makes the world go round? And who are the Jordanians to sell pleasure to anyone?

While I soaked in my pool, Sheba was groomed, emptied of dust and oily rags, vacuumed, blasted, waxed inside (with strict orders not to open the bonnet) and soaped and leathered outside. The hotel car valet had not had such a problem case in years. My Lady dropped a Piraeus gearbox on him at the handover, as soon as he climbed behind the wheel, but re-engaged immediately I swapped places, so that his eyes bulged at the witchcraft.

But he stuck with it. Amman likes its visitors to leave their desert behind.

I am rather hoping the past two days of taking liberties will be forgiven and that in the morning My Lady will be lenient with me.

Day 36

Repack, discard, dust, shave, some breakfast orange juice – vitamins! – and make a plan. Studying the hotel's wall map, the road to Petra looks a good 200 kilometres.

Send a telex to the British embassy in Cairo. But what to say – 'Nearly there'? And one to the Foreign Office in London too, in case a contact has been found for long-stay parking in Egypt, to be forwarded to the embassy. And a third to home to report that the distributor cap is good.

*

At 1,600 miles from Izmir we turn off the main highway, on the spur out west to Jordan's premier archaeological site, Petra.

More desert, with the occasional sand devil whirling near the roadside for light relief. What happens if you walk into the middle of one of these twisting spouts to investigate?

The Bentley gleams from her valeting, but she smells of the cigarettes of the young hitchhiker I picked up; he had fun in the back playing film stars with the cars we passed.

At the first check she gulps two bottles of water quite merrily into the radiator, but she has been running at between seventy and eighty miles per hour on a full-blown motorway for an hour and it's to be expected.

I refill all the spare bottles while I remember.

*

Petra – from Πέτρα, Ancient Greek for stone or rock.

Built into a valley ravine several miles long, accessed through slot canyons. Canyons mean water erosion, and this promises to be another fortified water tank. The hills must have had springs, a treasure since dried up. And the smooth walls of the serpentine canyons testify to a history of flash floods. Torrents have poured through, laden with scouring rock. Even now floods happen. Two dozen French tourists were killed here by such a freak of nature in 1963.

So the Petrans would have built dams and cisterns long before any facades.

Petra flourished as Rome to the west developed an appetite for exotic products from the East. These included specialities of the Arabian Peninsula – incense for temples and scent for ladies. The frankincense and myrrh growers then had demands of their own, for spices and silks from India and China.

And so it became sensible to cross this desert, and inevitable to collect water where it could be found in a defensible form. Such a spot would become a crossroads between the north–south route from the Silk Road to the Red Sea, and the east–west one from Arabia and India to the Mediterranean.

The car park is a dusty field populated by tour coaches and horses for hire. Access appears to be free – I find no turnstile or entrance fee. The signposts lead to a gully in which five men could stop an army; the canyon narrows to a gorge which tightens further to a slot, perhaps the very one where the Frenchmen died. The path seems endless and in places is barely wide enough for two horses to pass. A waist-high water channel, like a scale model of the Amalfi coast road, has been chiselled into the cliff face on the right. That it is so little damaged tells us how rare the flash floods now are.

The denouement is all the more impressive for this narrow approach: the Treasury, carved into the facing red cliff. The first glimpse is vaguely reminiscent of the west elevation of St Paul's Cathedral viewed up Ludgate Hill.

So much architectural rock carving, across a site stretching a couple of miles, says that water was profuse here. I count a dozen temple-like frontages and hundreds of porticoed caves. There would have been trees and gardens. Plants would have lent shade, oxygen and perfume, where today even a gross of tourists make the air stale and insanitary. Their roots would have held the soil together.

Nevertheless, for ancient Petra's populace of 20,000, princes and paupers, their livestock and pets, life must have required the strictest timetables, rubbish collections, curfews and standards of public hygiene. For example, the amphitheatre, with fifty tiers and seating for 3,000, would have required silence in the rest of the town for anything to be heard from the stage below. The difficulties of sleeping, with the noise of horses and street-callers ringing off the rock faces on every side, could only have been solved by curfews and earplugs. As I write, just two Jordanian guides shouting at each other, and one lachrymose infant, are enough to clog this acoustic sewer. How could Petra as a community have been physically bearable? And then, what would have been its politics? Was this an appalling place to live?

The fall of Rome seems to have been matched by the fall of Petra. The demand for luxuries collapsed. Also, this looks like an earthquake zone – any columns not carved into the living rock have been toppled. We are on the junction of the Eurasian and Arabian tectonic plates, so that is not surprising. However, such shocks are the absolute enemy of water management. Springs dry up, pipes break, cisterns leak, dams burst, and the effort of rebuilding makes no sense because the whole thing could be smashed again tomorrow. The other problem is extreme weather events. Even worse than droughts are the hundred-year flash floods where dams are strained to bursting point, compounding the catastrophe if an overtopping trickle starts to carve down.

Today the faces around are all fat white tourists. A busload of such women is arriving on horseback down the long gully. They sit astride their hirelings, rolling their bodies to the unaccustomed movement.

While the matrons stir themselves with romance, virile Jordanians canter through the ravine, hooves flinging dry manure into the air and threatening to trample everyone. They kid themselves in their Arab horsemanship.

But the biggest childhood fantasist is me. When I was four I had a favourite Dinky toy car, the length of an index finger. It was a Bentley S1, but the two-door James Mulliner Continental, black on silver. It disappeared, and someone wise and kind found me another within the week. I'm not sure you'd take a real, coachbuilt Mulliner Continental for a long drive like this. They are just too valuable. But a four-door S1 of the same vintage on the same chassis and running gear still does it for me. If you half close your eyes, the tail view of 15 XKN matches that nursery toy well. At the bow-end, her bonnet lines are the same, but higher because of the roof. Crucially, the fog lights serve as indicators, as on the Continental. To mock the delusion, My Lady is a wedding car, for goodness' sake. Where's the bride? What self-respecting girlfriend would be seen dead in such a thing?

Now, now. You are supposed to have left all that in Palmyra.

*

The road south from Petra to Aqaba is TE Lawrence country. This is the wrestling pit where the Ottoman Empire tripped up towards the end of World War I. On our 'Arab Front', we British were, to put it mildly, inconsistent. We had at least four policies running in parallel. Ostensibly we supported Lawrence's plan for a self-determining Greater Arabia, running from the Indian Ocean to the Med, under King Faisal of Saudi Arabia, with its capital in Damascus. However, the Balfour Declaration of 1917 excluded Palestine from the definition of Greater Arabia, in the interests of the Jewish diaspora. A third British position came from the imperial administration in India, which was more interested in protecting trade routes than fostering Arab national self-determination.

Finally, Bolshevik revolutionaries in Moscow revealed at the end of 1917 that France, Britain and Tsarist Russia had made a secret deal two summers earlier to carve up the Ottoman Empire their way – the Sykes-Picot Agreement. This treaty had room for several self-determining Arab countries between Turkey and Aqaba. Specifically, while Russia took eastern Turkey's Armenia, the French would help set up an Arab government in what is now Syria, and the British would sponsor what are now Jordan and Iraq. However, it withheld the Mediterranean coast from both areas, anticipating Balfour. Lawrence had no idea of Sykes-Picot's existence. The Arabs whom he had fought alongside saw it as a betrayal.

The partition settlement reached by 1923 paid lip service to the wishes of the 'indigenous populations'. But it ignored the Palestinian Arabs, the Kurds and Lawrence's promises of a Greater Arabia. And that was the start of it all.

A cocktail of long, grinding descents, and floating, arrow-straight traverses, takes us down to the Gulf of Aqaba and the Indian Ocean.

The mountains remind me of the Cairngorms; their outcrops of harder stone deserve to be a national monument park. To Lawrence, who was nothing if not sentimental, fighting his way towards Damascus, they must then have been the very gates of Valhalla.

*

DAMN.

So close.

That'll teach me to switch off for a rest within sight of success.

The starter motor is not engaging. It has been OK all day; and I thought the problem was over in Aleppo anyway.

Furious, I pack up my rations for a quick exit and run around in the gathering dusk, squirting oil, poking with the screwdriver, coughing in the slipstream of the passing road-trains.

What makes this happen every five or six times I stop? I don't understand. Perhaps the Bendix drive has just worn out again. Now I have to decide quickly what to do. Very bad spot to leave the car for the night – hard shoulder of a main artery through classic ambush country.

Not a pretty place to hitch alone in the dark either.

I take the oil cover off the almost inaccessible starter and tickle the mechanism with my finger. Then I release the handbrake and go for a rolling start, heaving the whale-like carcass towards the bottom of this gentle slope, slipping her into gear once she is rolling, and nothing. She needs to be doing 30mph for that to work.

I am exhausted.

I pour two cupfuls of oil over the non-engaging cog, which only makes it grind all the faster. Must I hitch down to Aqaba and pay someone to come and tow me?

Think now. Whenever you tickle the cog through the inspection flap, it is always butted right up against the flywheel teeth and you can even feel the teeth which are not meshing. They are somehow irregular. Then you pushed the car forward to turn the engine and nothing was solved. The engine wasn't turned, because it's automatic. Think. If the engine didn't turn, the flywheel didn't turn either; but if it had…

It is the flywheel which is worn, not the Bendix drive at all. The flywheel does two jobs. Most of the time it lends the engine a smoothing inertia. But it is also the lever by which the battery turns the motor to start. The flywheel is a giant cog, whose teeth have ground down in one small patch where the crank most often comes to rest. But how to turn the crankshaft without a starting handle? The engine would only need a sixth of a turn to push the flywheel to a less worn place opposite the starter drive. Think. Maybe turning the radiator fan…

Eureka! The cogs bite, the engine fires, we're saved.

How long before my mistress finds another way to show who wears the trousers?

*

Aqaba has many faces: a naval base, an army checkpoint, commercial docks, a ferry port and upmarket hotels on its beaches. After peering at each of these in the dark, I have my bearings and choose a travel agency to arrange the next step – a boat to Egypt.

As I am parking, the proprietor looks at his watch, spreads out his prayer mat and begins to pray. When he has finished, he tells me there is no boat until 11 a.m. and to come back in the morning.

In four days I have to be back at work. My Lady is just building up her rhythm. And bang goes another ten per cent of the remaining time.

Day 37

A sea view at seven. The Gulf of Aqaba.

Egypt lies opposite, across this finger of water. It is still and silent in the morning. Between the Egyptians and us in Jordan, Israel has a foothold on the waterfront too. Their town, Eilat, is at the top of the bay, to the right. Each country is marked out conveniently by a low range of brown desert hills. These slope directly into the bay, like fences between rival terraces at Stamford Bridge.

Some claim the course of the Great War was turned in the Middle East. If so, it was here. Lawrence attacked Aqaba from the Empty Quarter, the Arabian Desert side, and stormed the Turkish citadel, whose defences pointed out to sea. In much the same way, the Japanese took Singapore in 1942.

I need a ferry to take me over to Egypt. Even were an African transit possible, to cross Libya I cannot risk an Israeli stamp in my passport.

The beach is strewn with litter: tin cans, a sole sandal, a semi-submerged tyre, some battered clinker fishing boats and an iron barge. Another barque rests drunkenly on the sandy bottom about fifty yards out. Further away, I count eighteen ships at anchor on our side of the bay. They have the ordered look of a fleet under review, lined up from their moorings by the steady breeze; or frozen in the closing stages of a mad race for the hotel on the point. A glass-bottomed boat ticks past on its way to work, crossing where the cleaner seabed makes the water blue.

A young Arab couple walk hand in hand along the firm sand where the tide is coming in. The woman is broad and peachy. She still wears her impractical high-heeled shoes, suggesting an unplanned trip – they are not yet honeymooners. They smile at me with the particular assurance of the newly bedded. A ruffian walks past in the opposite direction, flip-flops flapping in the wet, talking to himself. He staggers back five minutes later, having found his morning remedy.

One day this beach, with its natural sand and profusion of palm trees, will be cleaned up and privatised for tourist turrets. It has been fun to know it still as common land.

A Royal Jordanian Airline Airbus, gleaming in the sun, hums low up the Gulf towards the airport.

*

My prayerful travel agent has overslept, but it's just as easy to track down ferry tickets myself by taxi. Then back to the Bentley, which spent the night in the mosque car park, to drive down to the harbour.

*

The border control shed is once again battleship grey and lit with strip lamps. If I ever reach the front of this queue for exit visa tax, will I have the money to pay it? There seems no way to find out. The line is very long, and the people are growing restless.

In Queuing Theory, a moment comes, just before anarchy breaks out, when joining the end is pointless, and new arrivals start barging forward. Whether they jump all the way to the front depends on the dynamics of the barriers, the purpose of the queue, the visibility of its length, the ambient temperature and a dozen other factors. One influence is whether those standing in the middle of the queue exercise their position for the common good, including their own, or beckon their friends forward, for a brief but disastrous moment of self-importance.

A particular destabiliser is if a new queue forms around a counter which looks about to open. If the booth stays closed, the people who gambled will not want to go back to the end of the queue they were in.

Forming a secondary queue is of greatest interest to those who can see the disused booths but are not in approximately the first third of their own queue. Those at the front of the old queue are just hoping that a new booth will not be opened, to justify the time they themselves have spent waiting.

In Aqaba this morning, we have people in the middle of the queue who regularly call new arrivals to join them. We also have disused booths in full view which occasionally prepare to open and then don't.

The result is every man for himself.

Sometimes it helps being tall.

*

Aqaba has disappeared behind us and now only the stern flagpole breaks the horizon line between sky and sea. The passengers are calm, exhausted by their ordeal by riot at the border post. The coastal range rises majestically ahead of us above the brume.

Powerful Egyptian profiles abound among the sleeping deck cargo; rounded chins, full lips open in sleep, hooked noses and straight brows, much darker-skinned than the peoples of Asia Minor.

A young geographer studies my maps. He has been on holiday for seven weeks and is 'mellow now', he says. Seven weeks! How do the West Germans do this and still be so productive?

We are all beset by the enforced contemplation of steamboats crossing flat, windless seas. The shore looks as distant as the world from space; as London from Egypt; as love from loneliness. Navigating between these points of perspective can bring a brief fix on one's own future. A sea voyage can show what we want to be doing with life, reveal the strategic heights. I must put flags on these peaks while the air is clear and bright. New job, wife, new house, family…

An Egyptian passenger wakes me. We have dropped anchor off Nuweiba and now wait for the harbourmaster to clear the dock. Over the rail, a passing school of pink jellyfish balloons its way north.

*

At Egyptian customs and border control we encounter the most arrogant and menacing police yet to present themselves on our tour.

My Lady is emptied of seats, carpets and door panels and driven up a ramp for a thorough under-body inspection. Among other novelties, I cannot enter unless I buy a Mickey Mouse fire extinguisher. Literally, it has a picture of Mickey on it.

The only way to handle these swaggering cops is to make life merry, to poke them immediately but playfully if they poke you, to act out an elaborate game of double-checking that they have looked at everything, to read every word of the customs carnet small print before signing and to take an immense time to pack up and leave.

In the process we gain a new identity; 1909 is the registration number for 15 XKN, and she is an honorary Egyptian.

*

Five miles of Sinai and the road has offered no trees, one bus, two cars and seven wild camels. The tarmac is good, but the desert is more hostile than anything in Syria. You could not imagine Special Forces surviving a long march here, let alone the Children of Israel.

Verdi's *Falstaff*, conducted by Bernard Haitink, heard live by this princess of picnics last summer, drifting over the car park at Glyndebourne, now rings in reproduction between the bristling, jagged mountains. The echoes rattle like pigeons in the roof of a customs hanger.

If Jordan was the Cairngorms, Sinai is the Alps.

Evening draws in. The peaks and chasms seem to exude a red beyond the visible spectrum, prolonging the sunset. The air is a passionate exhalation. Even after dusk the sky remains light enough to admire the endless painting which unfolds through this barren kingdom.

Our soft yellow headlights sweep the verges. A candle-wax charabanc slips sedately between escarpments of the mind.

Day 38

The pleasures of an early morning stroll: an orange in my pocket, bare feet on wet sand, warm clear sea lapping between my toes, a strong sun low in a cerulean sky, balanced by a cool steady breeze.

Two dive boats moored to the jetty are loading provisions. Wetsuits have been hung out under emerald awnings. The flashing windows and glistening varnish contrast with the rough peaks beyond. I lean forward, forgetting the spectacles on my lap, and they fall gently on my footprint. Their polished factory finish is similarly incongruous.

The truth is, I would so much rather be driving than diving.

*

Today is the first day of Ramadan. Thoughts of fasting, closed banks and scarce petrol stations pull me up at a holiday village. I need breakfast, Egyptian currency and water for the radiator.

It is as if twenty acres of Bavaria have been lifted from beside the Tegernsee and dropped on to some of the best scuba-diving in the world. With green artificial turf and black wooden furniture, this is home from home for the von Trapps. Some of the guests are Brits, including even one expat family from Cairo. The father helps me change money.

*

I am parked on another strand, bigger, wider, like a blank page, with an inlet of turquoise water. Before me, the flat unblemished sand runs gradually into warm shallows as free of weed and waste as they have been for millennia. The Bentley's stereo croons Chris Rea's 'On the Beach'.

Ras Mohammed is a name on the map, the southernmost tip of Sinai, but there is little else. A tarmac road, hot enough to melt tyres, wanders to it through the desert. But no building awaits at the end. Instead two sentry boxes greet you, one to take a small entry fee, the other to log your number plate so that they know to come looking if the allure of the place should addle your brain.

Then you are free to wander the dunes, inspect bay after empty bay until you find untouched sands which fit your own idea of paradise. And you may strip and lie on the saffron surface and sleep until the sun crisps you to bacon; or, if you have had the foresight, which I didn't, you could pull a hamper from the boot, lay out a damask tablecloth and sip chilled champagne while the cold salmon is sliced, without the slightest fear of interruption, even by flies. But please take away every last scrap of rubbish when you leave.

Whether Ras Mohammed is always as empty as this I do not know. I wade a long way out, naked. I swim to the far side of my lagoon, where some tracks indicate that a visitor with more courage than skill once put his four-wheel-drive machine into a tight corner in the shallows and had problems getting out. But today the world is paralysed by the start of Ramadan. My Lady is alone with her inheritance. She lifts her nose into the breeze. The air runs over her. In this blazing heat, her pale skin remains cool to the touch. The sun is so high that it drops though the windows only onto the back shelf and the very top of the walnut fascia. This weather makes a mockery of sunroofs – you would never open one.

Egypt. Above: Sinai, Day 37 (page 144); below: Ras Mohammed, Day 38 (page 145)

War and Peace is coming to a close: 1,200 pages gone, 100 to go. My journey is the same: 1,800 miles covered, just 200 left up the Gulf of Suez.

*

The tide is still going out. The softest lapping is all that can be heard. A solitary raven flies low along the waterline in front of me, big and black, the only living creature seen in hours. It beats off gently, like a regretful farewell, and I roll up my rug and leave just as quietly.

*

Away from the water's edge, the day is so potently hot that the vista crawls beaten beneath it. The unremitting blast is hypnotic. The margins of safety are wafer-thin once more – no detours to points of scenic grandeur. Now I understand that exhalation of heat and light which struck as dusk fell yesterday. It was a masterclass in radiation wavelengths.

The Bentley holds a steady fifty miles an hour because the temperature gauge has sprung a new trick, reading completely cold, which is more outrageous than completely hot.

The highway runs away from the sea, up into a shattered valley. The mountains on either side are stegosaurus spines. Like driving through dinosaur country, you would not get far here if your car broke down.

Later the sea reappears, bringing sand dunes. The larger ones threaten to block the road but never quite do. The Bentley lifts a dust trail as she clips each apex in turn.

We pass a refinery with three high chimneys topped with yellow waste flares.

*

The water situation is looking tight. My Lady will be parched again soon, but I would rather not stop to check now because she could just stall and not restart until sunset.

Three small children back there were standing by the road near a village, waving plastic containers. I thought they were selling water but, on reflection, perhaps they were begging for it.

Later, a petrol station breaks the emptiness. Out comes the heavy Allen key, the saucer-sized radiator cap hisses slightly as I free it off and four litres of bottled H_2O go straight into the filler neck without a splash. Fuelled and trying to forget the unholy lavatory I found around the back, I climb behind the steering wheel and take up the chase once more. I have forty-three hours to be in the office.

*

This must be the place where the Israelis counter-attacked across the Gulf of Suez before the Arab oil embargo forced a ceasefire in the 1973 Yom Kippur war. The terrain has been flattened into a wide park for mechanised armour, and here, where the road swings round to the left, is one abandoned straggler, a medium tank, rusted by salt air and desert dew to a darker red than the landscape. It is just too far away to inspect clearly without stopping, which would be foolhardy.

Mile upon mile we roll on. The lengthening shadow of the Bentley's profile runs along the wasteland to the east like a ground-skimming UFO.

*

In the evening, a first clump of palm trees arrests us with its verdant decoration. Reversing among them, the gearbox fades away into neutral. The Bentley takes five minutes to remember whatever she did at Piraeus and cure herself, while I stretch my legs under the unfamiliar vegetation as the day cools.

Then on to the Suez Canal while night draws the drapes. Fork left at the T-junction and enter a heavily reinforced tunnel. It is dark as we stop at the crossroads, now on the west bank of the canal, to check the compass and choose a route.

Which way to turn? Down to Suez to be near civilisation; and also to buy some sugar or coffee for my mother? That would play on a family joke: she still squirrels away a small hoard of such luxuries, 'Suez Stores', in the expectation that food rationing will be reintroduced, as it nearly was in the Suez Crisis of 1956.

Three DCP (desert camouflage pattern)-clad villains appear out of the darkness and make as if to climb into the car. They look only vaguely like the soldiers they say they are. The decision is forced on me. I drive off the way I am facing, which is south. When in doubt, one hitchhiker at a time, and none at night, that's the rule, thank you very much.

Minutes later, we are on the outskirts of Suez. I find a crumbling service station, a chance to refuel. With the engine mumbling, the attendant fills the tank. The note from the straight-six drops distinctly, as bad petrol mixes with the brew brought over from Sinai, Jordan and beyond and reaches the twin carburettors. This must be the 80 octane lamp oil which the handbook mentions. I wonder how the Mercedes desert cruiser would have coped with this.

From the far side of the garage, a train toots on top of an embankment. Then I see, or do I imagine, its funnel, lit up like a Christmas tree, passing along the ridge. But the funnel is many times too big for a train.

It is a ship in the canal behind.

A mile further down the road, the city gathers itself into suburbs and swells in amplitude. Rich odours, savage drivers, pedestrians swarming between arc-lit bazaars, vans and taxis breaking down all over the wide tarmac runways that have been driven through the slums. Suez's vehicle stock comes from beyond the grave. Among these zombies, the Bentley has the alluring bloom of life. Sorry, Mum, but I dare not leave such a flower to their mercy while I shop for sugar.

*

Back up the west bank of the Suez Canal about four miles to the crossroads. The soldiers have gone. Turn left, another tunnel, under another, smaller waterway, and into…

Africa.

Day 39

Dawn. A lay-by off the fast road from Suez, east of Egypt's capital.

No sudden movements. Sit up and let the knee joints ease after their third night folded against the door. The fire of sunrise kindles my urge to be rolling.

Much to do today.

Climb over to the front seat. Ten turns of the key, but bad petrol makes for a dismal desert breakfast. The engine almost catches, then stops in that roulette spot, with the missing flywheel teeth aligned to the starter motor.

I lift the bonnet and turn the fan, and the ageing Lady responds gamely. She is warming up as the sun breaks over the sand dunes to the east. It must be about 5 a.m.

*

The endless sprawling backstreets of Cairo. No place for a gentle Englishwoman. But she has timed her entrance well. The boulevards are empty because of Ramadan; the faithful are staying home late to conserve strength for their daylight fast; and the sky is clear.

Using the sun and the compass, we thread our way westwards, sometimes tracking back to dodge over a railway, sometimes disputing one-way streets, always ignoring traffic lights. One thing is sure. Not even I can mistake the Nile when we find it.

A train terminus appears. I saw it on my brief reconnaissance going home from Izmir at Christmas. The east bank of the river must be close now.

A U-turn on a flyover section, a right-hand exit from a left-hand slip road and the river is won. I park Pharaoh's daughter on the corniche and lean over the railings to gape at the limpid waterway. Among such reeds Moses was found. For five thousand years, this artery has pulsed with civilisation. It makes Sardis young. Man's rages, passions, dreams all pass. But not the Nile.

*

Breakfast on the terrace of the Hotel Intercontinental Semiramis. Here I had melon and guava ice cream at Christmas.

The Parker ballpoint pen which has held out since Vesuvius is packing up. The waitress gives me her equivalent.

After the thirsty plain, the sumptuous buffet is unbearably delicious, and I drink insatiably. Two glasses of – is it mango? A big glass of – passion fruit essence, if such an extract exists. An identical glass of orange juice; a cool, plump date, spicy hummus, Lebanese greens, purple gherkins in lemon juice, marinated nuts, unleavened bread, a croissant, a sweet yellow sticky bun, scrambled eggs, sausages, bacon, fruit salad with chopped strawberries, apple, green melon, honeydew melon, and orange and pomegranate seeds. Set against the oven-coast since Ras Mohammed, the wet fruit of Cairo is a personal aquifer.

As history undergraduates studying American slavery, we read of the obscenely indulgent breakfasts which British planters could eat in their evil mansions in the West Indies – hams, chickens, cakes, bottles of Madeira wine and all. We thought it exaggerated. In my present prandial bliss, even they seem possible. My gaze must be as glassy as the steel river below.

Empty passenger launches plough their way to their first calls. Near the far bank, beneath the palm and eucalyptus trees, two men row a boat standing up, with little progress.

*

I have rested the Bentley outside the hotel and taken a taxi to the customs building. This much was established at Christmas. Leaving Egypt is like leaving Turkey. Your car must first be impounded by the State.

Traffic, fumes, soldiers in red berets, hot sunlight, the blue eyes of a blue-wrapped girl in a blue car, weaving through the klaxonning, swerving rush hour. She noses in beside us in the jam but soon passes ahead.

The Bentley would have overheated long ago.

Poisonous exhaust to suffocation point.

We are now driving north. It seems to be a long way. The meter is not running, despite my protests. Policemen with white-chequered sleeves to their black uniforms; a flyover; a motorcyclist with pillion rider forces through, tooting, on the inside – no crash helmets of course. Pedestrians have to stand sideways and breathe in not to be run down. A six-lane highway pauses for a level crossing where the tracks have sunk like a dry Syrian riverbed – then immediately back to highway again.

Everything slows for a ridiculous speed bump built across the road. We are now driving into the sun.

*

At the car pound in Medina Knassre, Nasser City, the first sight through the gates is a Rolls-Royce radiator. It is reassuring, albeit dust-caked and on a set of burst tyres. The customs office does not open for another hour. The taxi driver agrees to sell me a bulk rate for two hours, and we settle down to wait. He traps a sheet of newspaper in my rear passenger window to keep the sun out. I prop up my bag on the back shelf to do the same. I miss my book. I could have finished it.

The customs pound faces through a linked wire fence directly on to the highway. All six lanes are jammed with buses, taxis, motorbikes and battered Peugeots. A few minibuses and delivery trucks are in the throng, but no heavy lorries.

The heat and dust are worse after a minibus takes to the rubble to round a stalled jalopy.

My taxi driver is a small, unshaven man with a short-sleeved shirt coloured like a decked coffee and chocolate sundae. Thin golden threads run across the shirt and round the sleeves at the junction of each layer of brown.

The trick for staying cool is to move as little as possible, to forget about the future and relive breakfast in the imagination.

*

We are now inside the car pound. More waiting. I pull a chair out of an office and sit on the walkway, watching the caretaker hose down the brick path. Against the sky, under the lemon tree, flies hang like toys over a child's cot, swaying gently in formation, bandits in the sun.

Their tiny bodies gleam black. Their wings spin silver.

Time passes.

The caretaker finishes with the hose. A soldier who was asleep under the wall wakes up, shoulders his gun and fetches the pipe to spray the dusty surfaces around his stool, then sits. You can feel the bricks and earth cooling as the water evaporates.

At first, of course, nothing is possible. Take the car out of the country, take it anywhere, back to England, we don't care, you are not leaving without it. But the combination of patience and an unusual story prove irresistible. Officialdom creaks into unfamiliar movement.

We agree that what I need is a six-month visa. Then I could leave the car here, or with a friend, or with a hotel. Mr Taha himself would do the necessary with the *Triptik* papers, 'most willingly'.

Outside, the taxi driver is waiting, asleep on the back seat. I know the feeling. I wake him.

We are off. I should be at work tomorrow. And how lucky I am, not to be driving.

What is this splendid fortress we are passing? The Citadela, he says, for the military.

The road back through the slums follows the course of a high stone aqueduct, built in the Middle Ages to last a millennium. Gaps have been knocked out of it to make way for mechanical life forms that drink a different fluid.

*

Six-month visas do not come easy; Mr Taha omitted to mention that.

For each month of extension you must show you have exchanged US$180-worth of hard currency into Egyptian pounds. Unfortunately I only discovered this on completion of my first application, which netted me twelve days.

The minotaur edifice where they issue visas is beyond Hollywood gothic. The Moggama building, literally The Combined, is a death trap from the moment you step through the door. Any daylight that makes it past the coarse-wired glass, blackened with filth, is lampooned by lines of jaundiced fluorescent lights.

Its eighteen storeys are reached by one round stairwell, reminiscent of the well at Al Taggibah. This unguarded central throat is vertiginous to the point of making suicide seductive. In a fire, the broad shaft would draw like a furnace chimney. The flames on any floor would quickly spread, ripping through the acres of matchwood pens which corral nigh-on 20,000 staff. The few lift shafts would fan the conflagration. In the decrepit lifts themselves, the buttons work only if you toggle them back out with your fingernails.

Waiting for the thrill of execution, the many-hued tribes of man surge and shamble between the floors, between the pens, and within each queue, in the struggle to reach the front.

Having done it all once and gained twelve days, I force myself to return, loaded up with money, to dance the slaughterhouse shuffle all over again.

*

Now my passport says I need not fetch the car until August 22nd, which is a plausible time for a holiday.

*

If anyone is looking for a doctoral thesis topic, *The Location of British Embassies within Urban Environments* would make for an erudite monograph. Presumably Britannia hung on to the best sites in all her ex-colonies.

In Cairo the embassy adjoins the Nile, looking out to the playboy island of El Gezira, just three blocks upstream from my hotel. The embassy clubhouse still echoes to the gramophone strains of a gentler time. Tall windows give on to green, well-tended gardens. A pretty, fair-haired young woman walks round and throws them open saying, 'Let's have some fresh air'. Three children and a mum pad through the bar area with towels over their shoulders on their way out to the swimming pool. The male diplomats all seem to sport beards.

The walls are decorated with framed newspaper vendors' flysheets of Fleet Street headlines past, and the coats of arms of forgotten warships. They are like the banners from football matches still hanging in the bedroom of a boy who has long since left home. Such sentimental treasures. The stomach knots to see them now, icons of a country frittered away in the 1950s, 1960s and 1970s.

To my amazement I meet the sandy-haired Englishman who helped me at the Schwarzwald holiday camp before Ras Mohammed by changing money from his own pocket. He tells me of his work out here. His charm and the enthusiastic twinkle in his eye show him to be a fitting ambassador for his country.

I tell him about my last week of travels.

'You missed a magnificent sight in Aleppo that first day in Syria,' he says. 'Their souk is the best anywhere. Covered alleys, so narrow, between miles and miles of stalls.'

He was one of our Foreign Office staff thrown out of Damascus when Britain broke off relations in 1986. I remember the case. It was a tit-for-tat expulsion. A Jordanian hitman, working for Syrian diplomats in London, duped his pregnant

Irish girlfriend to carry a 3lb bomb onto an El Al flight from Heathrow to Tel Aviv. The bomb was only found at the third and last line of security checks. The Jordanian was sentenced to forty-five years in prison. It was shown in court that the Syrian ambassador had personally provided assistance. But of course the Syrian regime had to protest its innocence or imply tacit approval.

'After we were expelled, the Syrians were punctilious about returning their British Council library books,' he says, 'even though they had only twenty-four hours' warning.'

We discuss the safety of long-term parking in Cairo. I tell my new friend how, twice now, I have made preparations to attend to the Bentley in the embassy garage here, and twice I have not taken up the arrangements.

Mr Storey, a tall figure, like a veteran sergeant major, appears.

I say, 'Mr Leach has had telexes and phone calls from me since Christmas. He probably suspects an elaborate hoax.' Mr Leach is their head of household.

'No, no, he was expecting you. He waited until just an hour ago but has left on two weeks' leave.'

Mr Storey settles me with a glass of bottled ale and even finds a greetings telex from my father; all's well at home. But sadly there are no instructions from an Arab contact of mine about possible private lodgings for my soon-to-be-abandoned mistress. Had Mr Leach been here, perhaps he could have made arrangements within the embassy compound. We conclude that the best option now is to try a big hotel.

From the French windows I feel the sprightly afternoon breeze. It is 4 p.m. Maybe I can still save today.

Let's go.

*

The air is hot; the traffic moves but the slipstream through the taxi window just roasts your face. The trip back to Medina Knassre confirms again how much more lethal for the Bentley African cities are than deserts. She would be burnt to toast if I tried to bring her even this far, let alone left her in the open customs park in the hotter months to come.

The broad exhaust of a bus is levelled at my face through the window. It will blast me with monoxides when this jam moves and we all gun our engines. Wind window up fast. If I make it out of here, I will park My Lady underground at the Semiramis.

What if I had caught Mr Leach this morning before he left? In fairness to the daily users of the embassy car park, he could never have given away a space there for four months, even for a fee.

The taxi weaves to avoid a car with a rear-wheel puncture, the third in just one mile. Back over the wadi-like level crossing. We must be nearly there. We are, and the compound is closed. It has been since 2 p.m. If I had come here before the embassy I might have made it. But I did not know how things stood there, whether they had the space. I thought Mr Leach was around. And I would have missed my diplomat friend from Sinai.

Another day lost. At least the customs office opens again tomorrow.

On the return leg the world is a furnace of overheating internal combustion engines, flogging into the eye of the sun. The train terminus where I found my bearings in the calm of morning is now the centre of the cauldron. The traffic lies like a fistful of straws dropped from a height. The taxi driver switches off, and we watch a tram try to cross fourteen lanes of stationary traffic. This pushes the envelope for conceivable human stupidity. Cairo city planning. Is that an oxymoron?

Despite buses ramming into the melee up the wrong side of the street, despite small boys being knocked aside as the traffic bounds five yards, the tram forces a passage. My taxi driver starts up, shrugs and switches off, starts up, shouts, inches forward. No. There is absolutely no room between us and that green car. The green car is having its own showdown with a horse and cart. The horse must be blind and deaf. On all sides the traffic roars and hoots at it.

Trams intimidate large lorries. Large lorries intimidate buses, buses intimidate taxis. Taxis intimidate private cars and private cars try to scare beasts of burden.

The horse rears pathetically and our taxi grabs the chance to cut across it. Now we are stationary and the half-dead creature hangs its head just above our boot. We edge forward. The carter appears to want to pass us back. We come up to a taxi boiled over, facing the wrong way on our side of the road. Its driver cajoles it back to life and joins our own flow, simply reversing along.

Five minutes, five feet. Five cars are fighting for the gap. Tremendous shouting. Yes, we will turn this one-way street back into a two-way street or die in the attempt.

A man wheels a barrow of empty Coca-Cola bottles across the leaping street. We miss him by an inch. Now we are moving, we attempt to kill a pedestrian every fifteen seconds.

The taxi blazes down the street, pulling up to a strange hotel. Here we are, says the driver.

Ah, my friend, I said the Intercontinental, near the Meridian, not the Continental, legend though it is. I see, says the driver, and the engine stops. It has boiled. He grabs his plastic container and walks away to find water.

With a rag he tentatively releases the radiator cap. Steam shoots out. He starts the engine and pours in the coolant. The radiator takes the whole five litres.

I have never mistreated my own wheels so badly. Ever.

Now we are moving, faster even than you would down the Rue de Rivoli on a night of wild existentialism.

I don't believe it. We have stopped for a red light.

*

Hotel Intercontinental Semiramis. The name is a password out of Purgatory. Cool air like elixir in your lungs. Marble. Plashing water. A tent of oxygen-rich relief, one, two, three strides from the world.

Day 40

The visa extension office in the Moggama building is in frisky mood.

Although we cattle this side of the security glass cannot feel it, a refreshing morning breeze blows through the windows behind the passport clerks. A small woman in light blue with matching turban has sole power to operate the visa stamp on the table beside her desk. She struts around berating her colleagues and subordinates.

I have a bottle of water tucked in my bag from the hotel, but even so, the foul air on our side of the screen makes me sick.

You have to force yourself to enter a hell hive like this. Earlier this morning I turned back, deciding that the heat of Libya in August would be preferable to extending my visa this morning a second time, by a month.

But I seem to be getting the knack of the place. Already my passport sits on the desk beside the stamping machine, and only the woman with the turban can stop it now. Her eyes are streaming from some infection. She stands with her hands on her hips, or leans masterfully on her table, and ignores my bundle of franked and stapled documents.

I should stop writing and look more contrite.

*

From the vile tower for visas, I scramble to the flyblown customs yard on the outskirts and back to the refrigerated hotel, where the room bill has been marked up by fifteen per cent and the cost of a long-term car space by nearly double. Both prices retreat to their original level only after an appeal to the general manager.

Then, with a pat on her nose, I tell My Lady to keep out of trouble while I'm away, hurl my cases into a cab and race for the airport.

From Terminal 1 I hop to Terminal 2 and secure a place in a standby queue for Brussels. This is the last flight to northern Europe today. The critical moment approaches. The desk manager, a grey-haired Belgian of archetypal roundness, beckons me from across the empty departures hall.

'Yes, I can let you go on this flight. Please show me your bank exchange forms.'

I show him this morning's photocopies and explain about the visa office taking the originals. He says only original forms will do. The flight is called for the last time. He will not relent. I try the airport banks. They want credit cards, against which I have so far made a stand in life, not Eurocheques.

It seems incredible that one can have such wads of legally obtained Egyptian pounds in one's belt and not be able to catch this flight. I grab a taxi, but while we are searching for a hotel with a cashier, the roar of the Sabena plane is heard. I watch it lift from the end of the runway and turn away to the north.

I will not be at work tomorrow after all. Meetings must be cancelled. It is too aggravating, disaster snatched from the jaws of victory.

I creep back incognito to the Bentley's ice-palace to lick my wounds.

Strange that this pinnacle of Cairo's pleasure domes, with no idea of the value of money, is the only place I can now afford. For here they don't balk at cash.

Just checking in certifies you as beyond all that.

*

By taxi at dead of night, the journey from the Semiramis to the Great Pyramid at Giza should take about half an hour. Seven miles by moonlight. The last four are dead straight along the Al Haram, a wide avenue with a line of single palms down the central reservation, which runs west from the old bridge over the Nile.

My mother's father, Bobby Loyd, came this way as a boy of thirteen, in 1900. He had caught the perfect illness: a nasty chest infection just before starting at a new school. The school would not take him, as he would be a danger to his classmates. His parents were departing on a long-planned and too-often-delayed tour of the Mediterranean. His mother refused to leave him at home. The doctor recommended a hot dry climate.

So they booked an extra cabin and he went with them.

The party came to Egypt, which the British had colonised eighteen years before. Bobby bought a 3,000-year-old mummified bird as a souvenir and kept the change, pierced coinage, which was almost as exciting to the boyish mind. He also made an early addition to his lifelong fund of anecdotes, catchphrases and punchlines, which were repeated around our home when I was little.

One day, he and his parents were looking down on a valley. A procession passed by below with cymbals, drumming, chanting and wailing. Bobby asked their dragoman what the celebration was for. The guide said it was in memory of an ancestor buried nearby. This ceremony had been paid for by the deceased, long into the future. Bread was brought to the graveside to feed the dead man's spirit.

'How often do they do it?' my grandfather asked the guide.

To which came the reply, now family code for uncertainty about a future date, 'Not velly often, sometimes seldom, Monday afternoon.'

*

My driver hesitates at the unmanned barrier in front of the Pyramids. He is as scared as I am. The monuments are still some distance away, pitch black, unilluminated, starless quadrants of a starry sky. The place is deserted.

I say to drive through. At the T-junction of the path I say 'Turn right', and we circle to the north of the most massive of these objects. We travel along its side for a while.

'Stop here,' I tell him. 'Wait.'

Opening the door, I run fifty yards to the first of the world's seven wonders, 4,500 years old.

Over six million tons in weight. How long would that have taken to build? I hold my palm against the first ground-level block, at face height; then my forehead. If each block is twenty-five tons, and forty blocks were laid in a day, at six million tons that would be 6,000 days of work, about twenty years. The long production line to carve, transport and lay just one block per day, plus their provisions, might occupy a team of 1,000 men. So, forty blocks, 40,000 men, for twenty years, should do it.

Although this is the north face, the stone is still warmer than the cooling air.

At just this time of night I once pressed my head to a sarsen stone at Stonehenge. That had a similar sense of the mind-numbing effort to put it there. The same gentle resonance. The caution in the face of the unexplained.

But here, infinitely more so, is the feeling of a mountain between me and the moon.

Chapter Three: High Noon

Egypt, Libya, Tunisia, Algeria, Morocco, Spain, Portugal
Saturday 26th August to Sunday 10th September 1989

Day 41

Another crescent desert moon, so low I fancy a pyramid nearby. The compressed hiss of big jet engines winding down. The humid August night breathes through the airside coach's windows as we sway across the runway. Will My Lady's new tyre be on the luggage belt or did the flight details peel off its elegant tread? It could have gone anywhere in the five hours since I saw it at Heathrow.

Passport control lingers over my multiple visa but makes no comments. Now, with the clocks at just past 2 a.m., our dazed gaggle from EgyptAir Flight 705 waits by the conveyor in the polished granite hall. No pressure from over-willing porters at this hour. Even the black-bereted Egyptian soldiers stay propped up on their weapons in the corners.

Surely the Bentley's replacement tyre, naked as the day it was moulded, will have pride of place up the baggage chute. Ha, my truck-sized rubber is indeed first off the plane; I jump through the advancing crowd, up on to the belt to grab the heavy carcass and heave it onto a trolley. My holdall follows and I steer towards the tax men, the potentially ruinous gauntlet of customs.

'How much did this tyre cost?'

'Not much. It's for my old car, it's an old tyre.'

The customs man smiles wanly and waves me through, between a twin line of stragglers from an earlier flight. These unfortunates are still spreading their bedroom secrets before the inspectors.

We're away, with the best part of a suspension rebuild tucked up in my bag:

- one new patent hydraulic shock absorber;
- upper and lower lever arms;
- bolts;
- rubber bushes and mounting blocks.

Not to mention a complete distributor, with two spare rotor arms and two sets of points for old times' sake, plus various hoses and belts – the straight-six ones this time – in all, a small fortune in customs dues, if I really had been importing them, which I'm not.

But try explaining that at 02:15 in Arabic.

I hate to think what El Al security would have made of it.

My precious cargo rides its trolley down the corridor and out into the night. Brace for the midnight cowboys. But the car parks are quiet too. Even the taxi drivers are beyond giving me a hard time.

The landing has been a complete success.

The bridgehead has been stormed.

*

My black-and-white taxi drops me beside the Semiramis. The Nile glistens like a luggage belt. Tooting cars, even at 3 a.m. on a Saturday, irritate the ears with a steady prickle; flags loll exhausted aboard the river steamer sleeping at the quay.

Everywhere stone, cloth and metal are the same colour they would be in London. Yet the world they form has warped in the copying. How can such contrasts of climate, language and manners exist in an imitation of home? A moment ago, yesterday, when I believed only in finance, in memos left on tape to be transcribed and circulated as 'Dictated but not seen', these flatbed lorries loaded with grain sacks were already pushing down the corniche, jostling and surging, as if this too was the only city on earth.

A man walks past me up the pavement dragging a running hosepipe. Clear water pours smooth and lazy from its tip. Beside me in the gloom is a ramp spiralling down to the underground car park where the Bentley awaits.

I feel like a young admirer hesitating to enter a girl's room for the first time, for fear of a mortifying scream. Would she be surprised to be woken? She has been asleep for 100 days. The grit of a merciless urban summer will rest upon her as thick as a century of palace dust. If I just creep away and say hello over breakfast… No, then there would be no sleep for me.

Walking down the ramp, out of the hot night, the lintel of the garage entrance rises with each stride, revealing a deep stage. The lights are on. I pass the black-and-yellow barrier, past the American saloons, the white Mercedes, past stares and halting challenges from several attendants, even at this hour.

A dusty, shrouded form is backed up to a wall, boxed in behind lesser spawn. Grey powder from some mummy-chamber has dropped over it, *ersatz* icing sugar. An attendant comes up and shakes my hand under the strip lights.

We approach the shape, a monstrous egg, a cocoon from a lost world, an unborn Thing incubating in a fatty cell, an essay in suspended animation, peaceful, unstrained, pregnant with tomorrow.

Suddenly I am exhausted. Sleep for her, and now some sleep for me.

Day 42

Fog on the Nile. Or could it be that the air conditioning, which froze me in bed, has also misted the windows? No, it is real fog.

Out on the balcony, in the dawn sauna, I warm up and clear from my head the dream of desert war, the topic of my book on the flight down from Heathrow.

The Father of Egypt is running deep, still as a millpond. The Aswan High Dam is open for the man-made flood season and the river level is at its peak. The corniche's blare has risen from a prickle to the whine of swarming mosquitoes. Deep below this, the heavy waterboats throb, churning upstream, past the palm-shaped Cairo Tower opposite, under the nine-span road bridge and away behind the neighbouring block.

Perhaps some breakfast would help my head.

Over olives and hummus I think of Brendan's friend, Bruce, the chief mechanic at Frank Dales, where I picked up the tyre and my bag of spare parts yesterday. I see him in his workshop, surrounded by the swept running boards, lacquered wings and chromed headlights the size of fire buckets, and feel again his handshake. He is wiry, puckish, with grey hair disdaining attempts to comb it back, and a way of looking up sideways at a question. He is as comfortable in the company of his old Bentleys and Rolls-Royces as the showroom floor they are parked on. His sympathy with excellence is that of the seabed for the sea. Injustices and intrigues have long since been dismissed with a shake of the head as irrelevant. What must be is solid engineering.

But Africa? He wished me luck. I feel braver to have received his blessing.

*

The assistant manager brings My Lady's key. It is still in the white envelope in which I gave it to him. Together we take the lift to the basement car park.

The Thing has become a monster of the deep. Its remora are cleared away. A smart attendant hooks the shroud from under one corner and slowly draws it back.

Like peeling a lychee, the rough canvas shears away cleanly from the surface beneath. The lower radiator emerges, then one big round headlight, then the wings of the flying mascot, the long bonnet and half the curved and tinted windscreen, then the central roof aerial, folded to the side, and the door handles, and finally the whole wedding-white crepusculance is free. The contrast between the underside of the shed snakeskin, which is clean, and its grimy outer surface emphasises the billiard-ball whiteness beneath.

Another attendant approaches with a red pail full of soapy water on a barrow. He begins to wash the sleepy dust from her eyes. The Lady looks rested, composed, strong, with her prime still before her, a match for the heat of the desert, that long military coast road, the Via Balbi, the *Rommelbahn*, fought for by men of legend.

The flannel-bath is finished. Now the attendant rinses her off, water scooped from his dustbin with a beaker. As a final devotion, he scrubs and checks the wheels, all tyres still rock hard, before drying her.

The car park supervisor takes the key, but of course My Lady rejects his advances. The driver's door is on the other side, and her key works only that. I do the honours, as I should have in the first place. Entering the cool dark interior, seeing the almond nuts on the floor, strewn as a telltale just in front of the pedals, the water-purifying kit, the old white shoes which climbed Vesuvius this time last year, I am certain she has not been disturbed. I reach over and down and pull the left-hand bonnet release.

I climb out and walk round, run a finger along her lines and check again the solid tyres. 'No problem,' says the man with the soft cloth. Raising the passenger-side bonnet, I tip a litre of oil into the rocker cover.

*

The hotel air conditioning ticks like a cricket. The bell boy has carried down the luggage. Inspired by My Lady's example I have taken a bath, gathered myself and am now ready for the truth. Will she start?

In the garage we wheel her forward. She has not been on chocks as I asked, so the tyres are slightly deformed, and it takes four men to push her off the flat-spots. Lorry jump leads from Izmir are hooked up to the meanest Mercedes, commandeered for the big moment. With the German car being gunned, I sit at my wood-and-leather helm and turn the key. Nothing of the starter motor can be heard above the Schwabian din. Then the Derby straight-six fires. The machinery is thirty-two years old. And before that the design had nearly four decades of steady engineering development – witness its eight rings per piston, thirty-nine high-tensile bolts just to hold down the cylinder head. But these are still the sweetest harmonics in the world.

Now she ticks over, blocking an amazed Fiat driver who has just screeched down the ramp.

I stall her. We repeat the process. She starts immediately this time, and I reverse her out of harm's way. As the battery accumulates its charge, the water temperature creeps up to normal. Column-shift gear lever down; wheel hard over to the right for the ramp; and we are off.

We burst up on to the street like a submarine crash-surfacing. The sun and the air pour over us.

Several times round the block to ease her joints, then along the road to the sheet steel gates of the British embassy.

A name and a handshake are enough to gain entry. My original letter of request last November, subsequent telexes and the visit in the spring are not forgotten. My correspondent, Mike Leach, is absent again, in England. Mr Storey is on leave. However, behind the long, high walls, the gardens are still their manicured selves.

During a careful inspection for bombs by the gatekeeper, I am introduced to the embassy mechanic, Mohsen, standing at ease by the barrier in his spotless overalls, like St Peter at the Pearly Gates. I am very aware that this service is not available to all British travellers. I invite him with a wave to climb into the passenger seat and direct me to the corner he has chosen for us. I imagine we will do the work at one of the open car park spaces.

He signals me ahead, round the back of a barrack-like block, towards some high, azure doors.

Inside is an expansive, white-tiled workshop, with two immaculate inspection pits. Tools hang neatly in rows along the walls, set by set, above pristine workbenches. An enormous gantry crosses the ceiling with tackle big enough to hoist the turret off a tank.

Mohsen points out a mirror placed against the far wall on the floor to help cars drive up centrally over the pit. In it we can see straight under the Bentley to the sunny garden… and steam puffing gently from the bottom of her radiator. Her water is just coming to the boil.

I cut the engine and it runs on for some seconds. Maybe for the first time in her life, the fairest of them all is absorbed with her own reflection.

*

Mr Ahab, the defence attaché's driver, introduces himself; long-limbed, with the bloodhound features of a Pharaoh's chamberlain. He wears light clothes and speaks in an ancient *basso profundo*.

Together, Mohsen and he walk round the cooling concubine, discussing possible problems of lubrication, hydraulics and electrics. I show them the parts I have brought from Bruce, also the relevant pages copied from the workshop manual, covering shock absorbers and upper and lower lever arms. Then the new distributor and other spares are inspected.

A welcome mug of tea is pressed into my hand.

I explain that the last major service was only 2,500 miles ago, but since then the whole system has crossed the Syrian Desert and been left standing in a basement for five months. The front suspension needs a rebuild, the ignition timing slips all over the place and the radiator boils, as you see.

Mohsen says he trained on Rolls-Royces. Now the ambassador has a Daimler, and the staff share half a dozen Land and Range Rovers. Around us are cylinder heads and engine blocks from V8 diesels, a compressor, a welding torch and a caged-off stores section. However, the tools on the wall are Rolls Royce and you can tell from the mechanic's manner where his real affections lie.

Ahab says things are quiet with the holidays. He thinks it will take Mohsen until midday the day after tomorrow, Monday, to do all the work described.

I have leave from my office until Monday in two weeks' time. So midday on Monday will give me thirteen and a half days to reach Portugal, where Charles Prideaux and Charles Whitworth, my former and current flatmates in London, among others, should be recovering from walking the Pilgrims' Way to Santiago de Compostella. If the Bentley could do 250 miles a day, we would be there with a day in hand to find a new parking place before I fly home.

Far better she receives expert pre-emptive treatment now than desperate running repairs later.

*

Ahab and I walk tall and solemn out of the embassy, past the sentries and down the street. At the Nile Hotel he helps me book into a spacious, quiet room – not as flashy as my previous nights' accommodation – but Cairo is in high season and his choice is a good one; strings are being pulled for me. Ahab tips reception with a fluid backhand gesture more like a street-runner's switch than a gift.

It is only 2 p.m. but I take to my new bed for another heaped trencher of sleep.

In the evening, I watch the Belgian Grand Prix in the hotel room – this season's Senna/Prost duel within the McLaren Honda team is epic. Today, Ayrton Senna leads from start to finish in the wet. It is a performance to reaffirm his magic in the rain – that first year, 1984, in the Toleman-Hart at Monaco, going from thirteenth into the lead; and the following year in the Lotus in Portugal, his first win, coming home a minute ahead of the second-placed Ferrari, having lapped the rest of the field. Seven cars span off that day, including Alain Prost's McLaren.

Day 43

Egypt, Libya, Tunisia, Algeria, Morocco, Gibraltar, Spain, Portugal. Cairo to Cape St Vincent. It will be quite a jaunt for *une femme d'un certain âge*.

This Rolls-Bentley marque, which set overland records in India; which was favoured by viceroys and governors because it could master without modification deserts, mountains, rivers and forests; which was the chassis of choice to carry steel plate and a turret gun when the armoured car was being invented; which lent its engine to the British Army's Saracens, Saladins and Ferrets; how strange that such a beast should be reduced to crawling from parish church to confetti-strewn reception, barely reaching fourth gear. Must such a lilied fate await all those who would ingratiate?

For me too, Cairo to Cape St Vincent will be a classic circumvention. It orbits London, where my heart is still in a test of wills. What does my truelove want? Our relationship neither advances nor retreats. She told me 'Be patient', when I proposed. But that was nearly three years ago. She wants my company, my adoration, even my body, but not a life together – yet. 'Yet' is the word I add, nowadays, not she. When will I dare risk asking her again to marry me – 'such a bore'? I thought I could wait forever. I thought that, real and human as she is, under all that beauty and intelligence and wit, she would crumble if I went on being myself, just loving her. This is why I run, when the pain of unreturned commitment becomes too much.

Once, every league I could place between me and her restored my certainty. Now I am turning west. The destination is not India. And something else has changed. Certainty has turned to circumspection. What if she did agree? What is a love if it does not meet you halfway; more than halfway?

This sweep around the southern Mediterranean will not bring her up the aisle. The farthest tip of Europe is no nearer home than here, within striking distance, but not the finish. She should want to be there in Portugal to surprise me, but the thought does not occur to her. How long shall I give it? How fair is it, to wait until her biological clock forces her hand? She should be allowed to make her own life. She is bright enough.

Or am I smarter than that? Will I, like a white-sprayed Bentley leaving its donkey path from church to reception, just once do justice to myself?

All will be well when the wheels roll.

I don't want to shop in the bazaars. The idea of tours to secret chambers deep within pyramids leaves me cold. I want an engine that purrs, a full fuel tank and an open road. Twice round the block yesterday, to the hotel and back, running the black Bakelite helm through my hands, piloting the distant prow, easing on the power to join the train of traffic, pulling up at the embassy – it was bait. Cairo is Essen or Pittsburgh for all the cultural allure I feel now. The Nile is as dull as the English Channel the day I first saw My Lady.

It was a July evening. I had caught the train down to Brighton, changing to the single-track coastal spur which runs the gauntlet of retirement bungalows nestled to the west. At Littlehampton station a grand old rogue called Tony Borodell Brown, who had advertised her in *The Sunday Times* newspaper, met me in his hatchback. He said he had been a Merlin engine fitter during the war, 27-litre V12s on Spitfires, Hurricanes, Lancasters and Mosquitoes. So his Rolls-Royce credentials were clean, but he preferred the Bentley badge. He had managed to own one pretty much ever since. I think he took against this S1 because her colour would have stuck out at the golf club, so he had never road taxed her. When I saw him last he was driving a flawless, two-tone blue S2.

Anyway, before demonstrating the white car, Tony showed me her documented history. The file went back fifteen years to the mid-seventies, and pretty well authenticated her low mileage. If she had only done 30,000 miles in the past fifteen years, who could say she had not done 60,000 in the first, as the milometer said?

Then he led me to a block of up-and-over garages and unlocked a door, mid-row.

Inside, with barely inches to spare, was the pearl I had been seeking. I fell in love as he reversed her out into the sunny concrete courtyard. The aspect from the back as I signalled him round seemed to me then, as it does still, one of the most successful shapes in motoring. Another such design wonder of that period is the rear window of the Aston Martin DB4.

Out on the bypass, Tony let me take the wheel. I had driven one Bentley S-Type in London, but this was different. This helm was pin-sharp. The car exuded decades of sympathetic attention. She was not mint, but then who should be at thirty? Her brakes were on the point of seizure. Her indicator switch had been mounted the wrong way up, and the old valve radio was on its last legs. But steering, gearbox and engine were sound, and my pocket magnet stuck to her body in all the important places.

I went back up to London by the same slow train, slept on it, confirmed her eligibility with personnel and returned the following evening with MAM's cheque.

Over the next fortnight I took the measure of my new conveyance. Two features stood out. She had a long-legged gait, which made even the journey to Scotland for the chance of a Macnab and a watercolour disappointingly short. I had thought the Bombshell Mercedes rangy – it had clocked 100 miles in an hour in the Franco-German borderlands with Christopher Hill as sleeping co-pilot on the way to Verbier; and the next year it toured ten alpine ski resorts, one a day, from La Clusaz to Schladming. But never did it drip with the distillation of Grand Touring, of harmonious momentum, as this big Bentley does.

Such qualities were inexplicable to others.

The fact that I had slipped under the Chancellor's radar for company car tax was conceded as clever. But the choice of weapons was showy. The more I protested, the more it was thought too much.

Between these forces of push and pull, a seed germinated: why not a long run on the Continent to stretch My Lady and rattle my own cage? After Pacha in Ibiza Town, the seedling grew like a beanstalk. This was more than an antidote to moping. I had discovered a panacea.

Who needed a car in central London? One parking ticket saved paid for several taxis. Tubes were faster, and you could read on them. Meanwhile, the holidays stood logic on its head. The further away from base, the cheaper the rations and greater the interest. In a word, the Bentley made me curious. If she drove a coach and horses through the company car rule book, and showed me more of the world than I would otherwise ever try to see, was that so awful?

Unlike the other lady, she says yes.

*

The heat of early afternoon is like a bludgeon.

Air-conditioned lobbies are the only defence.

I dodge from one five-star foyer to the next. The outside air scorches the nostrils and lungs. I can barely breathe in it. Pausing in each hallway, I drink the solid oxygen in deep draughts. Cold air. Here is a Cairo pleasure undreamt of by the Desert Rats or the Afrika Korps. How did they do it? Pinned under this hammering heat for two summer campaigns in 1941 and 1942, they acclimatised. It seems impossible. Salt tablets, crates of mineral water, fevered thoughts buzz around each other. But what preparations can prepare for such a fry-up?

Forget My Lady's radiator. It is me that will overheat. This is a far cry from the frozen backstreets of Karaman.

*

Sunset across the embassy compound. The high-tossed fountain catches the last rays coming through the trees beyond the lawn.

The ruptured shock absorber has been removed and declared dead. Now Mohsen is under the wheel arch preparing to fit the new one. He is a quiet, smiling man, working alone into the cool evening, in one of the most exquisite garages on earth. Doves coo arias to the immutability of life, the rule of reason. The tool racks from the days when His Excellency took the Rolls look down benevolently – they all fit the job now, of course.

My own part this afternoon has been to dismantle My Lady's distributor and replace the slipping baseplate with the matching section from the spare I brought from England. Although the body of the replacement was brown with rust, the baseplate inside was clear of scars. Now it sits, gleaming snugly in its new home, with a pair and a half of new points. The last half turned out to be yet another V8 part supplied by that daffy storeman in Hammersmith. So I have used the least pitted of the old points in my growing collection.

I also talked to the commercial attaché's driver about the long road west of El Alamein. He said it has a good surface, but many blind brows, so stay well to the right and don't exceed 100kph.

I wander into the workshop to find Mohsen.

He shows me how the shock absorber that came through customs has been designed slightly stronger at the end which burst before. He must drill out the four holes in the old backplate to a wider diameter and the drill is in another workshop. It means he cannot finish fitting it tonight. In consolation he hands me a bottle of 'Sport' Cola from his big refrigerator. Ah, wonderful.

We also talk about a garage nearby which has a machine for flushing out radiators. If I could moderate My Lady's hot temper the journey would be easier – but that means conceding that the work will go on beyond tomorrow.

*

After dark. I sit on a low wall.

Beside the mosque across the street, a ceremony is developing in a colourful marquee. Red carpet covers the pavement and the tent is decoratively painted with Arab squirls and minarets. Inside sit 200 men on high-backed gilded chairs with green padded seats. From the ceiling hang at least 100 beaded and lit lanterns, swaying in the night breeze.

A reception line of men in suits greets each new arrival as if he was a guest at a wedding. But there are no women. At the head of the line, two soldiers in white tunics, black berets and riding boots stand smartly to attention. Each wears, apart from his pistol, a dark-green sash across his chest, dropping down to a sheathed dagger at his hip. To add to the occasion, the loudspeakers of the mosque minaret sing evening prayers rather alluringly.

The mosque is now emptying. Some men descend its steps and walk straight round the front of the marquee, shake hands down the line-up and take seats. Some don't even bother to shake. A fat master of ceremonies reaches for a large glass of iced water and swigs it back. The event seems to be a public meeting, not quite political, perhaps Cairo's Rotary Club, or a business association. I was never yet in either. If the conclave was political, it would surely have more security. If it was religious, they would all have gone into the mosque to pray. If it was some Egyptian freemasons' lodge, it would not be so open to the street.

The few spectators on my side of the road are stirring. A big Mercedes and a Volvo pull up. A crowd forms around the handshaking line. Some people leave, others are still arriving. A lull follows. Another big Mercedes arrives and a rotund, bald man in a khaki suit steps out. He walks straight past the first six men in the greeting line, shakes hands perfunctorily with the last four and rolls off between the aisles of seated men to find his chair. After another pause an even fatter man arrives, wearing a similar but light-blue suit of immaculately pressed, loose-tailored cotton. He walks right down to the end of the tent and a man at the high table rises to greet him.

A very modern black Mercedes arrives, bristling with aerials, and the driver and guard leap out to open the door for a silver-haired man whom the senior greeter then escorts inside. He triggers a wave of departures. Twenty or thirty men are queuing to take their leave down the greeting line. One of them is the man who only just arrived in the very modern Mercedes. His chauffeur sweeps over from where he is double-parked on our side of the street to whisk him away.

Most of the seated men are in silence, listening to the chanting music which took over shortly after the mosque fell silent. Presumably these are also readings from the Koran. When a newcomer walks down their aisle, those seated make signs of greeting as if they know him, palms pressed together, or one hand like a blade vertical against the nose.

Now I see where the music is coming from. Two mullahs sit in the tent, one in each section, on raised platforms. They have red hats with white headbands and clasp their microphones like pop stars. After each verse, the one I can see more clearly dabs his mouth with a handkerchief. Each verse cuts abruptly, as if someone flicks off the sound.

Now the whole of one side of the marquee, the junior side, I think, rises to leave. Or at least most leave; the rest re-form into seated knots of discussion. The recital in the senior tent continues.

All the while, traffic passes in the street, the wind stirs the hanging lanterns and occasionally a Western passer-by stops to ask me what is happening. I don't know. Some kind of come-when-you-like village meeting, men only, a pow-wow in a tent, distantly related to the meeting of desert nomads which I gatecrashed in Syria. Now the senior marquee has sung itself through and the audience stands. Much shaking of hands, much sweeping up of Mercedes, hovering of chauffeurs and glancing around of bodyguards.

I could say it was all over, but the mullah in the senior tent is singing again.

This has all been a wild goose chase, and I am for bed.

Day 44

Midday on Monday. Back in the haven of the embassy. The morning has been a steamy, gaseous reminder of April. Out to the car pound at Medina Knassre, via various other customs offices. Thence back to the traffic police headquarters for an extension to my driving licence.

The traffic police say I am now legal to drive with my old plates. Medina Knassre say I have to bring the car to them tomorrow morning for new plates, and a complete re-documentation. Since their car pound is directly on the wrong side of Cairo for the Libyan border, and since they are now closed until 8:30 a.m. tomorrow, I am inclined to believe the traffic police. Always assuming Mohsen's work is finished tonight.

The embassy workshop is devoid of life. No sign of either Mr Mohsen, or Mr Gouel, whom I met this morning when I dropped by to retrieve the Bentley's papers. An evocative Spanish guitar plays over the radio of a Land Rover, stripped for a gearbox inspection. The fan on the garage ceiling potters like castanets. The hills of Andalusia beckon.

Habib Gouel arrives. 'Why didn't you say you were coming?' he asks. I show him copies of my telexes and reassure him that he is the man I want. We talk about the mounting plate that needs to be drilled out and agree that it will be too weak by the time it fits. A new one must be cut.

Ahab comes over. 'Mohsen was in court for a speeding offence this morning. I hope the judge won't be too rough on him.'

I show him my certificate from the traffic police. Ahab translates. 'It says you have no fines or penalties outstanding. Your licence is clean.' He smiles. 'You can leave the country with this.'

We talk about the old days at the embassy. Apparently the garden reached down to the Nile, before Nasser put the new road through. The section leader, David, number four at the embassy after the defence, navy and air attachés, comes over, looking skinny and bright, about my age. 'I don't fancy the idea of Libya,' he says. 'If the Lockerbie bombing was them…'

'It's the twentieth anniversary of Gaddafi's revolution on September 1st, four days from now,' I say. He sees the point. No one wants a diplomatic incident to sour the glorious celebrations. I can sneak through under cover of the fireworks. He asks if I will be passing back this way. I hope not, but who can say?

We wait for Mohsen. And wait and wait.

At two o'clock I crack and ask Habib to help with finding someone to cut the new baseplate for the shock absorber.

*

Habib Gouel knows an area in Heliopolis, on the far outskirts of Cairo, where the metal-bashers congregate. We set off in an embassy Land Rover. His wife is

British consul here and rides home some of the way with us. We drop by their flat, just over the Nile. She asks me in for a beer while he changes into overalls. Joanna Gouel is to become consul in Cameroon in October. There will be only eight at that embassy, rather than the forty-two staff, plus more than that again in wives and children, here in Egypt. The flat is spacious and the future looks bright.

Back in the Land Rover, Habib drives like an artist. I ask about the ceremony I observed last night.

'That was a mourning, a wake for a dead friend. The people in the greeting line were relatives, the readings were indeed from the Koran.' Such memorial services happen just once for each death and are advertised in the social columns of the newspapers, or by word of mouth.

In Heliopolis, developers simply bought the land and built apartment blocks across it. The street is filled with the cries of date sellers, washing hangs from unrendered breezeblock balconies, children ride bicycles, dogs lick at dried puddles. The architecture is pure Le Corbusier, the squalor pure Dickens, the people pure gold.

We pass the palace built for himself by the Belgian architect who designed this new city. 'It is still in his family's hands, but they never visit', says Habib. It stands alone, covered in brown dirt, on a vast scale, like some horror movie film set, too haunted to demolish.

Arab friends of Habib's meet us in a second Land Rover. They will deliver the template to the place where the spare part can be made. He says it is best not to show foreign faces there, because the price of what we want will skyrocket. Habib has lived all his life in Cairo. He was educated at the Jesuit School here. His mother tongue is arguably French, as his green eyes and swarthy beard betray. So even he leaves this brand of bargaining to intermediaries.

The other Land Rover returns. Two hours it's going to take to make the new part. 'There's no choice but to wait,' Habib says. I put my empty Coke bottle on the ground and settle down for a doze with my book on the Alamein campaign.

*

As it was, Habib and I got talking. We philosophised about destiny, politicians, love and survival. For two and a half hours we spurred through, from 'helping others' to 'fear', to 'money' to 'intelligence'. Habib is much more worried about the forthcoming move to Cameroon than he lets on. What will *he* do?

'Get the Toyota dealership,' I say.

When the new mounting plate finally arrives I am exhausted, but we have established that those who know themselves bend like roses. Something like that.

*

At the compound, Mohsen has been and gone. A phone call brings him back, but now it is after dark and we are in danger of running over into a third day.

Habib says goodbye and I pay him for help and time, only to find that Mohsen refuses to use the locating plate we have gone to such trouble to make. He files out the other one, which previously he had wanted to drill, and after a while he has the old bracket mounted on the new shock absorber. We fill the unit with hydraulic fluid and take it out to the Bentley.

Ants run around on the ground, attracted by the inspection light. Gentle adjustments of jacks, poking of holes and matching of nuts. Will it all line up? And if it does, what will the tracking be like? The idea of flushing out the radiator must go by the board. If we can roll tonight, we will.

Mohsen is leaning over the engine bay, balanced on the wing. His feet are high and he looks as if he is about to fall in.

*

Even the seven embassy cats have gone to sleep. It has been painfully slow, but the suspension is at last back together. Now, as we each sip our cups of tea, the question is, will Mohsen finish the job by checking the back dampers and then the timing? And can I pay him in dollars? My latest crystal-ignition cigarette lighter is about to be given away too. They seem to go to silent types.

The front wheel is back on, and My Lady is now square on the ground with a mightily improved sway to her landing. The tilt of the wheel looks very slightly positive when it should, if anything, be negative. While Mohsen is reinstalling the battery I read through my photocopies from the workshop manual.

Adjustments to either castor or camber can also affect the height of the side steering lever balls, and this can offset toe-in.

Yes, let's try it.

Ten minutes with the points and she's running. Then a master stroke with the timing, one straight from the Rolls-Royce apprenticeship box of tricks. Mohsen loosens the distributor bracket while the engine's on tickover and twists the whole unit to advance and retard the timing. By rotating it five degrees he achieves a tickover so smooth, so responsive to the turn of the key, that I thought for a moment he had just lifted the bump stop to increase the minimum revs.

God knows what time of night it is now, but we are indeed going for a check on the rear shock absorbers' hydraulic levels. Another pair of tea mugs from the nightwatchman. The rear driver's side shock absorber is empty, but the other one is pretty good.

Now we stash the many surplus parts, including the new tyre, still with its Hammersmith destination taped to the tread.

Mohsen has gone to find some soup from his car and to ask the front gate what the time is. I guess it is 11 o'clock. We'll see.

Day 45

It was 11:45 p.m.

At midnight Mohsen and I shook hands for the last time. He was overwhelmed, or else very tired. In his sixteen years working for the embassy no one had kept him going quite so late, or joined in quite so vigorously. And my dollars were worth twice as much to him as they were to me.

Then the Bentley trickled quietly back down the compound, out through the barricade and gates and into the night. She crossed the Nile three bridges downstream, filled up with 90 octane (one-star), which Gouel assured me is in reality 82 octane, and set off to find the motorway.

Eventually I fight my way out of the Cairo suburbs. With the briefest hesitation on my part about revisiting the pyramids, and after a minor ignition stutter from My Lady, I call a halt to load some music and write up my notes.

I am in high spirits and choose the complete symphonies of Beethoven, six discs, a match for the cartridge. The new shock absorber has fixed the clunking. The steering is straight; the water temperature is holding below normal, which bodes well for daytime driving; the sight of my first mosquito has even persuaded me to start the antimalarial course so highly recommended for all North African countries by the inoculation centre near my office in London. The trouble is that you have to keep it up daily for a month.

Motorways are the only hope for night driving in Egypt. They are free of potholes, and the leery onrush of dazzling juggernaut headlights is kept at arm's length by a central reservation. The road is flat and straight. I can't be missing much by way of scenery.

*

The challenge of course is to press on until the motorway runs out, so that all daylight is spent on tougher roads. And in my current euphoria to be back behind the wheel, with the Bentley in better fettle than she has been since MAM bought her, I could even do it. But then, why go for broke on night one? From now on I'll have an eye open for a decent lay-by. But not here. A big Olaf lorry has just pulled over in the road beside me and an Arab man in a nightshirt is pacing about it barefoot. Time to move on.

*

A truck-sized rest stop brings it up to eighty-seven miles since Cairo. I am settling into this. The feeling of unity, the pleasure of looking for the gap and the broad bows following automatically, the subtle shortening of the bonnet as you fix more and more clearly on the road rather than the car, the sense of correctness, well-being, balance, each clicks back into place. The feeling is of being carried, like a small child who has run out of legs on a long walk.

I trust these friendly sensations will still be there when I wake with the day.

*

Rude disturbance before dawn. A lorry has stalked close up behind me in the lay-by. Under its own power it could easily be driven round. I do not know what the shouting is all about. Another truck pushes into it from behind. The lorry jumps forward within an ace of me, and the foul-mouthed driver then goes off to foul the desert ten yards away. I can't be bothered and go back to sleep.

*

Later I am awake, and the lorry has gone. I try my Aqaba trick of engaging the starter drive by turning the fan blades. It works only fourth time…

On tickover, I change into clean clothes and survey the scrawny flat sandscape. It yields one mongrel dog, an unfinished concrete petrol station, a series of corrugated iron warehouses and a green billboard in Arabic. Time to set off.

After a few minutes the sun lobs up over a mist-wreathed earth behind me. A semblance of a pine forest shows on my side of the road. The bark of the trees is like more shed snake skin; and with every minute the golden orb changes from harmless glow to blazing glare. Local hitchhikers dot the dirt hard shoulder.

*

North over a causeway across an inland sea. We must be close to the Mediterranean now. A huge cement works belches yellow smoke. Gas flares jig above an oil refinery. Then west at last, through the hinterland of Alexandria, and onto the dual carriageway heading towards the Libyan frontier. To the seaward side, the north, stand palm oil trees and grizzled fig bushes. To the south lie opencast quarries of soft white stone, sawn into bricks direct from the virgin rock, then stacked in phalanxes at the roadside.

Finally we are left with the untilled yellow earth, itself sometimes engraved into mini grand canyons by flash floods that have a season other than this.

*

Farm labourers wave from the fields as I pull over at the 150-mile mark. Long may this good progress continue. And, at last, down there on the right, where it ought to be, the limitless lapis Mediterranean, stretching all the way to Turkey.

*

Twenty Egyptian pounds-worth of petrol. That's five English pounds for about ten gallons, less than a third the European rate. I walk into the shade of the filling station wall and look down. Between the forecourt and the sea are scattered grey bungalows. A woman in long blue robes carries a bulk of olive branches on her black-veiled head; a wind-pump turns listlessly; an ass swishes its tail in the scant cover of some tall grasses. Out on the billow, a fishing boat moves among its nets. The breeze is straight in from the north, and it has brought a high cover of cumulus cloud. There goes the blue woman with another bundle of olive branches. She dabs her face with her veil as she passes.

*

A hundred miles along the edge of the desert, we motor into El Alamein. Not a place I would call defensive. Its choice as a battlefield was all about the vast, impassable, cliff-ringed Qattara Depression thirty miles to the south, which creates a bottleneck with the coast; and the overstretched supply lines for any fuel and water trying to come from the west.

This is the spot where the British General Auchinleck barely stopped the German General Rommel from reaching Cairo in July 1942. Rommel's panzers seem to have gained the ridge at Alam El Halfa, the fulcrum of the battle, before his radioed order to retreat reached them. They even had enough fuel to pull back; surely they could have gone on to Alexandria instead? But Rommel himself had been bombed six times that morning, as well as shelled; he had jaundice; and it seems his iron nerve cracked for once before that of his troops.

Thus turn the ebb and flow of war.

Each army then paused to build up supplies from shipping convoys running the gauntlet of the Mediterranean. The German and Italian ships needed to sneak from Italy, past Malta, to reach Benghazi, while the British seamen had the longer run from Gibraltar via Malta to Alexandria and the newly appointed General Montgomery. The showdown came four months later, that autumn.

Some three miles inland from the road is an east–west rise, Kidney Ridge. West of this, invisible even through the field glasses, are a handful of small depressions in the dry, otherwise featureless plain. On the night of 26th October 1942, two posses of British gunners were ordered to infiltrate the Afrika Korps' forward positions. They advanced so rapidly in the dark that they became lost. Stumbling upon a couple of these dished-down hiding places, not the ones they had intended, they backed in and circled their newly issued six-pounder guns. Keeping low, they were able to position just the gun barrels above the rim. They remained like that, crouched below ground level like two little hedgehogs, to wait for daylight.

The southern of these two strongpoints, codenamed Snipe, was held by the Rifle Brigade battalion. They had nineteen anti-tank guns. During the night the enemy raised the alarm, and the gunners fought off a tank attack from a mixed force of Germans and Italians. While it was dark, the flash of their weapons gave away their position. But then the sun rose, and in daylight they became almost invisible to the Axis troops on the plain. They found that they had plopped themselves down in the middle of Rommel's vehicle marshalling area. Their position was so improbable that they were twice mistaken as Germans by the British, operating on a different radio frequency, and shelled by tanks and self-propelled guns which appeared on Kidney Ridge behind.

For a day the Rifle Brigade force was surrounded. A rescue attempt by Allied-driven American armour (El Alamein was the first deployment of Sherman tanks) was beaten back by the Germans. And anyway, the Snipe depression was too shallow to be defended by tanks, whose turrets were easy targets for the high-powered German 88mm anti-tank guns. But without air superiority Rommel could not shift the British gunners.

I studied this because I have grown up in the shadow of one of the heroes of Snipe. My dear father is a member of a pheasant-shooting syndicate in Buckinghamshire. As a child, most Saturdays between October and February from the age of four or five, I would be taken along as a beater, or to stand with him and mark, or as a 'stop' – tapping a hedge to encourage the game to fly.

One of Papa's fellow 'guns' is Tom Bird, handsome, trim, a few years older than my dad, tweed flat cap pulled down on a full head of boyishly cut silver hair, with an ultra-high-pitched dog whistle between his teeth or a spaniel at his gum-booted heel. His was a quiet smile, a kindly arm to help young limbs over a stile, an encouraging word when the rain-soaked kale was tipping down my neck, and an occasional source of dark, hard chocolate on chill winter mornings. Many a time have I stood with my father in the line below a beechwood, with Tom Bird one or two pegs away, and seen his timing at work.

A decade before I knew he had been a gunner at El Alamein, I knew Mr Bird as a superbly clean shot. He has a fluidity and economy of movement which makes it seem that he has not even raised his gun. To watch him is to disbelieve your eyes. He picks his opportunities, ignores low-flying targets, regularly takes a high left-and-right and makes every cartridge count. High pigeons, which anyone who has tried will know are the blue riband test of a good shot, are a speciality. If you wonder where Tom is placed in the line, you only need to watch the sky for 'an absolute screamer' of a pigeon shot, as my father would say with reverence. And the beauty of it is that Tom is so modest, he lets his trophies speak for themselves, barely even acknowledging that they are his, let alone with what accuracy and anticipation they have been won.

On 27th October 1942 Major Tom Bird was second in command of Snipe. He brought to this not only his remarkable precision and timing, but also tremendous clarity of thought and courage under fire.

Let me quote from RL Crimp's book, *Diary of a Desert Rat*, published by my former employers, Macmillan, which I have with me. Crimp describes Tom Bird and a comrade in a Jeep

> *quite heedless of the M/G bullets slashing the air around them and panzers potting straight at them, collecting odd rounds from knocked-out guns or the guns of knocked-out crews, and taking them to guns that can still strike back. One bullet amongst the ammo on board and the lot would go sky-high.*

Of that day, others have recalled how the Italian tanks had an unearthly way of still advancing once they were ablaze, rumbling forward with their ammunition exploding inside. As the perimeter of Snipe became littered with knocked-out tanks, the hulks became hides for marksmen on both sides, but the German infantry had to stand up to fire down into the British position, which often proved fatal.

Before nightfall an informal truce was called. Both sides effectively withdrew, exhausted, gathering up the wounded and burying the dead. Tom had been hit in the head and his few remaining six-pounders had fired their last round. However, he and his men had destroyed thirty-three tanks, five self-propelled guns, several 88s and a staff car, with another twenty tanks towed away by the enemy for repairs they never had time to make.

The Snipe survivors were awarded between them a Victoria Cross, a Distinguished Service Order (Tom), a Military Cross, two Distinguished Conduct Medals and seven Military Medals.

Better still, the action at Snipe had tipped Rommel into allocating his reserves too far south. Starved of petrol, that was an error he could not recover from.

Hitler refused permission to retreat, an order Rommel eventually ignored. The Luftwaffe managed a small fuel airlift from Crete, enough to save most of the Germans, but not the Italians. Days later, with a formidable combination of tank superiority, aerial intelligence and code-breaking, and not a few thoroughly British cock-ups, Montgomery burst through where I am, between Kidney Ridge and the coast. However, due to a lack of coordinated pursuit from the air, the Desert Fox got away.

*

I drive on like a fleeing Rommel, despairing of cover in the flat, featureless landscape, puzzled that no one is doing much to stop me.

Occasionally, we pass a hill with the old scars of foxholes and slit trenches, but the shelter just is not there. This was a field gunner's dream. A direct hit at 5,000 yards was possible, when the air was clear at the beginning or end of the day. Only when the desert was shimmering in the heat was the fun more with the tanks.

Fuel and water are the twin pillars of any advance in this terrain; distant ports and long supply lines the only way to get them. Up ahead are the harbours of Mersa Matruh and Sidi Birani. Neither was as key as the port of Tobruk, just over the Libyan frontier. The battles for those harbours, and for the sea lanes which supplied them, surely saw much heroics too.

*

Fog feints around all morning. Whether this is because cloud condenses over land, and so the air of the desert seashore naturally mists up, or whether it is photochemical pollution from distant refineries, or the dust kicked up by humans, is a mystery.

Of the tents and lean-tos dotted near the road, only the bird lofts have substance. These are built like tall thimbles, perforated by rings of holes, each hole with a peg-perch protruding beneath it. The eggs are collected from within, as a quick and easy source of protein, though judging by the desert birds, the eggs must be the size of hazelnuts.

*

My Lady has leapt a day ahead of herself, to gain the seafront at Mersa Matruh in time for lunch.

The ivory beach forms a crescent, with a beading of reefs between its horns. The entire shoreline is decked with coloured umbrellas, as dense as Rommel's later anti-tank beach obstacles in Normandy. A man in swimming trunks carries some rubber rings over the road, while his wife in shawl and floor-length gown follows with the heavier deck chairs.

Without the sun umbrellas these swaddled women would boil.

Viridescent, single-axle gigs, drawn by skinny donkeys with bells on their harnesses, provide transport along the paved promenade that loops behind the strand. Some of the animals have bald hindquarters where their child drivers whip them excessively with short, leek-thick crops.

*

Barely time to write. The Egyptians say the Libyans may close the border at any moment. My Lady snarls off like a dragster.

*

Phew. Stamped my customs carnet and returned the plates on the Egyptian side.

*

No-man's land between Egypt and Libya. Sun sinking through the African horizon, fear rising, still no moment to write.

*

Libya, a triumphal arch in the middle of nowhere. At the line, alone on the wastes, two guards read my passport out loud to each other. They wave me on.

Is that it?

More endless road into the glorious, lonesome sky. Gauges look good, road excellent, and the plain is a featureless board.

I am ready for 'The End' to roll up in Times Roman across the panorama.

The Lady with No Name rides out into folklore.

*

The formal frontier control is in the first town. Libya introduces itself with the familiar agglomeration of square-built, single-storey, check-in sheds, except these are cleaner; brilliant white not grey. The national colour, lead-free green, is universally 'in' this year.

'English in Rolls-Royce,' chants the man My Lady is queue-barging as discreetly as a limousine with a chrome GB on the back can on such a stage. Better oblige, as he waves us back to the end of the line. Glad-to-be-here horseplay and handshakes with the drivers ahead of me. The Libyans like coming home.

Pause. Breathe. That was twelve hours of forty miles an hour, even if my notes don't show it. Time to change the CD cartridge in the boot from classical to pop.

One last push. Stir yourself, find the papers that have to be completed.

The immigration form is in Arabic. I cannot read it. Trust Colonel Gaddafi to obliterate the Roman alphabet. At moments like this my cool companion and I have to stick together. I hunt through my file for the unused Royal Automobile Club (RAC) customs carnet, the key to this country, second only to the visa itself. The AA wouldn't issue customs papers for Libya, full stop; but the RAC had once, a long time ago, and they listened to my plea. Their expert, Mr Saunders, said 15 XKN was the first British-registered car to ask for Libyan papers in nine years.

Returning briefly to move the Bentley forward, I am ticked off for leaving her, and so letting other cars queue-barge in front of me.

I slip from the crowds into the police station. I am unsure how it happens. I extend a handshake into the building as its steel door opens and receive a brotherly grasp from the other side. The police open the door, pull me in and close it again. How can a handclasp across such a divide say so much? They clear my passport then and there.

So far, Libya is all friendly but sober faces, well fed, sleek even, and everyone is much, much richer than in Syria. Next stop, customs. When the Bentley reaches the front of the queue I'm passed into the hands of another of this brotherly breed of security officer, also dressed like an angel – no, an archangel – in long white damask gown with embroidered teal neckline and short-gathered sleeves. This one has the Berber face of Gaddafi's caste and he minces gently under the diaphanous nightie. Respect attends him wherever he goes. His office is prominently located and locked in his absence. It has an uncluttered desk with a duck-egg-coloured phone and two chairs, a filing cabinet and a bookshelf.

On top of the bookshelf sits his high-fronted, black-peaked officer's cap. Suddenly you can imagine him in a more sadistic role. It is like spotting a pair of handcuffs on the Angel Gabriel's belt.

With my passport, customs carnet and currency form stamped, I am free to drive on to Tobruk, about eighty miles. Thank God I have the petrol, because it is dark and the banks are all shut now. Driving away on the level, well-marked road, I hit button 6 on the CD remote control, dab the volume, and that unbeatable surge of pleasure wells up, as it did crossing into Syria, like a pyrotechnic gala under your breastbone, starbursts and Catherine wheels. *Bye, bye Miss American Pie...*

*

Cut the sound. A roadblock. Wait for it. No guns though, and no trouble with my papers. I'm in. I'm really in. What was all the fuss about? Where are these murderous IRA training camps, these jokers who mow down policewomen and blow up 747s at 30,000 feet? Where are these self-proclaimed scourges of capitalism? Well, in London Alford thought they lived in Marseilles. In Marseilles Hattie thought it was Naples. In Piraeus it was Turkey, and in Turkey it was Syria. In Jordan it was Egypt. In Egypt, Libya, and in Libya, you've guessed it. They look positively worried for me when I say I will be heading back to London. 'But you won't, for heaven's sake, take this magnificent car to a place like that!'

*

New roadblock. New games. No, he won't take my hand. Let's see if I snatch at my passport when he jerks it back at the last moment. But roadblock guys are just that. We know neither of us is very frightening.

We both know who is. The angelic secret police.

*

Roadblock number 3. I'm beginning to get the picture. Nobody moves in Libya without it being known about. Power is to be feared. But we both have power.

*

Roadblock 4 is unmanned. Roadblock 5 waves me through. I'm very sleepy now. Find a side track, reverse down it, stretch out on the sofa, back doors open, looking up at the stars, the riot of infinity. In the distance, headlights move on the desert road. From miles away they project the shadows of the scrub onto the silver-screen flanks of the idol. An endless silent movie of penumbral forest fleets down her, like sea-spray flashing the length of a speedboat, so that all night while I sleep she seems to be once more chasing the dreaming steeples of southwest Sussex.

Day 46

Sunrise in heavy desert mist. My Lady's windows are fogged over as if by nocturnal exertions. But on the outside; where one was open the seat is damp. A farmer walks past, not a desert Arab but a peasant in a floppy hat. He waves and says good morning. For all the world we might be waking up in Italy before Brindisi, the day the clocks changed. A scrawny dog trots past with a stick in its mouth. A flock of sheep stirs on the other side of the main road. Away in all directions rolls the same billiard-table plain.

Get out and wipe the front and rear windows. Reload the CD cartridge. A two-inch beetle strides from under the Bentley like an alien land-crawler. Now, will the motorhome start? She has been very good, most of the time. Come on baby! No. Grinding gears to wake the dead. Open bonnet. Turn fan. Try again. Even worse grinding. Repeat procedure with a sharp backwards pull on the rotor blades. More grinding. Try again. Contact, engagement, immediate ignition. Hold it steady at about 1,000rpm. We don't want to stall now. Watch the water temperature until it comes off its bottom stop. Gear lever down, handbrake off. Hit *Rigoletto*! Move out!

*

Fog. Headlights on. It is unseasonably cold.

*

Tobruk. A long elegant harbour inlet. No town walls. Rolling, shepherds-to-Bethlehem landscape, only a strongpoint if defended by professionals. Aussies, Kiwis, Brits, Poles, Czechs and Indians hung on here in an extraordinary siege from April to December 1941, forcing Rommel to retreat, before he overran them in June 1942. So they delayed his arrival at El Alamein until the Yanks were well into the war. With Malta, Tobruk was briefly a tipping point of world history.

Now it is a peaceful, domesticated place. The banks will open at 7:30 a.m., about twenty minutes from now. Two cafés overlook the small square where we wait. Families arrive in Mazdas, Volkswagens, Peugeots, Chevrolet pick-ups and even a Land Rover to park in the neatly ordered bays in the centre of the square, to wait. Tobruk or Torbay…?

*

The money house is air conditioned and marbled, with no protective glass or railings, just one long, wide, stone countertop, like an expensive German kitchen, and an atrium level reached by a double-helix marble staircase. There are several male bank staff. A cleaning lady wipes the spacious surfaces. I imagine an Italian bank in some coastal resort would be like this, at low season, if they had paid their protection money. And what do the people feel who sit watching life go by from the sides of the square, so soberly dressed? Are they content with their BMWs, Mercedes, Toyotas, Audis and Mitsubishis? Libya is too good to be true.

Gamal, who is one of them, guides me and My Lady to the British war cemetery on the outskirts. He is a mechanical engineer, with good English because he studied in Liverpool. Now he works on 'maintenance planning'.

He tells me about Libya, with its four million population, and three million foreign workers, its fifty years' supply of oil, which is piped up from 300 miles south in the desert to the tanker terminal here, among other places. Libya has two refineries in West Germany and one in Italy, where they also own a chain of 400 petrol stations. Libya's population is rising, but only slowly.

The British cemetery at Tobruk. Two Arabs are asleep in the shade of the massive front arch. They stand up and shake my hand. A ship's bell from HMS *Liverpool* hangs by the entrance. The place is immaculate. The gravestones march quietly into the distance. Tom Bird's Rifle Brigade, the 44th Royal Tank Regiment, the Fourth Air Formation Signals, the Pioneer Corps, the Lancashire Yeomanry, the South African Army, Czechs, Poles, Jews, the Royal Engineers, the Royal Horse Artillery. A soldier of the 1939–1945 war, known unto God.

This land belongs to England, British sovereign territory in Libya, and the salaries of these grave-keepers come in sterling via Cairo.

Hutchison, Mitsypoyc, Hatten, Van Heerden, Kennedy, Casser, Cotton.

Dunlop, Sergeant Royal Artillery, 10th February 1942, aged twenty-eight.

The youngest here is sixteen, I am told. The oldest fifty. There's even one from the royal family. The Queen came to pay her respects, say the gardeners in sign language.

So many Australians and New Zealanders died they have a separate cemetery. And what about the local people? Gamal says Libyans still get blown up where the minefield maps were lost.

*

Gamal navigates us to a hotel across the port to make a reservation for me tonight in Benghazi. The hotel here in Tobruk is big and air conditioned, but the swimming pool is empty of water. Built by the Department of Social Security as a long-term investment, I am told the complex has been in virtual mothballs since the border was closed to Egyptians. Tobruk has been dead, but now 'life is returning'. 'Next year' is their mantra.

A ring road is under construction, and the harbour will be redeveloped. The main flyover and some office blocks will be levelled to make way.

The hotel cannot offer mineral water, but the fizzy lemonade is excellent. Gamal and I sit admiring the manager's oversized 26″ Toshiba 'four channel' multi-speaker TV, while he phones his friend and fellow manager at the Benghazi Otu and writes me a letter of introduction. Then Gamal and I head back in the Bentley to the square, where we transfer to Gamal's Nissan, current model, to go to the main bookshop.

But they don't have any maps of Libya. Bump. We just walked into a piece of the Potemkin scenery.

We talk about the weather. The climate has changed, says my guide, looking at the overcast sky. The farmers need hot weather until November to complete their second crop, and here we are with winter in September. We talk about the currency. The Libyan dinar is one of the highest denomination units in the world, second only to the Kuwaiti dinar. Whatever you say about black-market exchange rates, sixty litres of petrol is a lot to receive for one unit of any currency.

Anyway, we agree as we part, who needs a map? There's only one road; even I should be able to find my way to Benghazi. And My Lady has behaved impeccably.

*

Fifty miles from Tobruk, blue sea away on the right; an old white Peugeot pulls me over. Two men brandishing pistols get out.

'Papers please,' says the older man.

'Why didn't you stop for station police?' asks the younger one.

'Which station police?'

'Back there,' they indicate.

'But he waved me through; who are you?'

'Police.'

They look like farm labourers to me.

The younger man, seeing my visa, says one word, very clearly, in English: 'Rich'. Then he asks if I am alone.

I am unsure how to answer and say nothing.

The older man notices a book on Rommel lying open on the passenger seat at the page with the crude map of North Africa, the only one I have.

'El Gazala,' he says, pointing at the page, then to the ground. He shakes my hand. 'No problem, I'm sorry.'

They turn back on the road and drive over the ridge the way they came.

El Gazala, Rommel's last triumph. Here, in May 1942, facing the new Grant tanks from America, he turned the Allied line, then punched through its centre and dug in, using the extensive British minefields to protect his rear. Various Allied HQs were captured. Tobruk fell within days, and the British did not stop running until El Alamein. Wags called it the Gazala Gallop.

I suppose the vigilantes would have snatched me for cash if Rommel had lost.

*

At the next roadblock I'm waved through. Within yards, a twisting wind spout whips up the roadside and steps out, straight onto the Bentley. A surge of air rocks the heavy body. If this car had been a convertible, we'd have lost everything!

I stop in the village to buy some juice and settle down.

*

But there is no peace for me today. Ten miles on, a nondescript orange pick-up stops me. More police. These ones are in a khaki uniform.

No problems.

*

Seagulls flying in close formation over the surf beach at Derna. US Marines marched here from Alexandria in 1805, to win the USA's first land battle overseas.

*

Coast road beyond Derna. Is this another heavy wind making the Bentley wander on the road? I play the wheel but can't stop the swaying movement. Could it be a puncture? Roll to a halt, right by the sea. Open door. Yes, rear driver's side. Out comes our old friend, the tyre that left the fifteen-mile skid mark into Karaman. It must have started out on the back axle because it still has the print of a snow chain on the side walls. Combined with a heavy-gauge steel wheel, these tyres weigh a ton. I can barely lift it into place.

A well-earned mango juice carton awaits.

*

One hundred miles from El Gazala, the hills drop sharply to the sea. Deep ravines and dried-up riverbeds. Rocks across the highway warn that a spating river has blasted away the bridge at the gorge up ahead. In all, in the past forty miles, four of the bridges have been swept away and not yet replaced. Each time, a detour has wound down into the wadi and back up the other side. However, Her Ladyship is at home in dried-up riverbeds.

A red pick-up has been racing us from one bridge to the next. He can accelerate faster, but we can take the ridges in the road where bridge repairs have been successful, without slowing. So we amuse ourselves in evenly matched combat until he turns away.

The cumulus is accumulating; the rivers will come early this year.

Susa, twenty kilometres ahead, says the road sign, Cyrene thirty-seven; and, they should add, avoid sharp objects until the punctured spare is repaired.

*

Susa, also known as Apollonia. A classical city by the sea, partly sunk by an earthquake in the fourth century AD. And not a tourist within fifty miles.

Five village boys are out for a swim. It is the summer holidays. One of them is older, a man of perhaps twenty-five, with a glorious Greek face, large dark eyes, long straight brow and nose and the swarthiest complexion I've ever seen on a non-sub-Saharan African. Some ancient Mediterranean civilisation must run in his blood, long lost from Continental Europe – Phoenician or Carthaginian, perhaps. He tells me he is the local English teacher. I ask him who built these ruins. He doesn't know, nor has he even wondered.

Once the closest natural harbour in Africa to Athens, Apollonia was first surveyed by the Cambridge University sub-aqua club in the 1950s, led by Papa's cousin, Nicholas Flemming. When the Romans moved in, the basilicas facing the sea must have made for a most dramatic landfall. Now Susa is only a base for decorated yellow fishing smacks. Several iron hulks rest on its sandy bottom.

Should I linger or return to the car? She has thrown a Piraeus gearbox at me, goodness knows why, and I do not recall how long these moods take to pass. She just waits until I feel apologetic. Well, OK, I apologise.

I retrace my steps, turn the key and select drive once more.

Apology accepted, she says. Gallant submissions are what real ladies live on.

*

Cyrene is named after a spring 600 metres up, on the lip of the escarpment between the sea and the Libyan plateau. The fount still trickles out 100 gallons of water an hour. It once gathered around it a Greek city, later extended by the Romans. From the sheer scale of these ruins, I would guess this population reached 60,000. It would have needed a water supply ten times bigger than today's.

188

The earthquake which did for Apollonia in the late Roman period also choked off this source. Nevertheless, a litre every few seconds is something. The scene achieves a state of nature only known from eighteenth-century travel prints. Young children in long smocks of bright colours lend the ruins a sense of scale as I look down from the pine slope above. The water flows from the side of the Forum, to run through a system of baths, among elegant, shallow flights of steps and between the columns of a small temple. The sea view to the north is clear for twenty-five miles, the width of the English Channel at Dover, and breathes a lofty quality into this idyll. The layout too has a sensuous informality.

The scarp cradles the garden sanctuary with protective zeal, like a hand across a breast, hastening to cover this Eden from the corruption of prying eyes.

If you ever go round the Med, do it clockwise. For beauty and the stuff of love, this citadel is head and shoulders above Amalfi, Pompeii, Athens, Sardis, Ephesus, Sergiopolis and even Palmyra. How can I see the Mediterranean, the world's greatest tourist lake, from perhaps its finest viewing spot, and yet, as a tourist be the strangest thing that anybody else here can recall? For the first time in 3,000 years, Cyrene, the trading capital, the 'Athens of Africa', has forgotten about the outside world, and has been forgotten by it.

Mohammed comes over. He speaks English. We talk about the remains, both here, despite decades of pillage, and in other unspoiled places, less accessible, to which you have to trek by foot. He knows such places. He tells me that he himself has objects now at his home in Derna, coins, statues, an exquisite head from a grave in the wadi on the right.

His cousin joins us.

'Look,' he says, 'down there among the ruins is a small railway track; that was the Italians in 1911. Can you imagine what they must have taken out? They just sawed the heads off the statues. And down there by the pool is a still-complete Apollo. The British tried to steal it during World War II.'

He explains that they got it by boat to Benghazi, but there was an air raid while they were transferring it at the docks, the crate burst open and the theft was discovered. Locals objected and brought it back.

We discuss the tensions between noble appreciation of a place, which we all feel, confronted by this landscape; and the lust of possession – the excitement we also feel at the idea that this entire city was abandoned after the earthquake, that the money is literally sitting here in the soil around us waiting to be collected.

'Look,' says Mohammed again, and he picks up a piece of pottery from the dirt between us where we are sitting. 'Here,' and from down the slope he pulls out the rim of a big jar.

*

Encouraged by talk of the snows that fall in winter, I climb higher to find the best panaroma. I wander through the derelict city at the crest of the slope, failing to find the Greek theatre of which Mohammed spoke. From the main rampart of Cyrene, northwest the vista is so vast you can feel the curvature of the earth. The encompassing seashore at its closest is a mere five miles away, at its furthest perhaps fifteen. According to the formula for a circumference, $2\pi r$, for a three-quarter-circle with us roughly at the centre, that equals a coastline of nearly forty miles visible from this spot. But then behind is the sea. If the horizon from up here is thirty miles away, that is as good as 140 miles of skyline captured in one turn of the head. The whole circumference of the world is only 25,000.

I take My Lady over the back road, inland, stopping for a while at the muscular Ionic temple that stands behind an unlocked wicket gate to the left. The rusting track and derailed mining wagons speak of that pillaging operation at the turn of the century.

Night falls, and I am still hours from a bed in Benghazi. Enough of shadows.

*

Heavy roadblock under arc lights. Pistols. Swearing. The Bentley had been flying; now we will have to build up to it again.

Most of the recent stoppages have been just formalities. This time a man called Agdir wants to show off to his friends. British! But no British get into Libya, and he gives me a mad brigand scowl that tells me he's getting out of his depth. First they crawl all over the inside of the car, then a long wait for the mood to calm down.

*

I am in a roadblock five miles further on, so why bang on about the last one? These soldiers demand to see inside the bonnet. Discipline is fraying at the edges. Here's a cocky kid who wants to get in on the act. I pat the pistol in his hip holster and jokingly put my hands up. It eases the tension.

How long will they hold my passport this time?

Between Agdir's roadblock and this one was a fearful descent. It was as steep as anything in Turkey, for several miles, with dozens of double-trailer road-trains inching, almost winching, their way down it, brakes smoking, gearboxes screaming in the dark. We all went down at the speed of the slowest, except for those who were brave enough to overtake. The impatient ones then had to fight their way back into the line when a vehicle came up the hill, which meant that the queue of monsters behind effectively had to stop to make the space. And stopping was not easy. The Bentley did some overtaking. At one point the whole road seized, the downhill lane static, nose to tail with no room to dive in, and us stopped on the wrong side in the face of a stationary lorry in the uphill lane.

We reached the front and put some distance between us and our lumbering companions.

Here's my passport back, so I'm off.

*

Near the city, all road users are passed by a high-speed cortège of cars with flashing lights and sirens wailing. In the last car is a rent-a-mob echelon, clapping and singing as if Judgement Day was at hand.

*

The roadblocks became more severe as night fell and Benghazi approached. Out east a roadblock is three farm boys, a rifle and an empty oil drum. Then, below Cyrene, I saw my first uniformed soldier, complete with smart red beret and Kalashnikov. Three is presumably the minimum number to keep an eye on each other, or, less cynically, for two to set off in hot pursuit while the third stays behind/goes for help/works the radio.

When a roadblock has a dozen men, two dozen empty oil drums and even the fifteen-year-olds are packing pistols, you are coming close to a city. This is urban man. Politicised, chippy, less aware of the struggle for existence which binds him to his neighbour, let alone to an Englishman.

Before the last stoppage, the Bentley reached a stable cruising speed of 80–85mph, a rhythm she seems able to hold indefinitely on Mohsen's tuning. It is as if the engine, gearbox and suspension relax into such rapidity once all parts are warmed up. To accelerate to that speed from cold would almost certainly break something.

Thereafter, the road ran onto a military-grade bridge as yet unfinished, leading nowhere. We had to turn back, lost, into the folded velvet night.

In the dark I saw a broken-down Peugeot. The driver did not want to leave it. Flouting my rule about not being outnumbered, particularly after dark, I gave two of his passengers a lift on the basis that they would show me where the Hotel Ozu was and fetch help for him. They squeezed on to the front seat beside me and we swung through the night-time suburbs.

Benghazi is an entirely modern town. Even the ten-year-old buildings have been repainted sparkling white for the anniversary celebrations. The streets are strung and decked with green flags. Only white lightbulbs are permitted for the festooning of architecture, road signs and palms, so the place has an enchanted, and even fairytale, aspect. Cars thronged the long one-way boulevard and my guides saw several friends in other vehicles, much to their delight. Even Libyans love to be film stars for a night. Imagine the fun we will have in Tripoli when the twentieth-anniversary celebrations reach their peak tomorrow evening.

As My Lady's water temperature reached danger point, we saw a distant elevated bridge, Venetian in its humpback lines but interstate in proportions and concrete, lit up in Cambridge blue for once. My hitchhikers disembarked and pointed to a large hotel across on the other side of it, beyond several unfinished buildings. The bridge rises high to give ships access to the inner pool of Benghazi harbour. From the top, the city was a silver-sequinned cloth. Six powerful searchlights around the wide inner pool raked up to form a white teepee of light overhead, Nuremberg Rally style. Near the far bank, in front of the Hotel Ozu, set out into the harbour 100 yards from the shore, a long line of fountains jet up from vertical red and green floodlights.

The Ozu towers over the waterfront as I approach. Reaching it is easier said than done. Between us lies a half-completed version of the spaghetti flyovers in Izmir. My Lady draws toots and curses as she circles the maze several times before seeing her way through.

Then the tensions of the day fall away as marbled porches lead to the hotel's chilled interior.

Nobody is going to question my existence here. My room looks out across the fountains to the harbour basin under its big top of searchlights and the bustle of the main town. A tall office block is reflected in the water. It has left select rooms with their lights on, so that the windows make a '20' in white. Standing on my balcony, watching the citizens promenade along the quayside, one has to admire the degree of party planning, and the elegance and effectiveness of the display. In nine months' time, when the lightbulbs need replacing and the electronically dancing fountains no longer come out to play, it may be a different story.

In the bathroom, over the steaming taps, the face in the mirror is unshaven and gaunt, not a man you would just wave through a roadblock.

Day 47

Daybreak has transformed my balcony view for the worse. The fountains still hose through their complex routine, and the fifteen-storey office block is still there on the opposite shore. But now the lights are off. The only colour is grey. In the brutal dawn, workmen are busy with desperate last-minute preparations along my side of the water: ponds that are soiled with building site slick; flowerbeds that are only a fraction planted out. Surely the organisers will have to admit defeat. But no. More workmen arrive, and a digger carrying a ton of sand.

*

Looking for a way out of Benghazi, I pull up beside an old man waiting to cross the street and ask directions. He waves me on, saying 'Tripoli Road, Tripoli Road' in passable English. You know where, or rather when, he learnt to say that... My father tells how, when he was posted to Germany in the winter of 1945, aged eighteen, the German civilians had a similar attitude to troops asking directions: '*Immer gerade aus*' – straight on, straight on.

Shortly afterwards I pass a road sign. The names are in Arabic, but the numbers are school numerals. Three of the places are over a thousand kilometres away. A thousand kilometres from Benghazi to Tripoli. I'm going to count the roadblocks. Sorry, but that may be the only way to pass today – you cannot play I spy in a sandpit for very long. I guess fifty. And only twelve hours to do it.

High time we were motoring.

*

Roadblock 1. Chance to check the tyres. We don't want another flat before I can put the new shell on to a rim. Karaman tyre running very hot. Must be a slow puncture – 220 pumps on the stirrup pump and throw over some water to cool it down. I cannot tackle the desert shod like this.

*

Checkpoint 2. While they have my passport, let me catch up with the story.

I found a tyre specialist. I asked him to fix my punctured spare and fit the fresh Hammersmith tyre to the Karaman wheel. However, it seems Libya has not yet met the tubeless tyre – maybe desert splinters just make tubes more sensible.

By the time I realised this, the boy had levered the punctured tyre off the spare wheel and was cutting out its perfectly good valve. I have neglected to bring any spare air valves from England. A tubeless tyre is useless without a valve. Now, after angry discussions in sign language, I am running the fresh Hammersmith tyre with an undersized tube in it. The Karaman wheel is back to being my spare, and the punctured shell is in the boot for good measure.

We await events with interest.

My passport is returned, I engage gear and we roll away.

The road has been south since Benghazi, following the coastline. The terrain is back to desert tabletop, no vegetation in any direction, just telephone and power masts, and road builders pressing on to make it dual carriageway. This a graveyard for tyres, on average one shredded and abandoned by the roadside every fifty yards. Fuel looks a bit low.

Holding a steady sixty, southsoutheast, straight at the sun as I write, the shadow of the Bentley's dash-mounted rear view mirror falls like a sundial directly in the middle of the bench seat, by my leg.

*

Roadblock 3. They want to see inside the boot, then they let me go to the adjacent petrol station, then to the tyre station next door, where all pressures prove to be reasonably correct. But I have to return through the roadblock a second time.

A middle-aged man in a pith hat has appeared and I am told to enter his patch of shade and explain myself.

'What do you think of Libya?'

'Wonderful.'

'What about the people?'

'Wonderful.'

'What about compared to Egypt?'

'Much richer than Egypt.' Big smile from my questioner.

'What do you think of our Libyan jihad system?'

'I haven't seen it, I'm just driving all the time.'

'OK, go,' and his attention turns to a new arrival.

But in the delay the engine has overheated, and she has stalled and won't start. Oh dear, oh dear. Midday desert sun. No cooling shade anywhere. Sunlight to fry your brains. How long will this take to sort itself out? Will I miss the big military parade in Tripoli after all? Open bonnet to let the airflow through. Go down the embankment for a wander. Turn on some music. Try again. Nothing.

Exasperating.

I thought I knew the water temperature gauge backwards. I thought she always boiled out through the bottom of the radiator before she overheated to the extent of not actually working.

*

Done it! She's going.

*

Roadblock 4, by a shady tree. They want to look at the box of CDs.

Now I understand the green paint – it's all wishful thinking, the colour they want the fields to be.

*

Roadblock 5, waved through. Hard, merciless desert now. You can only admire anyone who followed Rommel off this oven-like road to cut across the raw wasteland to the south for a week to surprise Tobruk the first time. But of course, in so doing, they avoided that escarpment east of Benghazi which we came down last night. That would have proved even deadlier.

*

Roadblock 6. Again a friendly smile and barely stopped. The country attitude is returning. A heavier scrub here, not dunes, as some miles back. The road sign warning of camels inadequately explains the miles of barbed wire fencing that parallels this road on either side.

The trip meter set in Cairo goes round to 000(0) miles and we start again. With no map and no idea where we are, the road turns back to the west – which gets the sun out of my side of the Bentley, and means I can put my arm up on the window without it being broiled.

*

I have not seen the sea for a while, only the ribbon of tarmac through rolling desert. Then up ahead is roadblock 7, in the middle of nowhere, magnificently decorated with green and white flags draped from green-painted steel arches over the road; and as the winged and chromed radiator draws up to the halt line, a towering portrait of Gaddafi, naval ensemble ablaze with medals, stands above us on the right. Once through the questioning, it is the perfect photo opportunity, the white sand, the white car and no-idea white uniform, the blue sky, the police compound's green steel doors and green barbed wire atop, the weird arches of the crossroads leading to nowhere. Arabic banners strung between them flap in the hot wind. This will be my Christmas card.

Stepping off the main road, I look through the viewfinder for an angle. The picture is framed, almost taken, when a pick-up bowls in from the south, blotting the shot. I wave to ask the driver to move forward. The gesture alerts one of the checkpoint guards, who comes over with his Kalashnikov. I extend my hand to him. He takes it and keeps it, pulling me with him towards the police compound. I am surely asleep. He holds my hand firmly, walking beside me with the gun between us. We pass the car and I grab my document bag. He takes me round to the side of the building, where another pair of high steel doors, also painted green and topped with green barbed wire, let into the stout, whitewashed wall. He clangs on the right-hand door with the butt of the gun and shouts for it to be opened. With each bang my freedom hops another step away.

Once we are inside, the heavy gate slams solidly behind us.

My captor leaves me standing in the glare of the courtyard while he goes in through a dark doorway. I sidle off to the right to find some shade. My feelings split delicately, like an amoeba reproducing. One part, my superficial self, says nothing is wrong. But the other, familiar coward, reels at such sudden powerlessness.

Several minutes later a tubby young man comes out, rubbing his eyes and ignoring me, followed by the guard with the gun. I am led in through the dark doorway, down a cool passage and into a room on the left, where I am told to sit and the door is shut. I am alone. The room has two chairs, a desk and a low cot, which is rumpled and still warm to the touch. I stand between the chair and the bed. A new guard with a machine gun comes in and tells me to sit. I say I prefer to stand. The tubby young man comes in, sits down and tells me to sit. I do. He says I have interrupted his afternoon sleep and that I must give him my passport, which I do. He takes it out with him. The room grows chilly from the air conditioning.

After several false alarms, when strange faces appear at the door and look at me, I am led out into the corridor and down to the door at the end. The layout of the complex is confusing, but I must grasp and retain it. It could be my one chance. This second room is long, with barred windows at each end and a narrow T-shape of tables down the middle. Four of us enter. The guard, with his backwards sloping forehead, whiskers and dishevelled, weasel demeanour, goes first. He sits on the far side of the longitudinal table and lays his Russian weapon on the surface in front of me. I have not seen one close-up before. The tubby young man takes the swivel armchair at the head of the T, with his back to the open window, so that his face is silhouetted against the white of the compound. A black-skinned man of about my age sits down on the nearside of the table. I am told to sit beside him.

At the bottom end of the room is an iron bedstead – no mattress, just steel springs, like some tool of inquisition.

The black man tells me that he is Sudanese and is to act as my interpreter.

'Cigarette?' asks Tubby through him.

'No, I do not smoke.'

'Whisky?' as if they had any whisky.

'No, I don't drink.' First lie; but will I ever taste it again?

'How many cigarettes do you smoke in a day?' I ask Tubby.

'It depends how many problems I have. Today I have had three. I was just going to sleep when you arrived.'

'I'm sorry to be wasting your time,' I say.

He lights up and exhales. 'My time is wasted anyway,' he replies. 'What is your business in Libya?'

'I am a tourist in transit.'

'Why are you here?'

'To drive through to Tunisia. I am driving round the Mediterranean.'

'Why are you here now?'

'Because these are the summer holidays in Europe. I have to take my holiday now.'

'Yes, but why are you here now?'

'Because I am driving round the Mediterranean, and this is the section I have reached for this holiday, which my employer says I have to take now.' I can barely get the sentence out, but it works.

'What is your business?' He leafs through my passport.

'I work in a bank in London.' It's an investment company majority owned by a bank, but try explaining that.

'You have a business visa – who invited you?'

'Here, I have the telex.' I look in my bag for the file, hoping they will not snatch the whole briefcase away and find my notepad; what have I said about Libya up until now? I cannot remember. It must have been rude somewhere. I pull out the file and find the telex. But Tubby wants the whole file, and he leafs through it with suspicion.

'This telex is from Germany, not from Libya,' he says.

'Yes, I was invited by this friend of the family who is Libyan but lives in Germany.'

'Have you met this man?'

'No, but we have talked on the telephone.'

'You have never met the man who vouched for you?'

The door opens. Three black migrant workers arrive to fix Tubby's air conditioning. It is like a ghastly break for commercials. I want to whisper to them, or shout, to say that I am trapped here, get me out and tell the world. But of course they are in some comic dimension of their own, and I am as dumb as a sheep.

The refrigeration unit is mounted up near the ceiling, and after much confusion they decide to take it away for repair. One worker tries to lift it down by himself. It is obviously too heavy. For a moment he buckles backwards, his spine about to snap. In the nick of time, his two colleagues move forward and catch just enough of the weight to save him. Then the three of them carry the mechanism down the corridor.

From my chair, I see through the end door into the courtyard. The main gate has been pushed aside for their lorry, and beyond it is freedom.

Then the office door swings shut.

The problem is that I never sorted out my papers for Libya. Tourist visas are like hen's teeth. The man who helped with the business visa did it as a kindness, and the other end of the process, arranging the meeting with his company in Tripoli, was never tied up. The more they dig, the weaker my story will become, until they could even convince themselves I am some kind of spy or hitman.

Alternatively, they may be looking for some excuse for a hostage-taking. Or this may be a provisional splinter group, left out in the desert, which needs a little local difficulty to make some bigger point. My brain races on the edge of control. If I am held to ransom, no one will ever track me down in this thousand-mile stretch of coast. I think about my happy telex home, sent from the Hotel Ozu only this morning.

Being separated from the Bentley, I have lost my alibi.

'Have you seen my car?' I ask Tubby.

'I don't care about your car,' he replies. 'I'll buy it from you without even needing to look at it.'

'But my *Triptik* papers prevent that.'

'No, everything can be arranged.'

'What is your name?' I ask.

Hesitation, then 'My name is Saad.'

'Where is this place?' I follow.

More hesitation, then 'Libya.'

The ploy works, and Tubby moves off the sensitive subject of the visa, to more general questions.

'Has anything bad happened to you in Libya?'

'No, rather the opposite; everyone has been very friendly. Of course there are roadblocks, which we do not have in England. I've been trying to work out if the distance between them is systematic. It seems to be every fifty kilometres.'

'No,' he says, 'there's no system. So what do you think of Libya?' he asks.

'Of the countries which I have recently visited, Turkey, Syria, Jordan and Egypt, this is much richer, more peaceful.' Plenty of oil to share between just four million people equals new roads carrying late-model Japanese cars. Tobruk was like Torquay.

'What do you think of Britain's attitude to Libya?' he asks.

'No one in Britain knows what Libya is really like, because no one has been here. What we think may be prejudiced. I want to see for myself. For example, I have been to Apollonia and Cyrene, and they are more beautiful than anything in other parts of the Mediterranean.'

Tubby pulls out his briefcase and opens it. I am expecting a blunt instrument, but he shows me a resort brochure for a holiday village in Tunisia, on Jerba Island.

The translator says, 'He has a house there… well, his family does. He says it is a fantastic place. But if it's archaeology you want, then Libya is the place. Go to Lubda, beyond Tripoli.'

I think, Oh God, if only, that would be great. But I say '*Inshallah*', which blows it, because Tubby detects insincerity and resumes his previous hauteur.

'In Libya we believe that women are inferior to men; what do you think?'

I reply, 'The records set at the Olympic Games are almost all held by men. So you can see that men are physically superior to women. But I also know some very fit and also very intelligent women.'

'What about Mrs Thatcher?'

Tough one. I smile and shrug, and to my surprise, so does he.

An older man enters the room, places a message on the desk by Tubby and looks at me. Tubby scribbles a reply, and the older man, who behaves like his elder brother, leaves immediately. It must be about me, I am thinking. What could be more important than me?

'So you are going to Algeria? Where the French murdered a million people. Like that.' He holds his fists in front of him and makes a schoolboy imitation of a tommy gun.

'I did not know that,' I say, almost believing it.

Saad asks, 'Have you seen the film *The Prophet*? It is on everywhere.'

I rack my brains, and up pops an image of Anthony Quinn in a trailer for a seventies flop.

'Not yet,' I say.

'You will,' says Tubby, ominously. I have a vision of a cell with round-the-clock, year-round screenings of *The Prophet* as an added twist to solitary confinement.

'You know Yusuf Islam, what was he called…? Cat Stevens? He became a Muslim. You have never thought of it?'

All this conversation is relayed through the interpreter, who takes his time.

'Well,' I say, 'I am interested to learn more about it. The people in central Turkey are very religious – they took me to pray. It was interesting, only men, and bowing down in lines. But you don't change religions without deep and lengthy thought.'

'You will never hear of a Muslim leaving the faith.'

Saad has put his finger on it. For me, if the choice is not made freely, it is not worth anything. For him, society must be protected from itself. But he wins this round, and I must scramble now to keep him away from discussing the visa.

'I am also interested by the philosophy of the Arab peoples,' I say. 'For example, I have heard about *tarab*, the spiritual appreciation of music and poetry. We have derived the word troubadour. What are the other manly qualities? What is the word for courage in Arabic?'

We discuss the definition and decide on *shaja'a*.

'Well,' I say, 'if Libya and England are to solve their misunderstandings, someone has to reach out. That takes *shaja'a*. So here I am, the first British car into Libya in nine years, and look what happens.'

'What can I tell you?' says Tubby.

The veneer of normality seems more convincing.

I say, 'Working in a bank, I would like to know how lending money works.'

Tubby bites the hook. Through the interpreter, we discuss the iniquities or merits of charging interest, *ripa*. If we keep this up, I may yet win him over. I am holding another red herring up my sleeve if given the chance: we could talk for hours about heaven. But Tubby has a brainwave.

'What you must do is read the Green Book,' he says. 'We will find a copy in English.' He pulls an Arabic copy of Gaddafi's thoughts from his briefcase and passes it to the interpreter to show me. Yes, I think. I must get one of these.

But in the pause, my crust of bravado creaks sickeningly. I am quite alone in his country. He will bore of playing with me. He must make a display of competence to his bosses. I say, 'If I am not going to get to Tunis, I must let my family know.'

'Things will be told to you one at a time,' he says, and my heart sinks into my boots. 'First I must report you.'

I want to beg him to stop, but how could that help? He has several grey telephones on his desk. However, one is that arresting duck-egg blue I noticed at the border. Comecon's answer to avocado. This he now picks up and attempts to dial through a six-digit number. But it does not connect. He tries again and gives up. He already has my passport, but now he takes the invitation telex, the customs carnet and the rest of the file out of the room, saying he wants photocopies.

I try to relax with the interpreter. He says he plays football to keep fit and goes to the beach on Fridays.

'Oh, the beach is near here?' I say.

'Yes, two kilometres away, just a beach, no buildings or people.'

My mind is again full of ideas. If I could reach the sea, could I swim for it? If I ran for the desert, would anyone give me help? My hands are sweating and my yellow desert shorts too greasy with engine oil for me to wipe them dry. I am wearing the wrong clothes, the wrong colours, for anyone to take me seriously. Certainly I would get nowhere on the run. I would stick out, burn and die of thirst. And there is no Resistance in Libya to give water or a change of clothes. The car would be equally impossible to hide.

My tormentor returns. He gets through on the paradise phone. A shouted conversation follows, where I only understand the word *Inglisi*.

Then he leaves again.

The interpreter's heel bites into the carpet, and a tiny plume of dust kicks up behind it. Are these going to be my last recollections of freedom?

He begins to talk in a low voice. 'I know how you feel,' he says. 'This happened to me in England. I was stopped for not having a visa.' He looks resentful at the memory, and I wonder how much I can trust him.

'What do you think of the situation now?' I ask.

'Never, ever give them an opening like that telex,' he says. 'Just be the normal guy, just say you applied for a visa and got it. You didn't ask for a business one. It was a mistake. Never mention anything like the telex.'

The shadow is climbing the wall outside the window.

The day is past.

Tubby comes in and says I must now make my statement. He will write down the answers I give the translator. The urge to cry grips me, throat tightening, a weight on my chest, ears ringing, head alternatively racing off through anticipated minefields and stalling, so that even a simple fact cannot be remembered. I promise myself never to be so stupid again. If only I could make a little squeak or sigh of misery it would be comforting, and once or twice I even do, before I notice myself. How ridiculous to be arrested for photographing some flags and a picture of a leader.

Try not to slouch.

And so the questions start again. Name, age and so on and again the question why did you come to Libya – it is a very bad time, lots of important people together. I am beginning to see what he means.

'Just chance,' I say. 'I am in transit, but when I found out there would be celebrations, I was happy, because it is good to be with people when they are celebrating. And you have the best flags of any checkpoint I have seen.'

Tubby leans back and adjusts himself contentedly in his executive chair.

'That is all I was trying to do. Have a souvenir.'

'Did you take the picture?'

'No.' I wonder to myself if I ought to offer to expose the film.

Tubby reads my statement back through the interpreter. At the passage which discusses my conversation with the Libyan in Germany, I change 'He also told me this was a good time to visit Libya' to 'He told me that my visit was coinciding with the twentieth-anniversary celebrations, which was an unexpected pleasure for me'. This means that Tubby has to write the whole thing out again, but he shows surprising patience. At the end I add that I have seen Cyrene (Shehad) and am looking forward to seeing Lubda. Also that I was sure Mr Agila at the Libyan embassy in Paris would not have issued my visa if he had not been satisfied with my credentials.

Eventually the correct statement is read out, and I sign it.

Shortly afterwards the angel-phone rings. Tubby holds a short discussion. Then he puts the receiver down and leans forward.

'In Tripoli they think your visa is a forgery,' he says. 'They have never heard of you. I must hand you over to the big police station.'

I ask, 'Can I wash my hands?'

'Of course.'

Kalashnikov leads me out into the courtyard and points to a corner where I can urinate. Actually I do want to scrub my sweaty hands under a cool tap. But maybe this will be my last chance to relieve myself, to scout out the compound, to see the free sky, so who is complaining?

'Is that a Libyan-made gun?' I ask, as Kalashnikov walks me back. Yes, he indicates, presumably incorrectly.

Back inside, Tubby says, 'I will tell you what I want to believe: there was just a simple mistake in Paris. This Mr Agila should have written down Tourist, not Business.'

'No,' I say, 'it was going to be business, to take advantage of the fact that I was here, but the contact never came through.'

'How do you feel about this man who captured you?' Tubby asks.

'He was doing his job,' I say. Tubby and Kalashnikov smile broadly.

'Very good answer,' says Tubby, and gives a thumbs-up sign.

*

Night has fallen by the time we are ready to go. Everyone is saying sorry.

Leaving the compound I make a joke of putting my hands in the air, and Tubby shamefacedly tells the guard to leave his gun behind. But what use my having convinced these people I am honest if I only have to do it again higher up? I keep thinking there was a moment at the beginning when I could have taken charge and prevented this accelerating slide to Hades, passed from boss to boss, each less interested, more brutalised.

'Do they speak English at the security police?' I ask my translator. We all suppose so, but nobody knows.

'Do you want me to come too?' he asks.

'Obviously I'm frightened,' I say, 'but look, it's late, you have been too kind already, and you deserve some food.' He says he will come with me.

Out in the open, it is well after dark. The Derby Bentley stands untouched, a tonic for me, and she brings a smile to Tubby's lips.

'Drive,' he says. 'Follow the police car. I will be behind you.'

We both know there is no point me running off in this. Our convoy's headlights turn back through the roadblock, along the highway for a mile, then to the north. Round two small hills the road curves, and then I see the big secret. Crawling up through the arc-lit arena into the black sky are the towers, flares and plumes of a massive industrial complex. It looks like a space programme, well advanced, or a nuclear reactor site.

We drive right into the base. I have seen too much now. At the central barracks, Tubby and my translator go ahead and leave me alone sitting in My Lady. The street is hard-packed earth, with buildings set back at varying distances, like a Wild West town. I swallow my malaria pill for the day, unsure whether to keep the bottle with me or leave it behind to be inconspicuous. The Paludrine still makes me queasy. Hell, there are no mosquitoes in this desert anyway. I leave it.

After five minutes they both come out, quickly say goodbye and drive off.

Nothing happens.

If I want this ball rolling, I have no option but to go in and give it a push.

Through the barred door is a spacious living room, complete with a table and two chairs, two sofas and a television across from them. Five young men stand up when I enter. Four leave, going deeper into the building. The fifth is another archangel, like at the frontier, but his nightie is not white but duck-egg blue, to match the telephones, I suppose. He speaks English.

This celestial being becomes my new case officer. While he is talking with me, checking the copy of my statement, the television chatters away, coverage of the build-up to a stadium display in Tripoli. Like his fellow seraph at the border, he has the tribal features of Gaddafi, the sloping Berber face, the high, slightly receding hairline, soft black curls, almost shaggy; the frowning eyebrows, coal-black eyes and slim nose.

After the questioning, I am given supper on a tray, with the feeling it might be my last. But then why should they bother to give me one at all? Surely a real spy would have a better story than mine? Is it OK to eat fish with my fingers?

On the TV, the presidents of African countries are shown being welcomed by Gaddafi at the airport earlier in the day and then arriving at the stadium. The cameras scan the floodlit ranks, which in turn applaud the arrival of the Colonel's motorcade. Now the performance begins. A girl and a youth run round the track carrying a flaming torch aloft between them, then up through the crowd to a high cauldron. The girl is bulky, with a thick ponytail down her back. She pants from the climb, while the boy lights the fire bowl.

As I finish supper, the whole side of the stadium opposite the presidential rostrum transforms. The 'spectators' begin a synchronised display using coloured boards to form a sequence of enormous pictures. Clenched fists bearing automatic weapons, Palestinians smashing rocks on to the heads of Israelis, and the general message that Arabs must stick together. The display changes to a new picture every twenty seconds and is sustained for perhaps forty-five minutes, without a single dud pixel. I cannot believe the discipline. At the same time the floor of the stadium writhes with several hundred young men and women in a gymnastic display of equally robotic precision. All were born in 1969, says my inquisitor. The rehearsals have gone on for a year.

Watching this huge show shrinks me down to size, as fascism does. I realise that Gaddafi would not give a fig for one small diplomatic incident like me.

My Gabriel leaves, and one by one the other four men drift back in. One of them, a fat former merchant navy cook closes the barred door to keep out the smell of ammonia from the industrial site now that the wind has changed. I preferred it when the door was open. He talks some English, some French. I ask him what the fish was.

'*Feu rouge*,' he says. '*Connaissez Grimsby?*' I blink. Grimsby? Grimsby?
'No, sadly not.'

He says in English, apropos of nothing and barely intelligibly, 'To be or not to be, that is the question.' He wags his finger at me, 'Eh? Eh?' Those are his lips moving but the message is from somewhere else. I gape. Can he possibly know Hamlet's soliloquy? But his words are better said, more apt, less obscure, than ever delivered in Stratford-upon-Avon. I repeat what he is saying in clear English. This opens a whole new window on the wisdom of choosing death over dishonour.

I am summoned into the bowels of the building, to the office of a yet more senior secret policeman. I walk warily, looking out for the cells. A tall officer greets me, with a long face like Mohsen's, a more gentle manner, but also more bureaucratic.

'I am in charge here,' he says. 'What is your car registration? Why do you have no Libyan number?'

'The car is in transit,' I say. 'At the eastern frontier they said I did not need a number.'

'Did you take a photo of the checkpoint?'

'Not quite.' I begin a complex explanation of what I tried to do, then change my mind. 'Come out and see my car.'

I am learning how. I take him by the hand and lead him through the building and out of the front door into the night.

There she is – Jolly Jumper is waiting for Lucky Luke outside the bar in Painful Gulch. The long-faced officer gives me a quizzical look, breathes in slowly and exhales. He pats my arm and walks back indoors.

'This is all nonsense,' he says to me in front of Gabriel and his men. Then he leaves me with them and disappears back towards his office.

I ask if I may read a book from my pilot bag. No, says Gabriel, then yes; but it means the others soon wander off, which is scary because of what they might be hatching. Perhaps they want to see if I will make a run for it.

I walk through the building again, shouting 'Hello'. There they are, eight of them, with a square of carpet rolled out on the concrete in the back yard, eating.

'Who here is married?' I ask. 'So this is the bachelor end. May I join you? Mint tea? Delicious. How do you make this onion soup?'

'Add tomatoes, carrots, peppers and salt.'

I am passed a plate of stewed mutton.

'In England we eat our sheep meat with mint sauce.'

'Really? So do we in Libya.' A silence descends, a slice of brotherhood, a hint of redemption.

Fried fish and sparkling mineral water; a second supper so soon must be a good omen.

The security police talk about the future. 'When you get to London…', 'When you are in Tripoli…'.

I fear that saying such things they will make them not happen.

After supper we stroll round the outside of the building. The wind has changed again and the ammonia reek has gone.

One of the eight, a bachelor, shows me where the clumps of wild herbs grow. He picks some from the shadows, saying rub them in your hands and smell the crushed leaves. The scent gives a hefty kick. He tells me he is the security policeman for an oil installation deep in the desert, up at the coast, on leave. I tease him about the security service using British cars, Land Rovers. He proudly takes me out to show me his. It is even right-hand drive. I sit behind the wheel, stroke the very English dashboard, and a wave of nostalgia for such familiar images floods over me.

The oilman says this Land Rover is on its third engine. Motors die on the 600 kilometres into the desert, where the sand is pure white and the sun so blinding that you wear a facecloth with just a slit to see through.

Walking back into the police station, I ask him, 'Have you been to the British war cemetery at Tobruk?'

'No.'

We sit down on the edge of the decking in front of the security office.

'Whereabouts are we now?'

'This is the refinery on the Gulf of Sirte. About 300 foreigners work here. Of course we must get you a map of Libya.' Sirte, I think, birthplace of Gaddafi. My new friend heads into his office. Failing to find a map, he returns with a poster of the Leader in traditional dress. He explains the clothes, the camel-wool cloak, the sheep-wool tunic, the black Berber cap. There are still 750km to Tripoli, he says.

Several of us are on the terrace now. I say I have stayed at Tobruk and Benghazi.

'Oh,' he says, 'So you have been to Cyrene? We call that province, in the east, Green Mountain.'

The phone rings and the chief hurries off. Someone jokes, 'It must be Colonel Gaddafi saying let him go.' To myself, I hope so.

He seems gone a long while. We go back inside. One of the lads starts playing with my camera. 'Take a photo of me and your friends,' I say. And he does. I wonder who will develop it. As in Damascus, we talk about Arabic and its different accents: Algerian and Moroccan, very guttural; South Yemeni very soft.

The tall officer comes through from his office and asks, 'Do you want to stay here tonight?'

'Well no, I have 1-, 2-, 3-, 4,000 kilometres to do in the next ten days,' I say counting on my fingers, 'so I'll be getting along, thanks.'

Then the supervisor comes back. 'You may go,' he says.

He leads us all out, pats the car and smiles again. The oilman from the desert offers to guide me out to the crossroads.

On cue, My Lady grabs the limelight by refusing to start. No spy or assassin would rely on a getaway car like me, she seems to say. Good for her. Only when suspicion has been thoroughly replaced by concern for a fellow driver does the straight-six splutter into life. Following the police Land Rover out of the oil refinery, it is an effort not to push up behind them. We meander along as if it was all the same to me.

We stop briefly at a civil police station for more photocopies. The small group sitting outside in the cool night leaves us well alone. Again the officer seems to take forever. The Xerox copier has broken. All the while, the Bentley's engine temperature is rising, but I am leery of showing even such a small admission of defeat as switching off.

We drive on. I have picked up a casual passenger, another English-speaker. He needs a lift to the photogenic roadblock. When we stop he translates the sign between the arches. It reads, 'Welcome to all Foreign Visitors'. We pause while the full absurdity of this sinks in, and then we both laugh.

Waiting for a last signature from Tubby himself, the oilman and I crouch by the Bentley drawing numbers and maps in the sand. We talk about the 'Unwatering Project', a 'Great Man-made River', or GMR. This is a buried aqueduct, 7m in diameter, with sidewalls 45cm thick, to pump artesian water from where it lies, 600 kilometres inland, a kilometre below ground in the desert. The water was laid down in the last Ice Age, supposedly enough to last Libya 1,000 years, at a tenth of the price of desalination. When it reaches the coast near here, the GMR will be split and the bore narrowed to 4m to carry water to Benghazi in the east and Tripoli in the west. This explains the hundreds of concrete pipe sections I have seen since Benghazi, lying in the distance, inland of the coast road, lined up for league upon league, unassembled. There is something Stalinist about such an infrastructure bet. At least buried pipes won't let the water evaporate, as has diverting the rivers that feed (or fed) the Aral Sea.

The oilman says this water will allow Libya to become self-sufficient in food. Today there may be five million inhabitants; in twenty years there will be ten million. With projects like this, he continues, Gaddafi is a popular hero. The Colonel came to power when the Americans were taking eighty per cent of Libya's oil profits, and now Libya takes the eighty per cent. In the meantime oil has become much more valuable too. The surplus is being invested in 'sensible schemes like this' for the future, he says.

*

Five miles. It must be midnight. Reverse the Bentley up a short side track, unscrew the interior light cover and take out the bulb. Climb over to the back seat, open the door, lie down and hang my head out, looking at the matchless stars.

Never, never, never do that to yourself again, Fergus.

I want to cry with the shock and relief of the thing, and perhaps I will.

*

Name me a fear: the fear of pain; the fear of frightening loved ones; the fear of being honest; of being dishonest; the fear of failure in the eyes of others; the fear of not explaining yourself; of putting your destiny into the next three words you say, and then the next three, for hour after hour, until you say a wrong one; the fear of fear; the fear of complacency; the fear of the symbolic gesture; the fear of guns, which are more than symbols; as are bars on windows; the fear of the new, the unseen, of being chased; the fear of being used, set up, betrayed; the fear of stumbling on to a secret; the fear of being hated; superstitious fear.

I left the poster of Gaddafi behind by mistake.

Day 48

A pink sunrise is coming.

The fear which welled to a scream last night is soothed by an operatic overture – the opening bars to Mozart's once almost forgotten, *Marriage of Figaro*.

Figaro was revived in the UK after World War I by war hero and former Eton schoolmaster John Christie at his country house. I close my eyes and am in the Organ Room at Glyndebourne, in the summer of 1930 before the first proper auditorium was built. Grandpa Fergus Dunlop is waiting in the wings to sing the part of the Gardener. It is the smallest solo role in the opera. *Figaro* was destined to become Glyndebourne's official launch vehicle in 1934, in which Fergus also sang that part. The overture would become the opera house's unofficial signature tune. That 1934 performance was cut on gramophone, the world's first recording of *Figaro*, in fact the first-ever recording of a full Mozart opera. A six-disc set.

Grandpa was then the age I am now, ten years out of university, but rather further into life, with a wife, two small boys and a budding singing career. Born in 1900 in Willesden, a modest corner of north London, his teens had seen the Edwardian pretentiousness savaged out of England by the Great War.

209

That should have been to his advantage, as an unpretentious farmer's son with mercantile ambitions. But his lovely baritone voice landed him a Cambridge Choral Scholarship, and there the problems began.

Fergus could never quite decide if he was a man of action or an artist. And it was hard to be both.

As a member of the Cambridge Alpine Club, he co-authored the charming, illustrated, *Roof Climber's Guide to St John's College, Cambridge*. His personal greatest night climb was to put choir cassocks on the four pinnacles of the John's chapel tower. The college authorities worked out how much it would cost to have them taken down and declared an amnesty for whoever had done the deed, so long as they removed them. My grandfather and his accomplices announced a time, perhaps noon, anyway, in broad daylight, and proceeded to undo their handiwork in front of an admiring crowd below.

Fergus also rowed, winning the Bateman Pairs in 1921 and becoming president of the Lady Margaret Boat Club, meaning he captained the college 1st eight, and the oldest boat club in Cambridge. His crew went Head of the River and competed at Henley.

With a geology degree under his belt, he looked around for a mineral for which to prospect. His uncles' firm in London had recently acquired, in lieu of an unpaid debt, a claim on a supposed coal deposit in India, just lying on the surface. So Fergus picked coal. He got to India in 1923.

Although the British Raj was adding 1,000 miles of track a year throughout the 1920s, the trains did not go where his coal deposit was. So transport was by motorbike. Grandpa told me of the amazement his machine caused in outlying villages. Asked how it worked, he would explain that the motor contained a little devil, which you had to kick awake.

Fergus' coal deposit, the Korba field, is now the largest opencast coal mine in Asia, and the second largest in the world. But the opportunity required massive investment, a railway to a port, or a local power station or steel works. It was beyond the British Empire, let alone Grandpa. He returned to Europe in 1924 and decided on a career in opera singing. The coalfield only began to be developed in 1940, and the rail link wasn't opened until the 1950s, after Indian independence and nationalisation. In 1983 the Indian government completed the Korba Superthermal Power Station, which generates 1,600 megawatts at full throttle and three growing holes in the ground.

Imagine what might have been if he had picked oil in the Emirates instead of coal in India, and had stuck it out.

I too was a boy chorister. From the age of seven to fourteen I stood in robes and cassock at boarding school Sunday services, and in the choir stalls in ordinary uniform every morning and evening the rest of the week. Asked by relatives if I had my grandfather's ear for music, I always said no. It seemed wrong to put myself on his level. My place was to love, not challenge, even if I could have. Tellingly, he never pushed me to sing – perhaps he thought it a dead-end career, even for those passionate about it.

Grandpa, having been just too young for the Great War, was almost too old for the Second. He had volunteered for the London Territorials (the 2nd Battalion of the King's Royal Rifle Corps, 'The Rangers') on returning to London; and in 1926 he won their Nordfell Cup for his machine-gunning. That year he also served as a special constable during the General Strike – I have his wooden truncheon.

At the outbreak of Word War II he immediately joined up as a captain. But his leg was in plaster in May 1940. He had been knocked off his motorcycle in the blackout. (When they stitched him together, a piece of brake cable was unwittingly sewn into his shin. The wire would gradually work its way down, without symptoms, until the tip emerged at his big toe, to great surprise, years later, at which point it was removed.)

Meanwhile, his battalion was sent to Calais to cover the retreat from Dunkirk. The unit was decimated, almost all either killed or captured, and had to be re-formed by conscription. This lowered its average age – and Grandpa at forty was suddenly too old. He landed up with a desk job in the Political Warfare Executive, PWE, learning Hungarian. The Resistance in Hungary became his speciality. However, we will probably never know what that involved. Most of the PWE's papers were deliberately destroyed at the end of the war, 'because it was a secret organisation' as my Uncle Robert puts it.

After Germany's unconditional surrender in May 1945, Fergus, as acting colonel, was present at the surrender of Klagenfurt, the regional capital of Carinthia in Austria, becoming military commander of the town.

Klagenfurt is on the southern border, where Austria bulges into Yugoslavia. This district of Kärnten Province in May 1945 was the scene of the chaotic 'return' of a large number, perhaps 100,000, diehard Nazi forces from various Eastern European populations. They were the supposedly lucky ones, the remnants of many more being rounded up by Tito's almost equally broad coalition of Yugoslav partisans. These Slovenes, Croats, Cossacks and White Russians crossed into Austria and surrendered to the outnumbered British, rather than to the Communists.

In hot pursuit, the partisans followed them into Austria and trapped many at Bleiberg, under the noses of a few British troops. Thereafter, in contravention, or at least a misinterpretation, of the Yalta Agreement, the British began sending what were by now their POWs back to Tito in truck convoys.

It was a dark chapter, and it ended in multiple massacres on the Yugoslav side of the border, with thousands more being handed on to Stalin for his own revenge.

To this day, Yugoslavia denies everything, so the scope for speculation is limitless. A pro-Cossack version was published two years ago by Nikolai Tolstoy, seeking to name British culprits. In his account, the British decisions were made at ministerial, general and brigadier level, with Harold Macmillan, as Minister Resident in the Mediterranean, and Brigadier Toby Low (according to Tolstoy) ultimately responsible for the 'betrayal' of the anti-Communist, non-Soviet, Cossack refugees. This claim is now the subject of a libel action in the UK High Court, although the book remains on the shelves in bookshops.

What is almost as bad is that the official files seem to have been culled or contain sanitised versions and what may be forgeries. The few victims who escaped saw only fragments of the truth. Grandpa Fergus had a ring-side view of this event. But I for one knew too little to ask him.

I was twenty-two years old when Fergus died. They could not fit all the mourners into the church. Granny was genuinely astonished. Who were all these people? I can see her now, walking up the aisle supported by a strapping son on each side, staggered as much by the turnout as the occasion itself.

Many at that service were musicians, members of the Philharmonic Society which Fergus had founded in nearby Slough. But others were old soldiers and former PWE operatives. World War II was a part of Fergus' life he did not discuss, probably because he had signed the Official Secrets Act, but possibly also because the last moments had been too painful.

Grandpa Dunlop used phrases like 'By Jove!' and 'Right you are!'

He had one particular way to connect with me. He started making 00-gauge model railway track. He was looking for a retirement hobby, something to do with his hands, for indoor days, beside his gardening and birdwatching. He had enjoyed playing at model electric trains with his sons and saw how my father encouraged my interest. So Grandpa set about laying miniature track onto jig-sawed lengths of plywood. Just when the Beeching Axe was cutting out hundreds of miles of British branch line a year, my grandfather was adding to my collection of yard-long straights and ultra-fast corners, left-hand and right-hand junctions, and parallel track crossover points; not to mention exotic fractions (¼-, ½- and ¾-length straights and corners, slow and fast), which allowed any track design to be looped back to itself without straining the fishplates.

Each piece had been handcrafted with love. Each was unique.

Grandpa Dunlop was also what they called an Advanced Driver – I understood that it involved an extra driving test. His every hill start was exact, every gear change spot on, every turn properly indicated in advance. The smoothness of trips in his Rover 90, and later his Saab 99, were family folklore.

On the sale of their house a year after my grandmother died, I received a minimalist desk and a gothic chest.

I opened the chest for the first time last year. The cheap Nazi ceremonial dagger in the bottom probably comes from the surrender of Klagenfurt. But there is also a rolled-up, poster-sized photo of Fergus in uniform, by a dusty roadside, head back, left hand out, right hand swigging an unlabelled dark bottle to his lips. The light and the vegetation are Mediterranean.

He told me, as a boy, how he had been in Italy, driving the length of the Apennines, on VE Day, the moment of peace in May 1945. When dusk settled, the bonfires winked into life across the hills as the celebrations spread over the Roman countryside. In the poster, he is drinking with such elation I like to think it was taken the day of that happy, madcap blast up through Italy. The joyous thirst in this image, before he reached Austria and its complications, is also the thirst for life.

If Driving is in my blood, it comes from him.

*

My Lady fires first turn of the key. The water temperature comes off the bottom stop. We are 1,100 miles from Cairo. Mount up! Move out!

Occasional dunes, no trees. Lone shredded tyres still dot every fifty yards – little testaments to the blistering power of this sun.

I soak up every trivial detail, but passively, like a labourer home in front of the television on a Friday night after a long week. Yesterday's fright has amplified the pleasure of freedom, and yet has sapped my strength.

The Bentley is on full song, just as a travel companion should be, raising your spirits, providing confidence in the shakier moments.

*

Checkpoint 8. Thorough search of car by a Camberley-polite corporal and a private in a red helmet with the strap up across his forehead.

*

Checkpoint 9 comes up quite quickly (Tubby was not lying), luxurious camouflage netting but unmanned. Three squatting Arabs signal for a lift. I sign back, 'I'm sorry but it would only complicate things'. All this open range. I think of the hedgerows of England and wish I was back there now.

Ah! The sea, the Gulf of Sirte, with three supertankers moored on the horizon, accommodation blocks at each stern gleaming white in the morning sun.

*

A checkpoint right on the beach with a polite young soldier in a red beret.

150 miles from my inquisitors, the GMR water channel is still under construction. Sections of 4m diameter pipe lie side by side for mile after mile.

*

At roadblock 11 a squaddy throws my pillow in the dirt while I am emptying the car for them.

I shout at him and in response the soldiers conduct the first full-depth inspection of the boot since Nuweiba.

*

A huge natural salt pan stretches beside the road, like the hard sugar on a school bun. I want to drive out over it, to see the wedding pearl against a smooth white skin, under a royal-blue sky. But a low, unbroken dune bars me from the crystal surface, for ever, a seamless ha-ha, with the laugh on me.

There is no point fighting it.

The next roadblock is a many-headed affair, with a search of my pilot bag (for documents) and also, a new wrinkle, the dashboard glove compartment.

'Where is Madame?' they ask.

'There isn't one,' I double-lie.

One is in front of them and the other hopefully at home, reconciled after her Easter jaunt to Paris. I try to watch all the guards at once, to stop them planting evidence. Or could some last wrinkle still have been overlooked up to now? Click. The barrel of an AK47 knocks against the open door. This is really happening.

*

No, Tubby was wrong; it's a checkpoint every fifty kilometres. At this next stop, we have seven Libyans peering into the engine, with both bonnets up like a cabbage white butterfly's wings. That's one way to stay cool on tickover. Also, for the first time, the words 'transit' and 'Tunis' appear to have meaning. I suppose we are halfway there. The guards release us before she boils, but after six miles the engine still runs hot. The radiator takes three litres of water. Don't get ideas, foolish man.

*

The pilot bag is searched again.

And now the road turns sharply from the coast into the desert. In an instant the climate renews its offensive. For league upon league, the tarmac runs straight over the featureless landscape. Your head begins to bulge with the distance covered – 1,300 miles from Cairo, and no idea where we are to the nearest hundred. Up ahead must be Sobrata and Lubda. The heat is ugly, at least as bad as Syria. Time for some heavy artillery. I risk a few seconds' pause to stack the Wagner CDs into the auto-loader in the boot, 'The Ride of the Valkyries', squeeze in plenty of bass on the remote control, and hit it!

The water gauge struggles to recover from the brief stop. Four miles at 60mph through the fan-oven draught brings the needle back. I pat My Lady's dashboard. Keep going old girl. Keep going.

*

Petrol station by roadblock 15. Perfect. The radiator takes another litre, and I refill two one-and-a-half-litre water bottles and check the wheels. The front driver's side tyre is cooking. Not even roadblocks can operate in this heat. At the checkpoint a man clutching a green-blue telephone receiver waves me through from the shade of his tent.

Keep the speed down to help the overheating tyre, 45mph. At this rate of progress, the pressure of baking air across the cooling system cannot stop the temperature gauge rising, but it's enough to keep it off the boil. We are in the critical band before fuel evaporation occurs, where the gasoline has become part of the coolant, flowing from the colder tank through the hot fuel line and twin SU carburettors.

If I stop, it may be hours before the engine bay simmers down enough to let petrol reach the cylinders.

*

Ten miles. Smoke in the rear mirror. Lean out of the window, look back, look forwards, look down. Front tyre on my side. Slow, don't brake hard. Stop. Clouds of smoke. Out. Run round the front. Crouch. Look under radiator. FIRE.

The driver's side wheel is on fire.

The tyre is burning on its inside face. Grab drinking water from front seat. Splash it inside the wheel arch. Six-inch flames. Only seconds to save her. I am counting. One. Two. Three, to the boot. Four. Five, snatch up more water, a bottle in each hand. Six, seven, eight seconds. Top off, fling the first spare bottle over the fire. Nine, ten, eleven. Second top off, fling the second bottleful. Twelve. Some effect. Thirteen, but still flames. If they get to the wiring loom we are finished. Fourteen, back to boot for third and last bottle. Fifteen, sixteen, kneel under front bumper, throw hard at flames, hard because this is your only water, your reserve for walking out of the desert alive. Seventeen. Flames out. Eighteen, nineteen, smoke returning. Twenty, hurl on last half bottle. Smoke dies down.

From the boot, grab the jack and wheel nut brace. Hubcap away. Loosen bolts, jack up body, cranking furiously under the death-ray sun. Whip the wheel off. What is that cracking, popping noise? Only the wheel bolts hissing in the water on the road.

Rest.

Ten hours or twenty seconds, a crisis knocks the hell out of you.

Look again. The Hammersmith tyre is singed, toasted in two places on the inner sidewall. God, if it had caught properly. Like tyres blazing on the bonfire on Guy Fawkes Night.

The fault is in the brake drum, I think. The fire appears to have been fed by a mixture of brake fluid, chassis oil and wheel bearing grease.

Is she immobilised? Is this the point at which I abandon her for good?

If I can just take out the whole brake innards and remount the wheel, she'll be rolling at least. But I need a screwdriver to loosen those drum screws. How come I do not have a screwdriver? And is that how the drums release?

I pack up the pieces as best I can and cross to the other verge, hoping to hitch a lift back to checkpoint 15. The road with its empty mirages stretches to the vanishing point in both directions. Approaching vehicles can be heard and seen for minutes before they arrive. Several lorries are heading west. Nothing east, in my latest direction.

Could there be a closer garage up ahead? Don't risk it. Or somewhere better to hitch? The sun is a blowtorch aimed at me. I curl up in a ball under the front bumper where a small shadow pools, and I can see the highway to the west.

*

A right-hand drive lorry rattles and grinds up the lonely return road from checkpoint 15, carrying me back to the stranded Bentley. Inside, the heat from its engine cover burns my ankles. The driver's arms are shaking so much from the steering wheel that I can't read his watch. In my bag I have a screwdriver borrowed from a young Libyan petrol pump attendant, thanks to the intercession of a Palestinian waiting at the filling station for a lift to his home in the south, near Chad.

From the exalted height of this cab, the road through the arid wastes looks even more tenuous. You see the shredded tyres more clearly. Our old truck is chucking us around as if it has lost several itself. So much for missing the Tripoli parade; we nearly had our own torch ceremony right here.

The driver stops ten yards behind My Lady, drops me off and pulls away with a wave.

*

I ought to travel in overalls. This shirt and these yellow shorts are a disgrace. However much I heave and sweat with the second screwdriver, I still can't release the screws. The answer is a butane torch, which I do not have. I tried matches of course. The wheel does turn, however, so the next best bet is to drive back slowly to the checkpoint village, without rekindling the flames, and see what other help can be found. I fix the scorched Hammersmith wheel back on. Will the starter engage first time, in gratitude for a life saved? No.

*

We limp back towards the desert service station, stopping every mile or so to check temperatures. Despite this, the roasted Hammersmith tyre deflates. The fire damaged it more than I thought.

Is it the tyre or the inner tube? Both probably.

Another wheel change coming up. Gather wits. Jack her up in the heat.

The poor old Karaman wheel goes back on the driver's side front. Also, it was the undersized tube that went, not the Hammersmith tyre: the valve hole was leaking out air. Will she start? The Bendix cog grinds on the crown ring again. Get out and turn the fan. Women.

*

Another pause to check the progress of the Karaman wheel; 30mph for six miles and the hub is stone cold. Whatever was burning in the fire (not asbestos I hope) is now so disintegrated that the friction has gone. So, of course, have the brakes.

We trundle on to the roadblock, two currently useless tyres in the boot, only one of them on a rim. At checkpoint 15, the guards have just been changed. I have to go through the whole 'I'm in transit routine' for them. And soon we see why. Here, somewhere in the Sahara, a cavalcade of black limousines comes charging through, longer than the first, sirens wailing, perhaps thirty Mercedes and a sleek, turbocharged and intercooled, all-black, double-decker bus.

Well, on revolution day the Leader has to be everywhere at once.

I got my parade after all.

*

The lesson about tyres, wheels and hot roads has not been wasted on me. My Lady is sheltered behind a north-facing wall at the service station and I am determined to sit the day out. In fact, it would be rather nice to sleep, but some maniac has just parked an old Peugeot pick-up nearby and left it ticking over. The day is so hot that even ten yards upwind of me it makes an intolerable heatwave. The maniac moves his car. I set up my camp bed tucked into the shade of the wall, trying to hide from the equally rabid, arid wind. I lie completely flush, feet first into it. This way I am desiccated noticeably more slowly and can breathe back some of the moisture being stripped off my skin. Even so, sleep eludes me.

*

When the sun is well past its zenith, say at 5:30 p.m., My Lady and I creep out of our pool of shade to find a repair yard. The garages here are manned by children, like any in such serious Mediterranean countryside. Surrounded by intrigued workshop lads, I sit on the vestigial running board while the front wheel hub is dismantled and reassembled.

Well served we Jedi are. A boy stands next to me providing a finger to hold down this page in the wind as I write. Another scampers 200 yards to bring me water to wash my hands. His family name is Fateh. Saalim is the eight-year-old chief who declares the Hammersmith tyre as good as new. He derides the first inner tube we had fitted. Quite apart from the fire, which would have fried anything touching the metal wheel, the tube inside was for a Fiesta-sized wheel, 12″. We

Libya, Cyrene, Day 46 (page 190)

Libya, Gulf of Sirte, Day 48.

Below: 'Smoke dies down.' (page 216)

Right: returning to the scene of the fire (page 217)

have a 15″ tube now. So the Hammersmith tyre is sent back into the fray, on the driver's side front wheel, and the Karaman spare returns to the substitute bench.

We attempt isolating the hydraulics to the burnt-out brake drum. We poke small nails down the two feedlines, nip them tight and clamp the metal tubes in the penultimate joints before the wheel for good measure. The idea is to hold back pressure in the system for the other three wheels. Now the Bentley is being jacked down, and my sitting place on the door sill falls correspondingly. Saalim's older brother, who had the idea about the nails, comes for a short ride to see if it works. And to my amazement the brakes do have some bite. By signs, he says I could get to England on three brakes if necessary. Well, out of Libya.

Then I drop by the garage to fetch some water. Beside the Calor Gas depot, two men are washing under the outside tap for evening prayers. In turn I too wash my head. Water running through your hair is blessèd stuff in a place like this after a day like today. Religious washing takes on a whole new price and pleasure in a desert.

*

It is late, late, late. The Bentley headlights show spectral vegetation, trees even; and the night air is like a long cool drink. Two more roadblocks have been passed, very relaxed. Crossing a country without a map has one advantage: no one can wave it about at checkpoints, making accusations. Against that, you rely on word of mouth. The place we are driving for through the night is Lubda, the ancient city suggested by Tubby. Sometimes it is the other side of Tripoli and miles away; other times it is nearby. The tyre repair village in the desert suggested 150km, ninety miles. Now we've covered eighty and the checkpoint outside this port town says it's a further sixty.

*

I must sleep. However, safe places to stop are few and far between. It takes fifteen miles to find an isolated side road. At last I pull over into a stubble field. Here the Bentley and I can ease our aching joints. I remove the bulb in the interior light so that the doors can be open without drawing the mosquitoes, wash in chlorinated water, put on fresh clothes and stretch out across the back with both rear doors open. From Tuesday's first minutes to Friday's last minutes: four days, 1,440 miles. That's 360 miles a day.

Can we be halfway to Spain yet? Have we enough time to complete what is left?

220

Just before sleep comes, I curl up, pull the doors shut and replace the bulb.

The Bentley takes hours to cool, occasionally wafting me with an oven-like reminder of the day.

Day 49

Pre-dawn over the cornfield. Click on the interior light.

I am still thinking of my grandparents and particularly Grandpa Fergus' wife, Gwendoline née Coit, also born in 1900, Granny Dunlop.

The word 'Grannyish' in our family denotes something small, intelligent, dangerous and cold. Granny threw immense emotional weight into getting her own way. To me she couldn't have been the attractive young woman Fergus married, or the Gwenny her friends knew.

I mentioned a chest of papers from Gwenny and Fergus' house, the one with the Nazi dagger and the poster-sized photo of him. It sat in their outer porch, brooding even before they died, and no one knew what to do with it afterwards. Since she left me nothing, it came to me along with Grandpa's desk.

This gargoyle-lidded box was full of souvenir editions of magazines and newspapers, programmes for events and several photograph albums. There is Gwendoline, the skinny undergraduate, Cambridge (Newnham), 1923, bandana, trousers and an open-necked shirt, on a field trip, normally in the middle of the group, next to the professor; then traversing glaciers on the roof of Europe in 1924; now with a different, more handsome geology professor from Geneva; and suddenly, skipping the wedding, a wife and mother, relaxing on a garden wall in Buckinghamshire. Finally she curls up with a book in the newly completed home of their retirement. That last image was the reality I should have seen as a child.

But I didn't. Was it a construction: Gwendoline the relaxed, Gwendoline in the forefront of modernity? Nowhere does she swig from a beer bottle under the Mediterranean sun, for the sheer joy of life.

Granny had received an independent upbringing, for a girl of her time. Her father, Dr Stanton Coit, was an American gentleman-philosopher grappling with the impact of Darwinism on ethics. Some of this was important stuff: equal education for women, votes for women, women in politics. His Edwardian prediction of the blow to trade unionism to be expected from female politicians would make a Thatcherite gasp. Other parts were grotesque, such as his dream of

State-run eugenics. But he was not just a theoretician. He was also a gifted linguist, gaining his PhD in Berlin. And he practised what he preached. He wardened slum refuges in New York and London before he married. He also founded the humanist Ethical Church in London, which provided ceremony without God.

In 1913, when Gwenny was hitting puberty, Coit's book *Ethical Worship for Use in Families etc.* was published in two volumes. The first volume alone ran to 600 pages of meditations and homilies. Gwenny, the middle of his three daughters, must have been right in the firing line.

Gwendoline's mother, Adela von Gans, was a German Jewish heiress. She had been widowed young with three small children, had moved to London and married Stanton (of his stepchildren, two eventually took the Coit surname).

In London Adela joined the Suffragists, the effective, law-abiding alternative to the militant Suffragettes. Granny's first memory was being pushed in her pram through the parks of London, festooned in the Suffragist colours – green, white and red, I believe; not to be confused with the green, white and purple bunting of the Suffragettes, their headline-grabbing rivals. By the time Gwendoline was a teenager, her mother was treasurer of the International Women's Suffrage Alliance.

Among these larger-than-life characters, Gwenny seems to have been reluctant to commit herself to anything unless it would let her shine.

In the chest I found two large, beautifully illustrated, 1880s science books in German, from her childhood nursery, flora and fauna slightly scribbled on; a teenage notebook, page after page of traced sketches and densely packed remarks on fossil urchins, ammonites and trilobites; her postgrad research paper, handwritten and typed, *Sur La Sédimentation du Lac de Genève*; her list of addresses of friends in America; and the enchanting little story, typed, of how she later told my Uncle Robert, by then seven-and-a-half years old, the facts of life, recording his precocious questions.

Geology sounds prosaic. Yet Gwendoline Coit, like Fergus at Korba, briefly stood on the very frontier of her field. Fluent in German, she read before almost anyone outside Germany Alfred Wegener's world-changing text on continental drift, *Die Entstehung der Kontinente und Ozeane*, the key second edition of which was published in 1920. She gave a lecture on the topic to Cambridge's Sedgwick Club geological society in 1922, two years before the English translation appeared. This was the equivalent of an undergraduate introducing the Cambridge physics department to Einstein's general theory of relativity. The idea of clearly immobile objects – mountain ranges, continents – moving, must have been laughed at. How could it not be? The causes of plate tectonics are still unexplained today. However, the club made her its first female president.

In line with her arriviste, independent upbringing, Gwenny was a staggering intellectual and political snob. She looked down on those who lacked a university degree (Papa, but not Robert), or an international network. She was incapable of conversation with my mother's mother, who suffered on both counts yet was somehow all the bigger for it.

In 1925 her Swiss professor, Leon Collet, sent two telegrams and a long letter asking for her paper on Lake Geneva so that he could present it at a conference in Italy. She drafted a reply (never sent?), fuming that he must not edit her text or place her name lower than his on the title page, usual even for male students – he was her supervisor, the topic was his suggestion and he had helped with the fieldwork (if that is what you call it on a lake).

At the same time, Cambridge seems to have been urging her on towards a doctorate, surely one of its first for women. Professor Collet also requested her comments on the first proofs of his lecture to the Royal Geographical Society in London in December 1925, on alpine folding, in support of Wegener's ideas.

Imagine what might have been, if she had only stuck it out…

Fergus, her fellow geologist and admirer from Cambridge days, on an impulse, stepped off the boat at Marseilles in 1924, en route from India to London. His plan to surprise Gwenny in Geneva found her more than receptive. He had picked the right moment to propose. I do wonder about that ceremony though – Ethical Church weds Scottish presbyterian.

Gwenny was marrying a man much poorer than her. But her major investments were in Germany and locked up through an English trust. Nobody took proper responsibility, her trustee blundered in the crash of 1929, and then the blow fell. President Hindenburg in Germany introduced exchange controls. At first the exit levy was only twenty-five per cent. People hoped it would be temporary. But by 1938, when Gwendoline capitulated and sold her German inheritance, Hitler had raised the rate to ninety per cent and it was called *Reichsfluchtsteuer* - empire flight tax.

Fergus would have to rely on his own wage-earning skills. It didn't make them love each other any less; in fact, it may have drawn them together. But their luck had changed.

Then World War II stopped everything. Fergus went away to serve and Gwenny suddenly had to run the show. Her world revolved around ration books and assembly line work in a factory during term time, since the boys were at boarding school – aircraft widgets in a bomb-proof tunnel, I think.

Afterwards they lived on Fergus' British Council salary and later pension from the civil service.

Unlike Grandpa, Granny was clueless about her grandchildren. A beach holiday to Alfriston in the mid-1960s was never repeated – I remember being called back relentlessly, before ever reaching the breakers, for a further layer of sun cream. Her idea of a present was a book token. When I was maybe thirteen years old she asked me what she should give Celina (in that case aged eleven) for her birthday. I suggested a five-litre container of ecologically friendly washing up liquid. And that is what Celina got.

Gwendoline died four years after Fergus. I was in the Alps at the time and was urged to stay there. Her memorial service, again in contrast with his funeral, was a lonely affair, according to the few witnesses. As a widow, she had taken in a lodger, a cranky bachelor who lectured at Slough Polytechnic. He was a Catholic and she still an atheist. He overrode her executors and insisted on organising a memorial mass a few days after the funeral. He and her immediate family, less than ten in all, trooped like sleepwalkers through the ceremony in the brooding vastness of the Brompton Oratory. At the appointed hour, I carved a little marker in the snow on a narrow sunlit col beneath two peaks under an azure sky. The place was closer to her heart than London SW7.

We must not judge other generations by the standards of our own. This tale may be a Parable of the Talents, and it may not. The lesson of the lidded wooden box is above all about mortality, about the easy parting of the individual from the collective memory, about the transience of me and you.

There, I've got that off my chest, ahem.

*

I kick open the rear nearside door to investigate the morning. More flies around. My feet fish for the shoes I flipped off last night. The footwear was too odious to sleep with in the car. That may explain the flies.

I did bring a guidebook for the next leg of the journey, Tunisia, Algeria and Morocco. From the map at the back, I guess 400 miles, 600 miles and 200 miles of road, respectively. Add 200 miles for inside Spain and Portugal.

Yes, I think we are halfway now. OK. Let's go!

*

Lubda is the modern name for Leptis Magna, Libya's proudest classical ruins. At some stage in the late Roman period, a huge investment was lavished on this town. The layout and adornments are properly imperial.

An oval necklace of columns runs round the sports pitch. Dozens of grey-veined marble piers once bore a shady canopy for those limbering up, resting or just spectating. Only the wooden roof and seats are gone.

The main outdoor pool is a neat rectangle. It sits in the optimal position between the sports oval and the indoor baths, and has its own marble-pillared enclosure for shade. *Natatio* is the Latin word, I think. My imagination echoes with the boisterous shouts of a school pool after a cricket match.

The *natatio* is empty. A stone diving platform stands at each end, and another in the middle of the long north side. Each is built out slightly into where the water would have been. The athletes would run straight off the track after a hard race under this sun and dive into the broad, refreshing expanse of water – as good a plunge as mine in Amman after the Syrian Desert.

The pool is long; I doubt I could swim two lengths underwater. With the kick-off at each turn, four widths would not be impossible. If only it was full now.

The *natatio's* location close to the pitch would have kept the young rowdies out of the formal baths behind. Nor did the latter buildings need much thermal boost in such a climate, so they could be bigger; more temple than tea room. Numerous four-foot diameter columns, twenty-five feet high, support the ceiling of the main hall. The interior walls are still dotted with stone benches for oldsters. Looking around, you can also fit chunks of fallen ceiling back on top of columns.

Toss your toga over your shoulder and luxuriate in membership of the most elegant and well-proportioned club in Africa.

All this time I am on my own. It is not the loneliness of Sergiopolis, where you itch for human company. The isolation gives an overwhelming sense of order, something larger than you. It is like being locked in a library at closing time – I once spent a night in the Radcliffe Camera in Oxford, too buried in my books up in the gallery to hear the countdown warnings from the front desk below.

The white-tipped sea sparkles beyond the grassy dunes. I have wandered through the main Lubda lot and climbed and scrambled on to a broader space. Between me and the Med are the colonnades of the market place or, to be precise,

225

three rings of pillars, a square surrounding an octagon encompassing a circle. To reach this idyllic, breezy terrace, you walk from the bathing area, down the column-lined street, which is seventy feet wide. An even wider dry riverbed has since carved a course on one side. Turn left into the forum. In scale and state of preservation this is more impressive than anything yet around the shores of civilisation's sea, even Cyrene.

(I ask again, how can the ruins on this journey just keep improving?)

Modern Rome is like multiple photographs, tacked together, compared with this seamless, panoramic exposure. Imagine the Roman British town of Bath without the Wiltshire loam of two millennia heaped upon it. Unaltered. Now add the bowed horizon of the sea. Cue the shady palms against the rising day, urging you to laze the hour away – none but you to know. That is Lubda.

Why was Leptis Magna abandoned? Did bubonic plague strike 1,600 years ago? Not an earthquake, or these pillars would have tumbled. Loss of an imperial sponsor? Maybe. Fall of Rome? More likely. Lack of natural advantage? If there had been a half-decent harbour here, would this site have been more looted down the succeeding centuries? I have no answer.

Walking back to the Forum, I hear hammering. Like a time machine, an old Peugeot pick-up is parked in the Roman street. Shady steps lead from it up into a theatre, open air, half-moon shaped, looking northeast towards the sea. Six workmen are building a sound stage. I stroll over and signal hello.

Two of them are students from Cambridge. The world springs forward. Stage-crewing in Libya is the new roof-climbing, glacier-crawling or underwater archaeology. From nowhere I am talking about Heffers bookshop on Trinity Street.

The chaps have been here four days. They are building the stage for an opening night on Monday (today's Saturday, I think). Gaddafi's Revolutionary Arts Festival season kicks off this evening in Sabrata. The Roman theatre there still has its three-storey architectural backboard, apparently. Then the show comes here.

This crew plays the pathfinder role, setting up stages ahead of the performers. They never get to see the results.

'Interesting,' says the more talkative one. 'Apparently that's the word for it.'

As if to remind us why, two Libyan Air Force jets streak low along our curve of the bay in close formation and turn above us. MIG 25 Foxbats. The fastest fighter planes yet built. With their twin tails they are a heart-stopping sight.

The modern world is back, and I take my leave.

*

My Lady's water temperature is doing a Syrian Desert on me. The dial reads fully hot, although the engine would have stalled from fuel evaporation long ago if that were true. A button on her walnut dashboard turns the petrol gauge into an oil-level meter when you press it. For some reason I can wake up the water temperature gauge by pushing this quite separate instrument.

Even more intriguing, by nudging me into that experiment, My Lady has drawn attention to her oil level, which is below 'min'. It explains her little palaver.

'I may not have an oil gauge staring at you; but you can still check the level from time to time. We have plenty of oil in the boot. Buck up,' she says.

I stop and obey.

*

First roadblock of the day, number 18 from Benghazi. The indicated water temperature has been up at its limits. It comes down, contrarily, as I drift to a stop by the painted oil drums. I am being given the runaround. Thanks for the oil, now worry about the water.

As for these checkpoints, the treatment meted out yesterday is just a memory. The policeman speaks good English.

'Lovely car. How old is it?' he asks, flicking through my passport.

'Thirty-two.'

'Older than you, eh?'

'Yes.'

'Well, have a good trip.'

And we are moving again.

*

Tripoli bypass, the urban hinterland. I am looking for a drink. Mineral water is a rare commodity here.

Just beyond the main city intersection is a modern, two-storey building, half hidden by crates of bottles. It is on my side of the road, draped with the ubiquitous green flags. But still no water. Instead, like some wine tasting, they allow me to try several different sodas and lemonades.

The yellow-canned lemonade is world-class, fresh, sharp and fruity. I buy a crate, 6×4, twenty-four, two dozen – that's honest Anglo-Saxon counting. Also their cartoned orange juice is good, so I clean them out of that.

The man says it is 25km to Sabrata.

227

Libya, west of Tripoli, Day 49, 'It's a selective earthquake.' (page 229)

Morocco, Quezzane, Day 54. The author with weavers. 'Four thousand domestic looms tucked away in the back streets.' (page 258)

The sun is at its zenith just now. Dangerous. Let's not rush into this. If Tunisia is less than 200km away, we can reach it today and see Sabrata too, assuming it opens before the festival; or we could go to the festival and leave Tunisia until tomorrow, Sunday. Count the days before I must be back at my desk in London: Tunisia, Algeria, Morocco is maybe going to take… five.

Thinking… comes… slowly, under this blazing sky.

Maybe I can do it all.

*

In the next village I find twelve litres of bottled Tunisian water. That's called curing your drink problem.

*

Oops! Missed Sabrata. The kindly roadblock man tells me it is back that way. How can you miss a country's premier national monument? Do we go back for it? In this heat? You are kidding. I wouldn't walk five yards to an open-air swimming pool.

Now, don't take that as disrespect, Dear. Just steadily on to Tunis will do fine.

*

Supposedly this is the last petrol station in Libya. Frontier about 30km ahead. Sun is dropping in the sky. I have too many Libyan dinars and there is nothing to buy.

Libya seems to have a problem with house construction. I've noticed it many times. The builders reach the first storey, always a flat concrete slab, and then the whole place just collapses. It is a selective earthquake.

Are people's houses knocked down as a punishment? Or perhaps, under Islamic bank rules, if a borrower defaults, the mortgage company must repossess and demolish.

Here, by the flattened building, stands a particularly ill-placed portrait of Gaddafi, already fading and slightly peeled.

I look around. No machine-gun-toting militia. I hurriedly squeeze off a photo. And another.

*

Hey, Libya is almost over. On the CD, Chuck Berry sings *'C'est la vie', said the old folks. It goes to show you never can tell.*

Volume to full. The sound nearly blows the doors out. You can't even hear yourself scream. The sweet ecstasy of triumph.

*

At the border, I take my customs papers to the man to be stamped. No quizzes here. I give him the RAC carnet, of course. But he wants to stamp the next page. We work out that we both speak French.

'Please stamp the Libyan exit page,' I say.

'No,' he says.

'Please.'

'No, this is Tunisia.'

'But I haven't left Libya yet. This must be Libya.'

'No, this is Tunisia. The Libyan frontier operation doesn't exist any more.'

Rather like a Marxist permanent revolution, Libya is a continuous frontier. But what if, in six months' time, the Libyans say the company car is still on their turf and claim the carnet bail bond? The collateral on that bond is effectively my main asset. They will be entitled to force me out of house and home in order to sequester the money.

The answer is to keep using the RAC carnet, not the AA one, to prove the Bentley went through Tunisia. Better still would be to get her back into Europe, so that the whole document can be cancelled before the Libyans catch up with their paperwork. They must not be given the chance to decide that I imported and sold her.

Dangerous things, transit papers.

I take some photos for evidence and go to the bank.

Next surprise. No Tunisian bank will take Libyan dinars, at any price. Some relationship these two neighbours have! No border; no forex. Back at customs my RAC carnet is returned stamped without ado. I am still reeling. This is probably the only place in the world where they accept a carnet without the previous page completed.

Thence to the passport police, who issue me with a white identity card rather than stamp my passport. 'Is this really you?' says the policeman, pointing at the photo of me in a suit and tie.

OK, so it was only twenty checkpoints from Benghazi, not fifty. But this is what a man will look like afterwards.

The Lady with No Name noses between the lines of incoming Tunisian pick-ups. They are all Peugeots, each loaded to the gunwales and being thoroughly searched. I am thinking that my flatmate in Bristol, Niall, had a Peugeot... Scrape of Bentley hubcap on the kerb, like fingernails on a blackboard. Horrified looks. Relax guys, you think I don't know the width of my own car? We checked this dimension in Ibiza Castle. She will fit the gap to the last half-inch.

Then we are through, like a bird, into the west, with the sun shining along the suddenly shoddy road surface. Narrow is the way that leads to salvation.

Where am I? Wasn't there a guidebook? Here it is, with sections for travellers arriving in Tunisia from all directions – except Libya. OK. The nearest tourist feature is Tubby's Jerba Island. Local industry: sponge fishing. Sounds good to me; anything to do with a bath.

*

We are back in Africa. The road from the frontier is a chicken run: head-on, single-track tarmac with wide dirt verges. My Lady holds her speed on the crown of the camber, winning more confrontations than she loses. Black-market currency changers stand back from the roadside, silhouetted against the falling sun. So this is why the banks don't bother. The slanting light glows through their waved sheaves of Libyan dinar notes like the sunrise across the honeyed backs of sheep in Cappadocia. I do a deal, pretty well one Tunisian pengo for each Libyan one. A right royal rip-off. However, mine are worthless to me now. Judged by the purchasing power parity with petrol, this is a new *Reichsfluchtsteuer*.

But was I too early or too late? In theory, the attraction of dinars must be falling the further you go down the turnpike. Supply and demand in action. Market equilibrium. Alfred Marshall would have been riveted. Old men and little boys, everyone's doing it.

First village in Tunisia. In the square, away from free-market economics, my trusty steed accepts a litre and a half of water.

Then we turn north towards Jerba Island. A stream of cars is coming out of a side road; I have right of way and cut in. They seem asleep and I force a few overtakes, much to the fury of the orderly Tunisians. They are crawling along. For heaven's sake, there is nothing coming towards us. Get a move on. My ample debutante shoulders her bulk round the front before we understand.

It is a funeral procession.

Apologies, apologies.

*

How serene to be able to read the road signs. And as for the advertising billboards, they are all 'cigarettes, whisky, madames', as Tubby would say.

The low moral tone is all around you. Gone are the banners with strictures in Arabic script. In their place are exhortations in the Roman alphabet for sun cream and hotels beside seductive cocktails or long-tressed girls.

*

The Bentley nudges up the coast. We explore a vast beach in the setting sun. The sand is firm enough to carry two tons with just half an inch of indentation, and the sea is so far away you might drive at it for minutes and despair.

Back on the road we mount a causeway. It must be three miles long. At the northern end is a short bridge for shipping to pass under. The road lands on the southeast corner of Jerba Island. The groves of indigenous palm trees, forests of them, would appeal to Libyans. I ask around for an hotel with an ace laundry.

When I find one, there is time for a shave and top-to-toe scrub before the restaurant shuts. The only clothes that are not presented to reception for cleaning are those I wore from the office to Heathrow.

Swiss and West German bankers choke on their chickpea soup to find a City gent has tracked them this far.

Day 50

The simplicity of the beach.

After a week of it, you have been nowhere, done nothing, met no one. You may even regret having gone away. But at the time, and particularly when it starts, what bliss. I sat here on the sand under my straw umbrella before the sun came up and have not moved since. Time is in the hands of the hotel laundry. I hope they take it easy. The breeze is soft, the bellies of the North Europeans softer, the strand is softest of all. Going soft feels wonderful.

The sun creeps over the rim of the straw shade and catches my eye. It says, lie down, let me stroke your brow.

Greek and Roman historians thought Jerba Island was Homer's land of the Lotus Eaters in his *Odyssey*. Little wonder.

*

Lunchtime. Clean clothes. Fresh start. The hotel coped admirably with the wardrobe of oily washing, but forgot to blitz the pillowcase in which it was delivered. So they have returned mine grimy with a clean, standard issue one of their own.

From the cradle it is but a step to the sandpit. Let's see how the toddler feels. Turn the key. Petrol pumps tick fuel to the carburettors. She likes it and fires first turn. OK. I'm persuaded.

Hear that swooping Elgar Concerto from the cello of Jaqueline du Pré.

*

Jerba island is served from the southwest corner by a ferry to the mainland, a ten-minute ride. It cuts an hour off the journey west, and the pleasure of being on water again will be unalloyed. I have stayed barely longer than Odysseus did. He dragged his men back to sea as fast as possible, having seen how quickly they were drugged by the lotus flowers.

We dive aboard. The launch is bigger than the landing craft that day from Chios to Cesme. It manages sixteen cars and a bus. The bus in turn carries a Cosmos tour, flown in from Luton – we must be nearing home.

The ferry pulls away. The captain sits up steel steps on the bridge on the port side, ready to steer the craft in either direction. A sturdy, white-haired woman from the bus comes over and says straight out, ''as she be'aved 'erself?'

Old men forget, but the girls remember their own. One of these days I'm going to meet a Sussex matron who was driven to the church in her.

*

I have perfected the knack of stopping with barely any brakes.

Poor aerodynamics is a start. Pulling the handbrake helps, of course. But the automatic gearbox is key. The tactical change-down from drive to third will decide the next thousand miles. Also, dropping into neutral in the last few yards means the engine tickover does not provide forward propulsion.

Still unanswered is what would be the effect of switching off the ignition at 40mph to achieve an emergency stop. Before, it was a theoretical question. Now it has become a serious possibility. The power to the brakes would shut down, but that would be scant loss in My Lady's current condition. More worryingly, the servo-assisted steering would go, making evasive action difficult. But what would the drivetrain do? The answer is – don't find out.

*

We descend into an arid plain, with gentian-tinted hills to the southwest. The road leads round to the north, through small strips of villages and towns, where fruit stalls crowd the roadside. After the monochrome national green of Libya, Tunisia is a rainbow. French-made mopeds, *mobilettes*, abound. They were absent

233

in Libya, perhaps because so few Libyans farm smallholdings. As in emerging Asia, the lowly moped is a first stepping stone of free enterprise.

Eight dark-skinned labourers are jammed into that Peugeot estate with boxes and sacks pressed up against the rear window and heaped on the roof. Their driver overtakes me and they turn their heads as one and crane to see backwards, despite each other and the boxes.

Do they feel anger at my waste of space, or at my comfort? Or disdain at the appearance of some absurd make of car that they've never heard of, as would the English at the sight of a Horch?

The point is, they are free to say what they want.

Interest? Excitement? Affection? My mind is in the meaning-of-life loop, like at Nuweiba. That is what ferry crossings do.

*

Night again.

Three packs of Libyan orange juice sucked through a straw. A long look at the page with the map. At a guess 1,100 miles from here to Cape St Vincent as the crow flies, 1,500 miles on the ground. It is a tall order. We have already hammered through the distance from Izmir to Cairo.

I would feel better if I could expel just one of these flies.

*

Lost again. In the dark. Somewhere on the coast up to Tunis.

The trip meter rolls over for the second time to 000(0). My Lady pauses.

Check the compass bearing and test a side road as a possible place to sleep. Hanging out of the door to reverse on the track, I hear the sea.

I am five miles further east than I thought. The lights over there are ships on the horizon, not cars on an infuriating, inaccessible turnpike.

Midnight stars of diamond intensity and snow drift plenty. Waves ever-rolling over sand and dropping explosively upon rocks. The Bentley has not broken down once. Even the water temperature gauge came back to life this afternoon, allowing much faster cruising where the roads permitted. It's as if the car is so fascinated by her lack of brakes that she has no time for other games.

For this reason I might be tempted to take the hilly inland shortcut to Algiers tomorrow.

There was only one roadblock in the whole of today. Two motorcycle policemen, about as frightening as zookeepers.

Day 51

We awake on a long rocky shoreline, with the sea struggling to be blue under an overcast sky. The next CD in the auto-loader brings Scottish bagpipes to warm the heart.

My family's enthusiasm for all things Highland comes from my mother's side. Whereas the Dunlops were merely Lowland Scots, the Robertsons were from the north, around Blair Atholl. Some say they are the oldest clan in Scotland, others not. Be that as it may, our Jacobite enthusiasm comes down the female line, my mother's mother's great grandmother being the Robertson for us.

Mother's mother was Olive Gladstone, 'Grandmummie' as she spelt herself for my sisters and me. She had more authentic style in her little finger than Gwendoline Coit could muster in her whole frame.

Both were the middle one of three girls, but there the similarity ended. Olive was as warm as Gwendoline was cold. We were her only grandchildren, and she offered each year a birthday cake for one of us in turn. So every third year you had a chance to order something extraordinary. Mine was once a marzipan fort, once a digger with 'sand' (a bag of icing sugar), and once a woven sugar basket of real fruit. Celina had a circular ballgown cake with a porcelain half-length lady atop.

Grandmummie's favourite colour was bright red. Red berets, red wet-look handbags, red shoes. If you wanted to feed her many cats, you just put on her red slippers and they came running.

During my last term at school she lent me her Austin 1300 – bright red of course. I would hide it in the backstreets and wear a headscarf and dark glasses to drive out of town.

Grandmummie knew how to decorate a dining table for Christmas (cotton-wool snow around an eighteen-inch silver stag) and Easter (daffodil heads floating over a mirror). She claimed to bet on race horses with fluffy nosebands.

She was from the caste that said 'clawth' for 'cloth'. Describing an occasion crossing the Atlantic by ocean liner, when my mother had been chatted up by an admirer, Grandmummie once declared, 'But my dear, he made love to you constantly.'

'Children, you know what she means,' shushed my mother.

Olive grew up in a fine country house. Its views to the west over the River Avon were improbably large, as was the pet cemetery – with room for favourite hunters. If she had been a boy she would have inherited a baronetcy from her father. So would her mother from hers, and the village of Bentley in Hampshire, strange to say. Olive wanted only to live in a cottage with roses growing around the front door. But it wasn't in her stars.

She had been a debutante in the summer of 1914 and once said the world stopped that August and never restarted. The boys were dead and the investments decimated.

The big deal in Ovie's life was the loving marriage between her and Bobby Loyd. She first spotted Bobby when she was sixteen and he a freshman at Oxford. She and her two sisters were looking down on their driveway from a bedroom when he and a friend walked up to the house. Bobby was staying at the time with his cousins, across the way at the neighbouring estate. Perhaps she knew. Perhaps they were expected.

'I'll marry the one on the left,' she reputedly told her siblings.

During World War I, Olive served in the Red Cross, working as a cook in Chippenham Hospital for three years, and wondering why Bobby never wrote. Afterwards he explained that he had been so sure he would be killed (as his little brother and almost all his male friends were) that he had determined not to lead her on, only to break her heart.

They married in March 1919, in the church her grandfather built to thank God for the birth of her father. Their guard of honour was formed by Red Cross nurses from the hospital. My mother was born in 1923, after Olive had suffered an initial miscarriage – a boy.

I remember Grandmummie being immensely brave at Bobby's funeral. The only time she buckled slightly was in the narrow churchyard when she looked down into his grave, which had been dug extra deep to leave room for her own coffin on top, in due course. In fact, she lasted only six weeks. The post-mortem said she had been dying of everything for years. She had not let on because she had been nursing Bobby.

Olive Loyd was the real thing. She went through life improving it. She wound clocks, filled vases with flowers, chose wallpaper with confidence and seized on any technical improvement the modern age could offer. Her house beside the Long Walk at Windsor had the first colour TV I ever saw, and also the first remote control. When the supersonic airliner, Concorde, introduced a Heathrow to New York service, passing daily over her home with an ear-splitting roar, she was delighted. If the weather was nice she would dart out to watch. Or if she happened to be on the telephone at the time, she would announce merrily, 'You will have to wait, ducky, the Concorde is going over', and maybe hold the handset out of the window, so you could enjoy it too.

I must write sometime about Bobby, 'Gampy', Ovie's husband, Mama's dad. But for now let's hit the road. Today is the day we need real miles under our belt.

Can that traffic running north behind these dunes indicate the main highway to the capital, Tunis? It will do for now. I have a five-litre engine to open the ears, and an unbroken horizon to stretch the mind.

Good girl! First turn of the key.

*

This morning it rained lightly, here at Carthage. Rain in North Africa is a major cause for rejoicing. The people in the streets are happy. The sun may have returned, but the ancient stones are cool to sit on, and a scent of herbs laces the breeze.

The cultural fulcrum of the Mediterranean swung 2,800 years ago from the Phoenician league, based in Lebanon, to North Africa. Carthage was even founded by a Phoenician refugee princess, Dido. For 600 years thereafter, this was the pre-eminent city of the central and western sea.

Some Carthaginian habits seem worse than Spartan to us, like sacrificing their first-born child to Tanit, the sun-moon god, in times of strife. But the underlying system is recognisable enough. A dock for the fleet, admiralty buildings, a queen's palace. Here Virgil's Trojan refugee, Aeneas, put ashore for pleasure (as Homer's Greek victor did at Jerba), before going on to found Rome.

Centuries later, humbled by Hannibal, Rome came back and defeated Carthage in 202 BC, going on to sack the city sixty years later. So, Cato the Elder, Rome's implacable anti-Punic senator, did not live to see his vengeance realised.

Physically, the Romans destroyed Carthage, ploughing the site and sowing it with salt. The wooded hillside looking east over the sea retains no two stones one upon the other from that time; only the indentation of the ship yard and the protuberant sea wall are evidence, but archaeologists have found the tombs of the sacrificial children among the groves and shrubs.

Today's biggest surprise is that the destroyers returned a third time within 100 years and built a magnificent city, with baths to match those of Rome, if not Leptis Magna. However, this city too has been demolished and quarried into minor-league archaeological status. For centuries, barely a ship left port without its loot of marble in the ballast. Even the baths now offer the tourist only brickwork foundations and heating caverns.

Ancient Rome ruled an empire for a shorter time than Carthage. It also copied Carthaginian economic precepts and technology: colonies, trade, sea power (those mighty triremes – triple-decker, oared warships). It was a formula that worked for later empires too.

Brits ignore Carthage solely because Carthage ignored Britain.

Twin spirals of barbed wire run along the north side of these historical excavations, fronting a glossy lawn where soldiers stand to attention under smart sentry awnings. Behind the barricaded greensward, a white rampart snakes over the contours of the land like a scale model of the Great Wall of China. Trees and radio masts stick up beyond, and the sound of construction work can be heard. This is the modern presidential palace, a work in progress. The president has his own little harbour, too; with a yellow beacon at the end of each mole and an MTB standing offshore.

*

Down at the Carthaginian naval lagoon, stagnant water loops around a broad ping-pong bat of land, which must have once carried the administration block. Triremes may be careened no more, but the fig trees, papyrus grass and exotic shrubs which drink from the C-shaped pool whisper of fleets once rigged and chandled here for mastery of the Med. The outer bank sang to the hammers of forty slipways, where now the rustling reeds filter silt – a marsh recaptured from ancient mariners.

Look up to the bosky knoll where Dido's palace was. Marvel with Aeneas that such a site and such a queen could have been found in all Africa. How could he leave her, who offered this, and her love too? For the million-to-one dream of founding an even better city? An Eternal City, to outlast time itself? That was foolhardy indeed.

*

Restaurant Le Pirate is named after the most fearsome sea-raider, Barbarossa, who once held the fishing village here at Sidi Bou Said for a lookout point. Among other Spanish soldiers stationed on this rock when he had been driven off was the young Miguel Cervantes, later of *Don Quixote* fame. No doubt the future author gazed down the coast, as I do from this terrace, aware that something in the character of life was eluding him.

238

I left My Lady in Tunis with the official dealer for Jaguar cars and for JCB, the digger makers. She was surrounded by curvaceous 1960s saloons in varying degrees of preservation or dereliction. This included a rare life form, a gleaming white, hard-top E-Type, with Japanese number plates, hence right-hand drive; a couple of Minis; and a stripped-out MG TC. The leviathan Bentley was jacked up next to these minnows and had both front wheel hubs disassembled.

For 900 miles since that fiery desert road, her foot brake has been vanishing and is now almost non-existent. The pedal clunks, and the subsequent grip can barely resist a crawl. Who dared hope even for that?

Having found a garage familiar with British engineering, and explained the possibilities as I saw them to the chief mechanic, I hopped in a taxi and said 'fish restaurant'.

Under the vines and palms, the eau de Nil-clothed tables are beginning to fill up. The waiter decides my order. First a sharp spicy *amuse-bouche*: olives, peppers, chopped cucumber and mango under a thick French dressing. Then a plate of three grilled *rouget*, small fish, and a second plate of punchy chorizo. Rich food on a stomach empty for thirty-six hours.

And now for the main course, *cert*. This fish is a clear foot long and with teeth unevolved since the coelacanth. Its flesh is juicy, browner than the *rouget*. *Cert* has a heavy, bittersweet flavour that transforms deliciously in the chewing, which can take a good while if you haven't worked out where the bones are.

A kitten chases a red butterfly through the long grass. A cat surprises me by scratching my leg. You can hardly blame it, the fish aroma must be maddening, but I am a dog fan, sorry. I toss a lemon slice and surprise it back.

Mmm, this is delicious. The last morsel, from down by the tail, had such a bouquet I'd gladly eat another. The breeze stirs the trees; laughter ripples among the tables; the cats stalk each other in the undergrowth. A Libyan mint tea would round things off nicely now. Sorry, no mint tea, or cognac, but fig and date liqueurs, yes. OK, Thibarine date liqueur. Yuk. Could this be the flavour they based that disgusting children's cough mixture on?

*

Long faces back at the Jaguar dealers. The rubber seals which are needed to repair the brake cylinders are not a Jaguar standard. We unclasp the green leather Bentley handbook for guidance. There are two separate hydraulic systems. System A, which works the front brakes, and System B, which works on all four wheels.

Both systems are gone on the burnt-out wheel. System A has only air in it now, but System B was plugged in time.

The trouble is that the System B seal on the other front wheel expired recently as well. Roughly speaking, at Carthage. That explains the latest all-round deterioration. The pressure to the rear pads through System B is now leaching away. It will take forty-eight hours to fly the parts here. That scrubs any hopes of reaching the two Charleses and their friends in Cape St Vincent. What if the Libyan trick with the nails could be repeated on the new leak? The rear brakes would come back into service. That might suffice as far as Algiers airport to meet a package of front brake seals the day after tomorrow, Wednesday. And the sprint for Portugal? Arriving Saturday morning? Maybe. And maybe is still enough.

The Jaguar dealer lends his telephone and I wait to hear whether Hammersmith have any such diaphragms in stock. Bruce is away today and the storeman, Ivor, is ill. They will look around... It's 4 p.m. in London. The international lines are busy.

The Tunisian manager tells me he hasn't sold any British cars for five years. They had a delivery of 100 Austin Metros in 1984, and that was it. His company has shrunk from 250 employees to sixty-five and now their main business is Japanese and Czechoslovakian tractors.

The problem is political. Britain has a trade surplus with Tunisia, and when this was politely pointed out to the UK, the British government declined to assist the Tunisian fruit exporters. Ah. The phone rings. The deputy storeman, Malcolm, comes through from England and is promptly cut off. Ten minutes later he comes through again. Yes, he has three diaphragm kits. Four would have been better, but three will do at a pinch because, guessing, the passenger-side System A front brake is still intact. My secretary, Dani, calls from work. The parts are being biked to her at this moment (well, it is a company car). We discuss possible routes to forward the package to Algiers. She says the standard time will be three to four days, which is ridiculous. I say send them to Tangier airport customs, where I should be by Friday. Please could she give me the consignment number so that I can identify them? I'll phone again tomorrow.

Then I collect the Bentley, brakes worse than before, if that is possible, pay my bill and roll away.

How can My Lady ever make it another 800 miles to Tangier? Just tracing a trail out of Tunis is a nightmare. The suburbs are full of pedestrians, cyclists, mopeds, vans, lorries and police. Each naturally assumes that all cars can halt, and that all drivers slept decently last night. Moreover, I become lost, or am misdirected, so that my two-ton package of perpetual motion, blessed with all the stopping-power of a grand piano, has to negotiate most of these streets twice.

The Bentley grumbles at me fitfully through the water temperature gauge.

Like all spellbinding women, deep down she hates to be seen in a state – no wash since the basement of the Semiramis.

*

Only twenty-five miles out of Tunis and night has fallen. It's time for a hard look forward at the next few days. I sit on the door sill with my head in my hands. The Tunisians say Algeria is a dangerous place at night. Men with knives leap out from the dark. Algerians hate all foreigners, so don't get caught alone.

What is certain is this: even if they turn out to be the friendliest people in the world, it will still be four times the effort to cross their country without brakes – twice the concentration for twice as long. If they turn nasty I can hardly hightail it in a cloud of dust – only to crash on the first corner; and one of these days I'm going to do that to a roadblock.

Time for a consoling Libyan lemonade. It is good enough to import to England. I tilt my head back and swig the last drop, and the cosmos overhead twinkles, as it has on far more serious dilemmas than mine. Every country you have seen, say the stars, exaggerates stories about it neighbours. Get back in and drive, they say, unanswerably.

Day 52

Winding roads, up hill and down dale, brought us to a halt last night 120 miles beyond Tunis. A tremendous electrical storm was brewing. After I had parked, the rain came, first torrentially, like a water cannon on the roof, wings, bonnet and boot, and then in lesser waves at regular intervals until dawn.

If the roads are not too slippery, we might actually reach Algeria – and this deluge should have cooled that populace's savage xenophobia.

Today deserves a change of clothes.

Sit up and look around. Crikey! A railway line. I've backed away from the road in the dark across a level piece of ground to within yards of a single-track railway. It looks disused. How I wish I could put Her Ladyship in a boxcar and let a train take her to Tangier. Today and tomorrow are Tuesday and Wednesday; I won't think about it.

Opening the door by my head, the fragrance of pines has been released by the night rains. Distant cockerels crow from three directions.

Is this the time to tackle my fourth and oldest grandparent, Robert Lindsay Loyd, RLL? He of the Egyptian mummified bird?

Bobby Loyd was a Berkshire lad, his father an eminent barrister and Member of Parliament, his great-uncle the owner of a bank. From a cosseted start, he achieved less than Fergus, although to meet them you would not have known it.

Born in 1887, Bobby rowed for Magdalen College Oxford, albeit less brilliantly than Fergus later did at Cambridge. But it was Bobby who proudly hung his oars in his library. Bobby was always addressed as Major Loyd OBE. Fergus, an acting colonel by 1945, immediately dropped the title in peacetime. I didn't even know Fergus had an OBE until after he was dead.

At the outbreak of war in 1914, when Fergus was fourteen, Robert Loyd had already been a professional soldier for several years. His regiment, the 16th (Queens) Lancers, sailed to France from Ireland as part of the British Expeditionary Force – 'contemptible' as the Kaiser called it – the Old Contemptibles, as they soon dubbed themselves.

The Lancers arrived on the Belgian border just as that front collapsed under the weight of two German armies, twenty-eight divisions, 450,000 men. Vastly outnumbered, the BEF held Mons on 23rd August, but the French to their east fell back. There followed a fortnight-long, 200-mile retreat, almost a rout, without transport or supplies, to the southeastern outskirts of Paris.

The impression I had from Gampy, as my older sister Tessa christened him, was of the overwhelming weight of enemy that August; the sheer exhaustion; the demoralising effect, day upon day, night upon night, of near-flight; the constant desperate need for water – 'first the horses, then the men, then yourself' (and 'a thirsty horse just loves a soda syphon sprayed straight into the mouth'); the leadership challenge, to find the energy for the counter-attack; the thrill when the world's earliest aerial reconnaissance saw the German First Army lose touch with their Second Army; the pride when the BEF took the bridges over the Marne between them, west of Château-Thierry; and the sheer relief when the German High Command blinked – lest his Second Army be caught in a pincer, von Moltke pulled his First back from Paris without a fight.

At seventy-five years' distance, the BEF's bridgehead over the Marne was a deciding moment of World War I, and possibly of the twentieth century so far.

Like Fergus and Gwenny, Bobby had stood briefly on the cusp of history.

A subsequent 'Race for the Sea' saw the Germans and the Allies each try and fail to outflank the other to the north. The British did not quite get back to Mons, but they made it over the Belgian border.

At the Flanders town of Poperinge, between Lille and Dunkirk, Bobby's younger brother was wounded by a shrapnel burst overhead. Geoffrey died in Bobby's arms, among the earliest of 50,000 British casualties in what became the First Battle of Ypres.

I once asked my father how RLL could have been at the Miracle of the Marne, gone through two World Wars and 'only' ended up a major. Dad said that Bobby had earnt a black mark as a young subaltern in Ireland. This must have been the Curragh Incident of March 1914. The officers of the 16th Lancers got wind of a plan to impose Irish Home Rule, furiously opposed by the citizens of Ulster. They collectively resigned their commissions rather than be ordered to use deadly force on their own countrymen. King George V intervened and the Asquith government backed down, claiming a misunderstanding. The officers' commissions were reinstated, from brigadier-general down to second lieutenant, but sixty principled military men had tarnished their records.

Bobby survived the full four years of France. Chargers were not pitted against machine guns much after 1914 so the Lancers did their time in the trenches. He emerged with a Military Cross and that OBE, both for gallantry.

After he and Olive married, Bobby transferred to the Life Guards cavalry and in the 1920s rode on formal occasions through the streets of London, sword drawn beside the royal carriage. I grew up thinking that was normal.

RLL was a popular guy. When he retired on an army pension in the 1930s he devoted himself to charities and worked on his freemasonry. Re-enlisting at the outbreak of World War II in 1939, at the age of fifty-three, he was put into the Royal Corps of Signals and helped run the training camp at Catterick in Yorkshire for the duration, writing a letter every evening to his wife.

At some stage during World War II, Bobby seems to have risen through the ranks of freemasonry to reach the 33rd Degree, the Supreme Council of the United Grand Lodge of England and Wales. He subsequently became Grand Master. In 1947 my grandmother stood aside to let my mother tour with him to North and

South America. For RLL the purpose was to re-establish links with his overseas lodges. For my mother, it was a belated finishing school.

The Gampy I knew was a portly, moustachioed, Father Christmas figure who loved complex jigsaw puzzles and the afternoon TV coverage of wrestling. Initially he was the most remote of my grandparents. Being the oldest put him culturally further away and sapped his energy. Also, being the clear alpha figure in his family circle for so long, he was more comfortable with my sisters.

Things improved after Gampy started asking me to change his heart pacemaker battery. He could not do it himself because the heart stopped mid-way. If he fainted he would be dead. This was quite a responsibility for a fifteen-year-old. Soon after, he dispatched me to take his gold wristwatch to London to be serviced. Again I felt trusted. As a schoolboy journalist I interviewed him about soldiering, and he wrote to me afterwards in praise of the British Tommy, 'the finest fighting man in the world'.

I find it hard to believe, but RLL does not seem to have suffered post-traumatic stress disorder. He was clearly sad to have lost his friends, and appalled by the devastation of World War I. Certainly he felt that Germany had an evil tendency deep in its culture. That was just the personal experience of having his life pulled down around his ears twice. It wasn't paranoia.

He had chosen soldiering as a profession and he continued to look at it as that. I never heard about nightmares, or mood swings, or an alcohol problem, or an inability to concentrate. In fact, he was the opposite, a source of calm, a fountain of jokes, a man with an orderly mind and tidy, accurate handwriting, who knew what he wanted, where every workshop tool had its place. The only odd thing was that he never visited me at Eton, not even on a Fourth of June, although he had gone there himself and lived less than two miles away. Too many ghosts?

His remoteness may have reflected other disappointments. I mentioned the still-born son. There was also a lost inheritance. He had been christened Robert Lindsay Loyd after his father's best friend, Robert Lindsay VC, Lord Wantage, one of the founders of the British Red Cross and then aged fifty-five. Robert Lindsay had married Harriet Loyd, a near relative who had inherited the bank. But they were childless. The implication was that my grandfather would become their heir. A very large fortune was involved. Lord Wantage died in 1901 when Bobby Loyd was twelve. But when his widow, Harriet, died in the autumn of 1920, she left the estate to a different cousin, one with young male heirs.

The name Aunt Harriet was rarely spoken in my childhood, but if so, always with a certain circumspection.

My mother set out to mend fences by making her surviving generational counterpart on the wealthy side my godfather. And I think by the time the matter got to me she had succeeded. He has been assiduous with Christmas and birthday presents. It is his rug I have been sheltering under from mosquitoes.

RLL liked big, comfortable cars. He drove a maroon Packard Super Eight 180 with a spare tyre on each running board and those 'suicide' rear doors. He read his Bible every night, so, end to end many times. But his chief pleasure was leaving fond gifts and notes around for Ovie, from whom war had twice parted him.

In old age they were as mad about each other as the day they met.

The trudge of feet is heard coming down the railway track.

So far six workmen have passed me, carrying their luncheon bundles and a stick or hat, going up the line or coming down it. We are all preoccupied with our various daybreak blues. A wave of the hand suffices. I have been writing, dozing and viewing the sweet-smelling woodland upside down through the rear door.

Again my vigorous Valkyrie fires with the first turn of the key. Mohsen's tuning has saved this transit.

Two birds, like crested brown woodpeckers, hoopoes maybe, search the stones around the railway for insects. A wild dog, as red as the soil, comes to investigate us while the engine warms up.

*

Of the various styles of customs post found around the Mediterranean – between the non-existent, from France to Monaco and Libya to Tunisia, and the military, at Nuweiba – this inland exit from Tunisia to Algeria is the sleepiest.

The barrier looks as if it hasn't been raised for a week. An old woman leads her cow round it over the grass. An even older man with his lunch bag follows along the verge. Like the road mender at Pompeii. Some borders only trap the tourists.

'No,' says the sergeant, 'the passport desk does not have a ballpen.'

I fetch this one, the waitress' at the Semiramis, from the car.

The scenery is a tree-clad valley, whose floor is dotted with farmyards. The mountains are like the Pyrenees. On these endless inclines I have been quietly appreciative of the low-speed second gear in the Bentley's four-speed automatic 'box (the later V8s only had three-speed automatics; in other words, harder climbing and even less braking coming down). The drizzle is turning back into rain.

Clunk! The solitary sound of a rubber stamp rings out across the vale. It can only be mine. 'Dunlop' they shout, as if a milling throng was concealing little six-foot-six me from in front of them. I present myself, then step across to customs, where the officer has clearly never seen a carnet docket before. He literally needs his hand held to tear off his portion and stamp the stub.

*

Up here, in the *maquis* between the two countries, is the classic defensive territory that Rommel yearned for east of Tunis. A guerrilla band, with tacit support from the locals, could hold out for ever on this coast of foggy, spinney-strewn hills. Wild cork trees abound. Some beside the single-track road have been peeled of bark up to their first branches.

Crossing the frontier line into Algeria, the lane descends now through rolling woodland. Here, virtually all the wild cork has been harvested.

The Algerian customs post is rather grand, in the Moorish architectural tradition, with six times as many staff as its Tunisian counterpart. However, the workload is the same. So each man does even less, if that is possible, and everything takes that much longer. After an hour and a half we are still around. During the ritual, repeated reference is made to a colleague who wants a lift down the road. He says it is only nine kilometres, but a policeman not in on the wheeze warns quietly that in fact it's 900. The colleague is left behind.

French is an easy second language here.

*

The road climbs along the hilly coast, with the blue sea nuzzling into small havens between the headlands. The scent of pines is strong, and cattle graze as free as they might in Switzerland. The tarmac ribbon sweeps back down to run round a broad marshy plain. A road sign warns of slippery surfaces and has written underneath the one word *Grenouilles* – frogs. Sure enough, 200 yards later the road is hopping with these green amphibian pedestrians. Even if I had brakes, the worst thing would be to try to stop. What a mess.

After that, another plains town, and a chance to refuel. The sudden absence of 'Super' suggests we are now back to European standards for petrol quality.

*

My Lady is about to head into the city of Annaba, 2,300 miles from Cairo, where Super is supposedly available. I calculate it is 900 miles to Tangier. Progress is proving painfully slow.

246

A motorway! Is it true? Yes. It says 600km to Algiers; how marvellous. So the Bentley has a puncture, but immediately, half a mile beyond the slip road. Should I be grateful she waited until now? You bet! It's the Hammersmith shell which has gone flat again, the one that caught fire – this second Libyan inner tube was no doubt still too small. How many lives can one tyre have? Out comes the loyal old Karaman wheel, up goes the driver's side on the jack – and the familiar routine leaves me familiarly filthy again.

The block of stone which I used to chock one of the back wheels has split open and is all silvered inside.

*

The motorway peters out and the next petrol pump attendant informs me it does not start again until Algiers.

*

By mistake I now steer away from the coastal rat-run, up into the hills towards Constantine and beyond. However, the roads are good, if not better, for having been built by French engineers with few landowners to consider (i.e. the roads are straight).

The population being sparse means no pedestrians at risk. So we bowl along merrily. I hear of a car wash just up ahead before Setif. It turns out to be the rural bus depot, complete with high-pressure hoses. They give my road-streaked ride her long-deserved bath.

The wind blows as solid here as it does on the high plains of Cappadocia. The mosque stands tall above its surrounding flock of homesteads. The people dress in dark blues and greens, and the workmanship and prices are on a par with Karaman in midwinter. I would say Algeria is what Turkey will be like in five years' time. As for the countryside, it matches Scotland for ruggedness and romance. The climate may be different, but emotionally, if Scotland had won independence in the mid-1970s, the screams from many Englishmen would no doubt have matched the wails with which France finally submitted to Algerian decolonisation in 1962.

The milestones with their red-painted tops, the avenue of trees beside the arrow-straight road, the spacing of the villages all, however, speak of France. Had Mary of Guise, the mother of Mary Queen of Scots, had her way, this is what Scotland would have been like, run by its Auld Alliance with Paris.

The Algerian harvest is well in and the sheep are being grazed over stubble that has yet been spared the plough. Arable farming here is prairie scale; nevertheless, the contours are Grampian and I have even found a convincing loch, complete with a mist as might creep up the hill at Coulin to conceal the stags. This will be the scene when ozone depletion bakes the Scottish Highlands.

*

That must be the fifteenth time in a row my helpmeet has started first turn of the key.

*

Three hundred miles today, by daylight. Can't be bad.

Pull off the *route nationale* into a steep village just as darkness is falling.

I park. A child conducts me around the ramshackle buildings to the shop. I assemble an offer of jam, biscuits, anchovies, dried figs, cream cheeses, red sausage and chocolate.

Everyone seems to have a squint or a crooked limb. Those who could leave left long ago. What can I alone do? I indicate that this is a takeaway and drive on down the road to a safe hard shoulder to eat.

My Lady attends in silence. How many travelling companions would wait through a menu like that without a word of criticism?

*

It proves tough to find a side road for the night. A confrontation with a pair of tractor headlights puts an end to my first choice. After another seventy miles, and nearly 2,600 from Cairo, a suitable spot appears.

The Bentley's feeble, tungsten-filament main beam makes driving at night on winding roads in busy traffic without brakes rather draining.

Day 53

Still the same dried-out Scottish scenery.

Not much sleep last night. The trucks whined like mosquitoes, and the mosquitoes hummed like trucks. Also, lying across the front bench to make a change proved less than effective. The dustbin-lid-sized steering wheel was in the way. This morning my shoes, which are put out at night because of their rich odour, had been invaded by an army of tiny ants.

I try the cheese and red sausage. Can I have ever eaten anything so disgusting? They are tossed into the ditch for the ants as consolation.

Another first-turn start from my nifty noblewoman.

*

Algiers is closer than I thought. A long highway with few exits leads down a mighty gorge to the coast where the capital sits. It is now too late to traverse the plateau behind the city. Defenceless without brakes, I fear to enter the imagined hurly-burly. I should have turned back, but instead try to cross a series of ravines by cart routes. At one moment the track is so narrow and the drop alongside so steep that a lost cow, or is it a bull, causes a five-minute stand-off. I persuade him gently with the front grille and bumper that he wants to go back downhill, there being no hope of us passing each other.

Later, I reverse away for women carrying bright plastic containers of water on their heads up a similarly steep slope.

*

The past three miles have been a descent held in second gear at about 10mph. It was a long quarter of an hour to be pinning one's hopes on the handbrake. However, I tell myself that this is one function the Bentley can't possibly have worn out during her spell doing weddings.

*

As always, things turn out differently from the plan.

The dendritic pull of Algiers proves too great and leads me to a glorious bypass heading west. When this runs out I crawl into a petrol station with the needle well past empty and find we are at the foot of a fine route back up on to the plateau, to hook round to Morocco. Sometime today I must phone Dani and learn the consignment details of the package landing in Tangier. Also, one of the punctured tyres must be repaired – currently I have no spare. But which?

*

The Algerians are the most demonstrative nation on the Mediterranean's shores. When My Lady passes, they whistle and shout. In plenty of other countries the people gape or smile, or wave approval; as indeed some do here. But in Algeria they make a lot of noise too. The cars toot, the shepherds screech-whistle, the boys cheer and the girls scream. It is not malevolence which makes you jump, but the sheer fact of the outburst.

*

Two hundred miles so far today, but by no means as the crow flies.

Regretfully I have had to miss a second town of ruins, after Subrata. From where we parked overnight we could have stabbed south to Timgad. The colonnaded streets, with their views of the Atlas Mountains, are supposedly Africa's finest desert ruin.

It was our friend, Emperor Trajan's, idea to build an R&R city for his army, somewhere for the lads to unwind, and for the veterans to take up their entitlement to a smallholding on retirement. The Maghreb was cooler then. Eventually the garrison of Thamugadi, as it was known, was withdrawn to defend Rome itself, leaving the place to the Vandals, and later the Berbers. In the Algerian south, the fall of Rome hastened an oblivion which a changing climate soon made inevitable.

I would have liked to see Rome's last word in town planning, as Pompeii was the first. But life holds other pleasures, as many as there are fears, and for me now the urge to reach Tangier in Morocco, or even Europe, is profound. The excitement of the race to Cape St Vincent trumps all.

The trip never had much breadth of vision and who knows ultimately what is for the best? Can anyone say whether the brake kits will arrive? Or if they'll fit? Or if the rear pads worked by handbrake will collapse in the next five miles? Or which of the other dozen things we know can fail, because they already have, will fail again?

It is as much to know one's limits as to find when there are none. So, stuff Timgad.

Yet again My Lady starts first turn of the key.

*

A place that might do road rubber. But no, he has no inner tubes…

And again she starts first turn of the key.

We reverse back across the tarmac to a pile of tractor tyres, where an old man catches my eye, as if he may be able to help. Indeed, he has small hot presses in a workshop the size of a photocopying room, and here he patches inner tubes, all day long.

What luck. A master craftsman. The Hammersmith tyre is OK, he indicates, despite its roasting; so is the other one with a tube in it. He whips out the Libyan inner, mends the leak, checks it in a bucket of water and pops it back in the tyre. Fifteen minutes flat, no pun intended. While we are waiting, his assistant shows me his collection of football centrespreads stuck up on the wall. He asks what my sport is. I can only answer 'Driving'.

The puncture repair maestros take a while to say goodbye. They have found a man aged thirty-two among them and are remarking how ill-preserved he is compared with my sprightly S-Type. Apparently 1957 was the year of the cockerel. This alone takes a minute or two to explain.

I must drive on. And again My Lady starts first turn of the key. The red leather is soft and warm. We have the second movement of Beethoven's Pastoral Symphony on repeat.

*

What is this sport of Driving?

When the road is fast and clear of traffic; when the surface is even and its temperature moderated by an avenue of carob trees; when the orange groves march away in lines and the ancient olives are silvery in the autumn sun; when the bends fall like grass to a sharp and well-timed scythe; when every brakeless overtake is judged to blueprint tolerance; when the needles on the gauges all point harmoniously towards the dead clock in the centre of the dash and the speedometer is reeling in a steady sixty miles an hour; when the view ahead is clear, and promises to remain so for 800 miles to the Atlantic; when the music picks up the sweeping rhythm of progress, faster, swelling to thunderous pitch; when your arms and knees and feet and the interior surfaces of the car tickle with the vibrations of a full symphony; then the spell of such a *trajet*, the crossing of Africa, winkles through your doubt and caution and plain suspicion and grabs your lungs, your heart, your shoulder muscles and the spiral of your guts; and your whole body howls.

Then every turn of the land, every ripple in the road is romance.

Then you know, remember, feel you will always remember, why. Why you do it. Why you did it.

You can hear the laughter and the cheering, the gasps, the astonished whispering among the ancestral spirits, among the poets, the travellers, the soldiers, the engineers, the politicians, the writers and inventors and dreamers and even those in England now a-bed; all, all would think themselves accursed they were not here... etc.

*

The main post office in Mascara, high in the mountains behind the Gulf of Arzew. I am trying to phone through to my office.

While I explain the telephone number to the operator, a young girl with a veil and mask comes up and interrupts, talking boldly to him.

I turn to her, she turns to me.

Flash. They don't need mascara in Mascara.

My call to London comes through. I have misjudged the time. Algeria is on GMT. We have driven through two time zones, not one. Dani has gone home. So the package code number will have to wait until tomorrow. The girl with the eyes has gone too. And again My Lady starts first turn of the key.

At the petrol station I ask the only question there is to ask in a town of this name. What do you call charcoal along the eyelashes? And the first answer is no, never heard of it. But then yes, we call it '*Cire*'. Maybe. Wax.

*

A tiny mosque is painted turquoise and green. It is only ten feet by ten feet, and the front opening does not even have a door. But it stands in the middle of a wide vegetable patch beside the road. The layout of the irrigation channels around it recalls the Taj Mahal on a rustic and miniaturised scale – as I imagine it, I have never been to India. Needless to say, the garden is lush beyond reason, abundantly, bounteously fruitful. I drive up to investigate. The tranquillity marks an interlude before we run to the frontier.

Reversing back to the main road, some passing traffic forces us to stop across two broad puddles; and that puts Her Ladyship into a combined fit of Aqaba starter and Piraeus gearbox, from which she threatens not to recover. After I have tried everything else, I offer to take a picture of the undignified pose for all the world to see if she doesn't pull herself together. And she does.

Beyond the little mosque, the road follows a river. Its floodplain supports three magnificent colonial estates, now fallen into neglect. The dates on the gables of the agricultural buildings are from the early 1930s, and the avenues of carefully spaced ancient olive trees and noble palms, mile upon mile, testify to the wealth invested here when the rest of the world was in economic crisis.

Further along the road stands a deep wood, planted with European varieties, grown huge from the proximity of water in this muscular marl and rarefied climate. Some trees billow up towards the sky like great bonfires. Others stand as tall and skinny as catwalk mannequins. It is a forgotten arboretum, a tree garden, someone's dream from the far side of politics and time.

The white haze of the highlands, which struck me as so Scottish yesterday, glows off the backs of the farm animals. It suffuses the bell-less bell tower. It coats the crumbling homestead in a varnish of peace. No hard sea-level light would so forgive their decrepitude. Up here at 3,000 feet the crisp, clean wind and the rich, red soil promise only prosperity.

We press on, speeding westwards into the sun. A flock of white doves flaps low, jockeying the pressure wave either side of the Bentley's alabaster bonnet. The blur of wings, backlit, makes for one adrenal instant of outrageous photogeneity.

Day 54

For the third time the trip meter is on 000(0). I parked up for the night to mark the exact occasion. The number sits there while I write.

Daytime is just too short. We need the lamp. This log exists thanks to the Bentley's inside lights – as the king of the monkeys sings in Disney's film *The Jungle Book*, in 'I Wan'na Be Like You', *What I desire is man's red fire*.

Once upon a time there was fire. Fire for hardening wooden points, cracking stones, hollowing logs, signalling – all of which made hunting easier. Fire for cooking – roasting, boiling water, smoke-preserving meat. Also fire to make the evenings less of a struggle – defence from wild animals, cauterising cuts, relaxing after the meal; warmth which dispels the need to bed down, which extrudes postprandial yarns; charcoal face paint; torches carried deep into caves, sooty sticks to conjure plenteous prey; dancing shadows to ignite the imagination. Fire can even be the story, how control of fire spawned language itself – that's another of Stanton Coit's theories. And storytelling is the mark of man.

Over the rim of the mountain, the sky turns from black to darkest blue. The stars fade. A donkey brays.

In the valley a hand pump begins to squeak. A dog barks, and a crow (or maybe another donkey) caws back.

My foxy jalopy is parked on a wide alcove in a ravine, perhaps forty miles short of the crossing into Morocco. I wonder what to do if we make it as far as Tangier today and the brake parts cannot be cleared through customs until tomorrow afternoon.

*

Algerian passport control.

We are back to queuing like cattle behind a steel fence, waiting to be allowed across the tarmac to the Portakabins where the rubber stamps ring out like shots at a casual abattoir.

The herd stands in turn for its place at the window, but before our queue is half processed, the next wave of mammalia is released into our corral.

A police sergeant with grey hair and the bearing of a man with his booty already stashed, cuts in ahead of me and slips two passports through the window, while stamping a pair of emigration cards with his own pocket rubber insignia. The cleared passports come back in a trice, and he hands them to an unctuous but otherwise innocuous fat man in blue, who shambles off without a sign of thanks.

*

Customs on the Moroccan side. Bigger lines waiting, one for men and one for women. There are more men. If you lend a pen to someone in the queue you can wander off, park properly and reclaim your position. It's a juggling act, moving the car forward and also keeping my place in the line. We could be here for the day.

This is not the sleepy place I walked into an hour ago. The police must have been waiting until 08:00 and I cruised through at 07:55 thinking 'nothing to worry about here'.

Thirty-two men stand in the queue behind me now. The line is becoming fidgety. The red Moroccan flags flap aptly in the sun. Beneath them stands a man wearing a striped nightshirt of cornflower, pea-green and white, down to the ankles, which would have done credit to a deckchair on the *Titanic*.

A second counter opens and the crowd surges. Again that instant of hesitation between order and chaos. It is the moment of opportunity.

*

In the Moroccan State Bank in Oujda they are dealing in stacks of notes. My presence is not welcome. 'It will take a long time,' warns the cashier.

Who do they think they are kidding? I argue – it says Change/Cambio/Wechsel on the brass plaque outside, and on the brass counter here. They take the dollars. I am given a smart, brass, queuing token. It is hexagonal, with the number 80 stamped through it. Beside me, coinage is being poured from one sack to another, and big bundles of notes are being counted out with astonishing dexterity.

Theatrically framed, with a lofty ceiling and long, wide skylight, the bank has many empty, brass-fitted booths destined never to hum all together again. I imagine the floor of the London Stock Exchange to be like this, now that screen-based dealing has scattered most of the brokers to glass and steel towers.

And already my pile of dinars is ready.

*

At this instant I'm connecting through to Dani for the air bill number, 775279886 by DHL. The brake seals should be there today. Many thanks.

OK. Now we just have 500 kilometres to reach them.

At the news stand, I see that Prost won the Italian Grand Prix at Monza yesterday. Senna still needs a win to retain his title.

Chewing some salty white marrow seeds (well they aren't nuts anyway), I spy my Derby flyer in the distance where she rolled to a halt outside the bank. Two small boys are washing her down, uninvited. They've pretty well finished. Ten local pengos for each of them. They do not want to stop but reaching the middle of the roof has always been an issue.

*

A bridge over the Ouad Bourdim River, a funnel of scarce water. We have taken the road southwest towards Fez, accepting advice in Oujda that the highway crossing the central plain of Morocco, although fifty per cent longer to Tangier than the coast road, is twice as fast. When you have no brakes that equals ten times as safe.

After the first few miles, the influence on the Moroccan countryside of the tidy planters of Algeria dwindles. Then comes an orderly French provincial town, to correct the balance.

Now we are heading back to the desert, and small nomad encampments pop up, the first since Syria. The road is good for 60 or 70mph, and with all instruments on minimum alert, motoring is a joy.

Little pleasures are everywhere in this last riverside grove; in this unexpected ricochet down to Fez; in the continuing theme of neighbour hating neighbour (now it's what the Moroccans say about the Algerians); these will become the corners of a wistful smile in years to come.

*

Zabubaa – sandstorm.

I have taken another hitchhiker, a princely man of the desert. He wears a maroon *shesh*, a Touareg turban-cum-shawl, and he is looking pensive.

A dirt cloud closes in on the right, and another is out there on the left. I say, 'We'll make it through the middle for sure. *Inshallah*,' and he chimes in.

I'm glad he's here; this storm front is like nothing I've seen. The truck straight ahead in the distance disappears, then comes back into view, like a lighthouse in a gale. The road grows a skin of sand, sheeting over the tarmac. My foot is down. The white rhino charges across liquid land. Keep going, aim for the truck, aim for the truck.

The road was straight, so there must be blacktop under our wheels. Despite the towering walls of grit closing in from left and right, ahead only the inch of air nearest the ground is in sandstorm. Raw desert flows flat under the car, then swirls up in the mirror behind, blending with the merged, sand-coloured plane of the storm we hope to outpace.

I glance at my guest. His jaw is set and his eye steeled. He has been caught by sandstorms before and evidently does not want to repeat the experience.

If either of the snarling banks of cloud catches us, I guess I must immediately stop and switch off. Quite apart from keeping sand out of the engine, I would like to stay on the road.

We plunge on for what seems like minutes. I try my damnedest to drive at the truck ahead. We are hauling them in, but the canyon between the two walls of sand narrows.

Then suddenly the air is crisp and blue. The road is black tarmac and we pass the lorry. It takes our place as the morsel for the monster behind. Possibly the truck driver does not even know what he has coming.

My passenger sighs. 'Hammed', he says, giving me his hand.

The road beckons onward. New bridges cross rivers next to the remnants of earlier engineers' overpass attempts, dismissed by torrents more violent than European colonialists could conceive. We soar to ridges from which the distant mountains reveal themselves, in aqueous tints, to the south; and swoop down into an occasional *oharzeese*, as my companion calls the pools of water standing among trees – each rimmed by a wide raised earth ring, the detritus of centuries of nomad camps.

*

And now Taza. Halfway to Fez. 3,200 miles from Cairo.

Hammed is still along for the ride. Nevertheless, in the town square he insists on calling a halt and sitting me down for a mint tea. No ordinary mint tea is this, but a glass beaker, four times the normal size, a thimble of strong infusion, a branch of spearmint rolled up on itself in a bundle and a half-pint of boiling water poured over the whole. Add a sugar lump if you must.

'Speciality of the region,' indicates Hammed with a nod.

*

It must have rained hard here south of Taza, when it was showering lightly on me in Carthage. The rivers are running, the drainage culverts overflowing. Boys gambol in the muddy irrigation sumps beside the road. The land seems more amenable to farming. The hills and valleys are planted with groves or ranged out in tracts of plough waiting to be sown.

The river that runs to Fez itself is approached from the north in a series of descending corners, not quite hairpins, but dramatic enough for one local bus to flip over today – the spot is already attended by police and ambulances. The panorama from the top of this gradient, with the torrent glittering away to the southwest in the afternoon sun, has all the scale of Africa, and water too.

Among such immensity, Fez comes up like a blip on a screen. We thread in to the eastern, oldest part of town. Somewhere in here is the world's first university. You must learn the Koran by heart to qualify for a place. Hammed is heading on to Casablanca, while time dictates that I turn north. We sip a second, valedictory tea at a pavement café by the post office in the old city, considering ourselves lucky to be alive. The two glasses come with a small yellow flower.

Afternoon sunshine strikes the tea, the tray, the tin table, the folding metal chairs and the 800-year-old clay walls opposite. All are as buttery as the flower.

*

My Lady and I are into the hills again, with half an hour of light remaining. I have stopped on a col, a saddle in the range, to stretch again and enjoy the view. The breeze dusts a gentle powder of earth from the plough into every crevice of the car. Soil erosion. That must be why they leave the stubble in the ground as late as possible.

A gang of ten small boys approaches. They are wild, a pack of jackal pups – they want to be dangerous but are not sure they are big enough yet. The leader has a rabid glint in his eye. One or two of the others look ashamed.

'No, sorry chaps, no cigarettes. I don't smoke.'

*

That, my friend, was one of the drives of my life. Precisely sixty miles from the ridge to Quezzane. If you are looking for a piste to put an older Bentley down, with single-track tarmac winding like a private drive through scenery sometimes as intimate as a medieval illumination, sometimes as crude as an opencast mine; for corners that do not quite need brakes; for blind rises that might hide a car coming full into you, but never do; for cattle, donkeys, sheep and dogs that wander off your trajectory just before you need to throttle back; then this is the road for you.

If colours of sunset so flat they pass clean under the car appeal; if that Sinai shadow of speeding coachwork, projected far out over the landscape still amuses; if you seek homesteads and farmyards of simplicity and order; or narrow bridges over broad rivers that gleam in the westerly light; if you have forgotten why big wheels and a massive chassis make fun of verges at 60mph when the truck looming down clings to the crown of the road; if you desire beauty piled upon image of beauty, too fast to register; if you appreciate a fine tool ranging back and forth across its extensive tolerances; then race a Bentley S1 up the road from Fez to Quezzane on a cool September evening.

And when the storming charge is over, sit outside a café with a final mint tea while the stars come out to join you.

The flash of cameras bounces down the street. The townsfolk are posing for pictures with My Lady. In the Kingdom of Morocco they still appreciate a Visit.

Trickle up to the town square, among the throngs out for their evening stroll. Offer to drive the first person who approaches you to their favourite bar and see what they come up with.

The town's industry is handwoven rugs and coverings. Four thousand domestic looms are tucked away in the backstreets, I am told, weaving wool and camel hair, home-spun and -dyed.

After your purchase, dawdle in the workshop beside the loom. Prop yourself up on wool sacks and carpets, and discuss (in French): the hope for mankind; the Moroccans' hopes for themselves; their fear of the 'European virus' – our distancing between individuals in a community, our high divorce rate; our unemployment benefit; their urge to have sons; and their dependence on the wholesale production of *kif* – marijuana – and in particular the highest level of purity, which they call sputnik, and how they weld up cakes of cannabis pollen into dummy caravan gas cylinders, with a little camping cylinder fitted inside the top, for the Dutch and West Germans to take home, and how their friend has four hectares under marijuana and last year sold 258 kilos in one shipment to some Dutchmen who brought in a boat at night.

Cannabis is the subject Miranda most mocks me about. She proudly enjoys a social spliff at house parties with her Cambridge friends, and tells me when I disapprove that I have 'a chocolate finger up my bottom', whatever that means.

If you had been there in Quezzane you could also have heard my ill-practised response to their drugs industry, my questioning whether they themselves find pleasure in chemically concentrated oils and cakes (they don't); whether they thought these to be a healthy symptom of society (again, they don't). That for me to be here, among the looms and carpets, discussing with strangers, was an active, intelligent pleasure; whereas the man who lolls in a drug-fuelled dream world fools himself that he is intelligent or lively or handsome or witty, but is stupid, dull, ugly and boring.

And secondly, that such an industry, being illegal and yet involving much money, becomes immediately dominated by a criminal element, which is even prepared to kill in order to maintain control of its territory; that protection offered by this mafia corrupts the people's understanding with their police, so that the attractions of having laws and law enforcement and a policeman nearby when you are attacked are forgotten.

You would have heard my worldly new friends insisting that in their untreated, natural state the drugs they grow are just herbs like any other, and that, in their community, live men of 120 who chew such plants every day and still have all their teeth. But that the condoms filled with narcotic oil hidden in the rectum, and the sachets of pollen-cake swallowed and later regurgitated, or pressed into bricks stamped with the king's head, were items Moroccans themselves would not touch with a bargepole. The locals just do what the crazy Europeans give good money for. What's more, they said, there are many pleasures in life, and each person finds his own.

But I argued that it is not enough to be responsible only for oneself. Given awareness and energy, one has responsibility for one's surroundings, for making the world a better place, which means putting one's opinions to others, particularly to one's children. Not in a prejudiced way, but based on experience; the values and insights into human nature and human needs, formed in reality. Such commitment and leadership were made from the solidarity which they said Europeans lacked.

Did they not see their own hypocrisy? Ultimately, one should be prepared to fight and die for one's principles, but usually one did not believe anything so strongly because such things are rarely clear. Not even one's own loves.

Then I talked about the knowledge of being clean, of knowing when the Libyans separated me from my car, that if they had walked in and said 'We've found it', they were trying it on; or they had planted something. Being clean was quite a trip in itself.

Day 55

The coastal plateau before Tangier. Mule carts and pack-donkeys pass my side-road hide while it is still dark. Sounds of awakening rise from farmyards in all directions, and a hard, mustard-earth plain emerges from the gloom.

That was my fourth night in the car since my bath and shave on Jerba Island, or was it the fifth? I can pull at my beard. You quite forget that it hurts.

Today is the big revelation, down at the airport. Mount up! Move out!

*

To the east a watery orange sun shines through spent rainclouds. To the west the Atlantic.

We are on a ridge between the rolling, tree-dotted contours of Africa and the dense green fringe of the ocean. White gulls circle the road, and two rustics walk past on their way to work. The ocean is coming in to the Continent on a swell. Its colour is grey, a straight rebuff to the Côte d'Azur. Even from a half-mile distance on a calm day, the surface is chopped and brutal. It has a force beyond even the sandstorm yesterday, a gravitas not seen since Vesuvius.

*

As the sun was rising, the road led into town. I thought I had arrived. There was confusion while the compass would not tally with the port and coast. In fact, the place name was Larache, fifty miles down from Tangier, still facing west, not north.

Now we are back on the drying 'pike through fields of yellow melons, past piles of the fruit stacked waiting for the buyers' lorries. Local transport continues to be on four feet or two, with or without a burden of water or firewood. In response to the rain, the shepherds have pulled out long brown cloaks with pointed witches' hoods; the same style as in mountainous Turkey, 5,000 miles away by land, 2,000 by sea.

Clouds of fluff are blowing in the wind, for mile upon mile. An explosion at a cotton mill? Wind up the windows against the blizzard.

After ten minutes I have to stop to work out what it is.

The rain shower has hatched a swarm of four-winged maybugs. How many must be flitting, nose up, close to stalling in their first day of flight, like a billion biplane prototypes? How long will they live? How quickly must they mate and lay before the dry weather locks their race back into the pupa stage of its lifecycle?

Towards the low sun, a herd of cattle and sheep flows over the hillside. Sunlight haloing off the backs of animals is this journey's leitmotif.

*

Tangier airport. No bigger than a Home Counties' flying club. The customs and freight terminal is a hut with cars abandoned up against it.

8 a.m. The office opens – a battered pair of rooms, with no record of my parcel. Have we been here before? Except this time it is more dangerous. I won't be walking away from a dead car, but into the dock for not stopping for a crowd of schoolchildren.

I insist on seeing inside the customs man's padlocked cupboard for storing smaller items. It has three prayer mats rolled up in it for official use, but no package for me. Checking at the airport, a flight landed yesterday evening direct from London, 7 p.m., the 917 London to Tangier. But my brake seals were definitely not on it, so everyone tells me at the freight office. How can DHL, who advertise themselves as being fast and competent, take three working days to miss a flight from Heathrow?

If the package is not yet on the ground, it will not be cleared today. The customs office shuts for the weekend at noon. No flights from anywhere in Europe land before then. This is worse than Adana.

I will double-check the air bill number with Gibair, the transit agent. This is the last shot.

After an elaborate runaround I have the right change for the payphone. I call the Gibair number in Tangier to give them a piece of my mind. They don't answer, and when I hang up the coin box swallows my money.

Oh well, who needs a foot brake to stop two tons? We still have the gearbox, the handbrake and the headwind. Not to mention the still untested ruse of killing the ignition on an automatic at speed.

*

Down at the docks a fair-haired vagrant flags me down. What on earth does he want? Why me?

With his rummy face and his one good eye, he tells me the times of the ferry boats across the Straits of Gibraltar and where to buy a ticket, and he changes pesetas at the bank rate from his pocket on the spot. He points me to the garage and suggests I spend what remaining dirham I have on petrol, because the Spanish price is so much higher. Then he leaves.

Have I seen one of these before, a guardian angel made flesh, on the road from Cesme into Izmir? At the Turkish/Syrian border above Iskenderun?

261

My Lady bursts into the docks and pinballs through the system. One moment I spot the raised bows of a vessel facing onshore like a great white biting the jetty. The next we are inside its belly. I give my long-suffering steed four more litres of oil. All this manual down-changing smokes the lubricants.

3,500 miles from Cairo, the Bentley is leaving Africa. 3,500 miles indeed! And more than 2,100 since the fire. The ferry is backing and twisting away from the dock. The funnel smoke and the stern flag dance gentle rotations over the deck. They were flying astern, now they blow towards the bows and now they hang limp, as the ship picks up speed to match the wind from behind. We will slowly suffocate in our own diesel exhaust.

The beacon on the point slips past in front of me. How can I have underestimated this drive by the distance from Land's End to John O'Groats?

*

A sea mist surrounds us. I have been asleep. I don't know where we are and don't care. Wandering around the deck reveals nothing. There is no past and no future. Only the sun at high noon and the nearby teal-grey in all directions where sea and ocean meet fog and sky. A school of dolphins or porpoises, fifteen, slick black backs and lightning action, breaks the surface out on the starboard side. Now on both bows, like the doves yesterday evening. It is an omen of good fortune.

And then, as if in response, an outline suggests itself through the haze, more immense than cognition bears, coming towards us, higher than the prow of our ferry must seem to the dolphins. Gibraltar. The Rock. It summarily dismisses that formation south of Sergiopolis. Yet its most astonishing quality is that it remains, even in today's world of guided missiles and satellites, a simple hill fort, impregnable, murderous to conventional attack from land or sea.

If the brake parts had been couriered to Gibraltar they would have made it by today. That was one leap of imagination too far for me, after a good lunch outside Tunis.

*

The ferry turns west and docks across the bay, in Algeciras. From here to Cadiz is a mere seventy miles; we did more than that before breakfast.

Put your hand out of the window. The air is cold. Not just cool, cold. Look at the road. It is smooth and free of lorries, like some funfair rink with only bumper cars. Here are Fords and multi-cylinder motorcycles, neither of which are known in the half of the Mediterranean from Egypt to Morocco.

Every building is a hotel or restaurant. How can there be so much food? The place is canopied with wires and power lines and telephone cables. The roof of every building is mocked by its television aerials. The fields are abandoned to thistles; occasional attempts to plant avenues have left dead trees in all but the hardiest cases.

The countryside feels driven over; nothing moves on foot. Even the air has been thrashed, like the ringing ozone at an autocross track.

Not until we reach the Andalusian *frontera* do the hills begin to compete with the impression left by Algeria and Morocco.

*

I was a tad offhand, dismissive even, about the task that remains.

Today is actually going to be another long haul. This corner of Europe is not yet blessed with the straight connections I have enjoyed since Cairo. I want to loop west round the coast, but after Cadiz the road will backtrack to the northeast, to Seville, before it strikes towards Cape St Vincent. However, I hope to fly home from Seville, so this offers a chance to research hotels which might garage My Lady for the autumn.

The pride of Sevillian hostelry is apparently the Hotel Alphonso XIII, between the river and the Calle San Fernando. It has gardens on three sides and, more importantly, extensive parking beneath them.

*

Cadiz, Plaza España. I am here partly to say I have been. Cairo to Cadiz in ten and a half days, and less than ten per cent motorways – that is an Ultramarathon. But also this is where to organise an air ticket home and acquire some more pesetas for petrol.

The harbour site is a phenomenon of the natural world. A slim finger of sand, tipped by a bastion of rock, shelters a port and lagoon from westerly and southern gales. Here Phoenicians from Tyre, the other end of the Med, built a trading post. Here Hannibal sacrificed to the gods before his long march over the Alps. Here a young Julius Caesar reflected on his own shortcomings before a statue of Alexander the Great. Juvenal spoke of the Roman Empire as stretching from 'Gades to the Ganges'.

Cadiz has had more Golden Ages than most. It was the third-richest city in the Roman Empire at the time of Augustus' census, rose again as the home of the Spanish treasure fleet in the sixteenth century and flourished a third time two centuries later, when the maritime route to Seville silted up. These days it is back in the shadows. The Cadiz boats just run to the Canary Islands.

One travel agent is still open at the siesta hour. The brochures in the window beckon the browsing holidaymaker to Turkey, Egypt and Greece. All so tame. The only cover I like is of Big Ben. The cheaper holiday magazines proclaim those strutting, near-naked Western women. Two weeks' of veiled faces make these somehow shocking; frightening, rather than enticing.

The travel agent herself is perhaps the most drop-dead gorgeous woman I have seen in my life. My head tells me this is a natural overreaction to the single-sex world I have left. But my heart is in love. I am once more a sixteen-year-old boy on a school sailing expedition to the Channel Islands, fumbling for coherence in front of the busty seventeen-year-old with a golden S on a chain round her neck, selling ice cream at the St Peter Port go-kart track.

I flirt with my gorgeous travel agent and she flirts back. My flight from Seville to London with an open return becomes a subtle foreplay. Her hand is so close to mine, one move of a finger and we will touch. The skin over her collarbone is soft and flawless. Her ear is unpierced and delicate, her breast moves under her shirt, she is so completely adorable, so perfect, that it is all I can do not to propose marriage on the spot.

As she hands me my blue-and-pink APEX multi-leaf ticket, she looks into my eyes and we are on fire. I am sure that she would say yes. Only the robotic response of my feet to a direct order from my frazzled brain gets me out of the door without a serious mistake.

If that is what a North African male goes through when he arrives in Europe, God help us all.

Plaza España in the afternoon sun; lovers kiss; lads' litre bottles of San Miguel stand empty; a young girl pulls up her mini skirt to show her friend a mark. We Europeans have learnt to wrap invisibility around things. We are not voyeurs. Our park benches are widely spaced, facing the fountains, in a way which the Arab world also rejects. What is it about personal space in public, the value of elbow room between park benches, that Europeans understand and North Africans do not?

I think of the girl I say I love.

She has a way of blinking slowly when she is content, looking straight at you, so that one eye closes after the other.

The pigeons land on the ground around my feet. Each puffs up a brief, sunlit plume of dust with its final wing beat. It is like the spittle of dirt kicked up from the carpet pile in Tubby's office when the interpreter stretched out his heel.

I am not myself today.

*

We are still in Spain, 130 miles from Cadiz, 130 miles to go to find the villa by Cape St Vincent where the two Charleses should be.

Even a small European city like Huelva, set back from the Portuguese frontier, seems bigger than the capitals of Libya or Tunisia. Algiers and Casablanca I did not see, but Fez is definitely smaller, as are Oban in Algeria and Oujda in Morocco, each regional capitals. The investment which European cities represent must be unmatched in the world.

We have been travelling on unfinished motorway. Even in that state the artery is a revelation of simplicity and smoothness. My Lady touched 85mph for fun, remembering how her steering goes light at that speed. But she is of an era before motorways, a Grand Tourer for the Great North Road, and although she packs a punch between 60 and 80, nowadays that is 20mph too slow.

Today just happens to be a carnival in Spain, the big fiesta, the first Friday in September. Huelva's main street closes over us like the Red Sea upon the pursuing Pharaoh. From nowhere, a carnival float of the Virgin Mary appears, and My Lady is in danger of becoming a Popemobile.

A rubble-strewn building site presents itself as a possible escape route on the left. With memories of Syrian riverbeds, the limousine takes the kerb in a stride and sets out into the night across the strewn bricks, to the consternation of the men on the pavement.

I am pressing on because the ferry over to Portugal may close shortly.

*

Ayamonte, the border town, is also in carnival. The sky is lit with fireworks, and the narrow cobbled backstreets are jammed with diverted tourist cars wanting nothing more than to find the quayside and the ferry. Lost in this warren, drivers with British number plates consult each other in despair, split up and search for clues, yet miraculously reconvene on the dock at the right moment. The surge of cars when the riverboat arrives matches the rush of humanity when a new passport window opens in Aqaba or Oujda. With luck we should all be together on the next shipment.

The border police have not asked for the Bentley's customs carnet.

265

Day 56

The crescent moon of Cairo has reached a semicircle. It stays wonderfully fixed in position through the windscreen over the heads of the passengers leaning on the rail, as the lights of the riverbank stream by.

Fifteen cars and fifty people perch together in a coracle on the Rio Guadiana, somewhat fewer than in the Jerba Island ferry. It would take a Dunkirk calm for this boat to be safe on open water.

The captain spins the vessel in the stream to bring its disembarkation side up to the Portuguese jetty. An old sensation, the horizon and moon are now revolving, with the immediate distance, the cars, the wheelhouse and the guardrails all fixed.

Bump. Bump. Bump.

Dry land. Vila Real de San António.

As she comes up the ramp, the Bentley receives a tremendous cheer from the pedestrians waiting to cross back from Portugal to Spain.

In all honesty, she deserves it.

*

3,867 miles from Cairo. Perhaps three in the morning.

This must be the track down to the beach. No placard, but we've run out of road. Beyond Salema is only the Cape proper, the end of another continent, King Henry the Navigator's command centre for Vasco da Gama's explorations, the launch pad of European imperialism.

The roads of the Algarve are marked out by nice white lines, the buildings decked with neon signs for chainsaw hire and used car sales. The air is so chilly the crickets barely sing.

Yet here, just for this track, the law of the jungle rules again. Surprise is on our side. The leopard pads stealthily down the stony path towards the sea, turning to investigate several sidings before finding the steep upwards incline we seek. The last one. All the signs are right. However, the angle of the junction is so acute and the side road so narrow that she cannot make the turn, so we go on to the beach to face about.

With a rush we remount the track. The sheer grunt of the straight-six demolishes the ascent. I cut the lights and trickle silently through the bottleneck gate at the top. My Lady waits on the back terrace of the villa, while I search for a door, then for a candle and matches, and go from room to room looking for a free bed.

The scene has the reassuring bomb-site shambles of a student digs.

My friends realise they have an intruder. The girls are the first to raise the alarm. And no, Miranda is not among them. The boys emerge. Charles Prideaux is here and my flatmate, Charles Whitworth. I present everyone with small gifts. They have just walked the Pilgrim's Way to Santiago in northwest Spain so have many adventures of their own to relate.

The two Charleses insist on going for a drive later today, in daylight.

We do not turn in for some time.

*

The tide advances and ebbs out. Our tyre tracks have gone. The sand dries clean and level. Squeeze its softness in your fist and watch the white grains flow over your knuckles. Each grain can be seen fleetingly, for itself, and then drops to the beach.

So it is with the days of a journey. The arc of travel outweighs the detail.

My Lady's circumnavigation is still a work in progress. Only the grail complete will chime with the thrill of triumph.

This afternoon I must head back to the Alphonso XIII and put her to bed for the autumn.

Chapter Four: Circuit Closed

Spain, France
Thursday 2nd November to Sunday 5th November 1989

Day 57

Heathrow. Iberia Flight 621. Doors to automatic. Sunset over grey cumulus. The passengers embrace the journey south with all the relief of migrating birds. Beg a ballpoint from the air steward.

My flagging London spirits rumble down a runway of their own and soar above the week's grimy cloud base. I have been verbally warned by the personnel department that the Bentley must be home by Christmas. Something to do with the new leasing company (my idea), Velo, needing physical proof that their vehicle still exists. If his people have to waste valuable man-hours tightening the policy on company cars, says the friendly HR director, heads will roll.

Two cans of brake fluid are on board with me, between my feet. You don't need to tell me the stuff is flammable – I learnt that the hard way in Libya. Not for carrying on civil aircraft. But the staff at Heathrow were understanding. Each telephoned ahead to the next security check and then said to me, 'Smile nicely to so-and-so.'

'It's Castrol RR226. As the label says, extra heavy duty, only to be used for Rolls-Royce and Bentley cars. Otherwise I would buy the stuff in Seville.'

I unscrew the caps on the one-litre cans to prevent them bursting in the event of a decompression, I tell myself with doubtful logic. No need to go into a crash with your legs daubed in lighter fluid.

Electricity runs within the clouds below. In the dusk it looks like pearly underfloor strobes in a foam-filled Pacha. The steward brings a brandy.

I remember how another storm swept in, towards the shore at Monte Carlo, a black hand reaching to shake some sense into mankind, and me in particular. The Principality was girdled with Armco crash barriers, but heavy rain could still have cancelled the race. It was my nineteenth birthday, the night before the Monaco Grand Prix. I had driven down from the factory near Dijon, where I was on the assembly line, and slept the night in the sap-green Fiesta.

All through that Saturday evening, the storm stalked along the coast, out to sea, playing grandmother's footsteps with the 100,000 people eager for the morrow's joust, stretching its menace so close that by nightfall it had humbled us all.

I put on my dinner jacket and walked down the big mole towards the lighthouse to see if I could get lucky. The biggest hulls, like social warships, were moored up at the far point, nearest the harbour lamp. When I reached the end, with the lightning out to sea, I just turned right and mounted the last and biggest gangplank.

We were all equal before the state of nature.

Today it is the same. A cognac and a storm. A cocktail of anomie and elements.

*

The tarmac at Barcelona glistens with recent rain. The hot, wet night makes you cough. The foreign voices seem quaint – like Gaelic or Welsh in a world that increasingly talks money and English. The neon transit hall, the computer-driven departure board, the whistling in your ears, which turns out to be shopping mall muzak, show how far globalisation has already conquered. I sit in transit for Seville beside a glamorous Italian girl and find that we have haunts and bars in common. We imbibe the same messages – *Der Spiegel*, *The Economist* – and manifest the same habits – a jog before work, a salad at lunch, a whisky in the evening.

*

Another plane, another flight, another terminal. My mood has lifted like the thunderstorm outside. At least I have cleared the in-tray I brought with me.

Here in the Deep South, in the capital of Andalucia, you ride with the taxi window down even at 11 p.m. in winter. We pass under the tower of La Giralda, the twelfth-century Moorish minaret, floodlit sugar piping, a birthday cake basket of tracery, buttresses and rose windows. By midnight my head is on the Alfonso XIII's pillow in the heart of the old *frontera*.

Day 58

A tense and disorganised dream ends with an old English car being found with the driver dead at the wheel in the jungles of Vietnam.

I am relieved to be awake. I lie on my bed and reflect that today must hold fewer horrors.

I phone cousin Simon, who co-drove on the first leg from London to the Balearics. He has just begun a work experience job in Madrid. I suggest we meet for supper, if I can fix My Lady's brakes.

Madrid can't be far. But where in Madrid?

Simon says the steps of the Prado.

'At 9 p.m.,' I say. 'But does the Prado have steps?' Neither of us knows.

'Well, in the middle of the west side of the Prado then,' says Simon, and we leave it at that.

The clock of the Giralda chimes 9 a.m. I have twelve hours. I hurry for the lift, which has been clunking and buzzing all night.

*

Signor Dunlop has come for his car. But this is the Hotel Alfonso XIII. We are the monarch among the pesky generalissimos of Seville hostelry, we have our routines, and he must wait. What are a few minutes after fifty days?

My scalp goes hot and cold with frustration. The only hope is to sit back and appreciate the museum I am in; the gorgeous tiles, royal blue and golden yellow, take me back to the terrace of the Hotel San Pietro di Positano. But these marble floors and glazed brickwork arches have their own distinctive Spanishness, equally resistant to the omnivorous glass and steel world outside.

Eventually, the general manager, Andres Hidalgo Cruz, passes on his clipped, quick-fire morning inspection. He has calculated a queen's ransom, presents me with a bill with my name correct at the top of it and accepts plastic. (I now carry a credit card since the horrors of leaving Cairo last spring. And to appease Miranda, who didn't notice.)

Down in the hotel's long, empty underground car park, the Bentley stands in her corner. She and I are alone together. A carpenter has been working in some bays to the right. I approach slowly. Covered in her Smyrna sackcloth, nose to the wall, she is fearsome still. It is a while before I have the temerity to touch her. We have survived so much, I am drained just to meet again.

Would we both be happier left to our memories than taking up the cudgels once more? Do I have it in me? Does she have it in her? Will she let me strip down her front brakes and make her safe for European roads? How can I heave this crushing mass from inertia into life? I roll back her cover. The soot of Izmir and the sand of Cairo are now topped off with the sawdust of Seville. The tarpaulin has done its job.

I release her handbrake, bunch my back up against the wall, place both feet on her front bumper and force her over the flat-spot on her tyres.

Like a reluctant carthorse she shifts her weight and backs into the middle of the car park.

Lubricant has pooled on the concrete beneath where her engine was.

I busy myself clearing the empty cans and cartons from her boot and laying out my tools and the photocopies of the workshop manual Bruce gave me. It is too soon to attempt to start her.

Is she real? Is it really her? Can we trust each other? Can we trust ourselves? Slowly the telltale shapes and sounds, the blistered paint, the rippled front wing, the slam of the door, the faulty catch on the boot, the dust-streaked chrome cowl of her radiator, tap their passwords into my memory of her. I take the spanner and pliers and reconnect her battery. Her interior light glows warmly in the gloom. The oil level is good, despite the puddle on the floor. I pour in more and then quickly turn the engine over. It fires at the third twist of the key. The lazy sound of the Bendix drive is always a shock after a month or two of hearing only the busy whirr of modern starter motors.

One more turn and she is running. Well done old girl. I manoeuvre her round under the central row of strip lights, to give better visibility for the front brake mechanisms. She is blocking nothing that might be needed for the next few hours.

Cut the engine, pull out the jack and set to work.

Off come the Karaman wheel, the bearing cover, the split kingpin, the crown that holds the heavy ring of roller-bearings in place and finally the wheel hub itself. Slowly I work my way round the guts of the design, poking and tapping, trying to understand how the blackened parts conspire together to be a braking system.

Within each front wheel are two half-moon pads, located by a socket at one end and a spring in the middle. These shoes are squeezed out against the wheel drum by hydraulic plungers. So each wheel has two plungers. On the driver's side wheel, the rubber seals on these plungers are all but burnt away. Even with Bruce's illustrations there is going to be some guesswork. I spend a while undoing the mischief we caused deliberately in Tunisia to stop brake fluid leaking, and puzzling out the best way to stop airlocks behind these rubber vitals.

*

I have repaired and reassembled the first brake and wheel, and am struggling with a bent split-pin on the second one, when an elderly American from the hotel parks his hire car at my end of the garage. From my grease-stained arms and black hands he mistakes me for the house mechanic. He tells me in awkward Spanish that his Renault is playing up. I say I am an English guest but will help if I can. Another new life for the taking: working on foreigners' hire cars in Seville. While I tinker with the Renault's timing, my new friend tells me with relish how yesterday's car broke down in the hills, and how he was forced to hitch, with five suitcases and 'my chic wife'. He is obviously having the time of his life, although I cannot speak for Miss America. What is it that makes such holiday diversions a challenge for one person and a misery for the next?

*

His problem with this hire car may or may not have been the timing. I can only say it ran perfectly well when we tested it out, and he tipped me generously.

*

The brakes refurbished, I retreat to the hotel's panelled and mirrored men's room to scrub up. The ivory-handled brushes and crisp linen towels make an odd setting to wash brake fluid out of your hair.

*

It has taken me a whole day to rebuild the front brakes and then find a workshop to help bleed them. First, Seville was in siesta until about a quarter to four, and then I fell foul of the European main dealer mindset. No, this is a Seat dealer, a Peugeot dealer, a VW dealer, and we do not touch other marques.

'But I only want to use your inspection pit and bleed the brakes.'

'Sorry, we wouldn't know what to do.'

'But I know what to do. All I need is someone up the front to open and close the bleed hole while I pump the master cylinder from underneath.'

'Sorry, we only handle…'

But then I am used to being infuriated. Infuriation is what I live with in London. Be patient…

*

A depot for delivery vans proves humble enough to listen. In exchange for letting several mechanics drive a Bentley round their forecourt, her hydraulics are more or less free of air. Now she needs oil. I throw in five litres, far too much of course, but that is the manic mood.

*

Fifty miles out of Seville, 5:30 p.m. We must keep moving.

*

Madrid. 350 miles from Seville. 11:15 p.m. I lean against the front door of the Prado – well, I think it is the front door – between the statues which line the long, western facade. You cannot but admire the four fountains that frame the boulevard running north–south – their vertical spouts of water squeezed from the mouths of dolphins by merciless imps. It is too chilly to stand here for long on the off-chance that Simon comes past to check if I have made it yet.

Round the side of Spain's premier art gallery I find a bank of payphones.

Simon is still at home. He tells me to drive north, to the edge of town, and to phone again. After a further delay while I lose my way and the gearbox goes, I make a second call from a box at the intersection of Pio XII and General Franco, and shortly afterwards my cousin's figure is in the headlights, running down an embankment to intercept me as I take the slip road off the highway.

Neither of us can believe that such a rendezvous has worked. He climbs in, positively slapping the walnut dashboard and red leather armrests, and we drive up to the tower block where he is staying for his first few days until he finds a more permanent arrangement.

'Everyone lives in apartments in Madrid,' says Simon.

Day 59

The night is still young, and we head for the Old Quarter of the city. We catch a few nightclubs with their guard down – Friday night is hitting peak romance hour. Kissing in corners is at saturation point. For ten minutes, we leave My Lady alone with the windows down and 'Yellow Submarine' on the Beatles' *Revolver* album on repeat and she starts a street party. Rather later, we discover in the Via Maison de Paradis a pick-me-up made with rum and cubed lemon which has you wide awake in no time.

Madrid must be the only European city where people are leaping in the alleys at four o'clock most mornings of the week. The night owls leave their cars just about anywhere in their hurry to be in on the act. My Lady forces her way through the parking bottlenecks in the narrow one-way system, her front bumper and heavy rear wheel arches nudging aside occasional offending Seats.

We wend our weary way home, and I carry my newly acquired Moroccan blanket and camel-hair rug to Simon's flat to roll up in on the floor.

*

Breakfast and family talk. We agree that all our friends and relations are certifiable; that girlfriends stop you reading; that Spain is a complete mystery; and that we should have gone back to that first party we crashed last night.

*

At 11:30 a.m. I am on the streets queuing for petrol, then off to find the new motorway to Zaragoza.

Just as we come into a contraflow for roadworks, clunk, clunk from the front end, heavy steering.

Here we go again; the Karaman tyre has finally died. But stopping, I see that all the tyres are OK. There is nothing trailing under the car. If anything the engine is running quieter.

Perhaps it was some rubbish I just did not see lying in the road. Moving off, the steering is again heavy, and now I see the generator warning light on and the water temperature soaring.

By the time the next petrol station comes up I have pretty well worked out it is the fan belts. They were new on in Izmir, thanks to Brendan.

Nevertheless, the sight of them tangled round the immobile fan is a shock.

In fifteen minutes the spares are fitted, and my hands are oily black again.

Will there ever be a day when this car just drives from A to B without a hitch? Surely there was one. In Algeria?

*

Spain is vast.

Time is slipping out of control again. Worse, by accidentally wearing a watch I have made this journey seem less magical, more pressed than before, a straight race against the clock.

North Africans would call these roads superb – motorways interlaced with long sections where the old turnpike weaves back and forth either side of the levee that will be the new road when the next EEC grant comes through.

The wilderness is in autumn colours, with the grandeur of Wyoming or Colorado. Occasionally a ruined castle stands atop a volcanic plug, to remind us that this is the Old World.

Passing Zaragoza, the cathedral, with its central domes herded between corner minarets, seems closer to Sultan Ahmed's Blue Mosque at Istanbul than to Christian tradition.

*

However much we fly, however well I balance bulk and momentum to wring more miles from each fleeting hour, there is no escaping the sheer scale of what I have bitten off in today's journey.

I told my goddaughter, Fleur, that I would see her just inside the French border at 6 p.m. But I have underestimated the distance by 150 miles, probably three hours, just as I did yesterday. And I don't even have a phone number for where she is staying. Fleur is now five years old. It is altogether less clever to be late for a five-year-old than an adult.

I face the facts and call her grandmother from a service station, leaving a message in case they speak between now and then, that I will be an hour and a half late.

In the petrol station shop, by the phone, is a CD of Tchaikovsky's ballet *Swan Lake*. I snap it up. It has taken me too long to see my odalisque as Odette.

*

We blast down onto the coastal Valencia–Barcelona motorway, heading for Perpignan. I am carried away by the speeds which the Bentley is holding. Never before have we breached and held 100mph.

Then I begin to notice my surroundings. I feel that we have been here before. Fifteen months ago, this very road, this same direction.

At the Barcelona filling halt, throwing in another ninety litres, the truth dawns.

My Lady has done it.

She has gone round the Mediterranean.

The idea absorbs me but we press on. It was one of those notions, so simple, so obvious, that it did not need a map to think about. If it couldn't be done, the world was grim indeed.

A weight should be lifting from my shoulders. Surely the hard part is behind me now.

I have lived. I have seen something few alive have seen, if any. When I have time, perhaps in my old age, I will have something to reflect upon.

However, I do not feel elated. If this was do-able, perhaps I aimed too low. Should I have turned left at Raqqa? To Nineveh, Babylon, Persepolis. It would put me the far side of Mount Everest by now... about at the Turfan Depression, that oasis below sea level, just north of the Himalayas in western China... the most fascinating spot in the whole school atlas.

The truth is, I have been playing the game for the game's sake. I may have closed a circuit, but I have not found closure. I do not want this to stop. Emotionally, I cannot afford it to.

I have built an alternative reality. Which one is real life now, and which one the distraction?

I try to set myself a new goal.

My employer has said I must bring My Lady home to London by the end of the year. If not I will be, 'Laughing on the other side of my face'. I guess the chairman will no longer ignore me. One of the founders will flick me with his pitiless gaze, like the Eye of Sauron. But if I can pull it off, what is done is done and will continue to be a good joke for everyone.

Well not quite everyone. At least one girl is unimpressed.

Into these thoughts comes a trespasser. A steady, resonant tap, tap, tap, tap from deep in the engine. I have been going too fast. Pulling over, I lift the butterfly bonnets and listen, my ear against one end of a large spanner, the other probing around the cylinder block like a stethoscope. Not the rocker cover, not the distributor. It seems this could be the dreaded broken valve.

But with visions of goddaughter Fleur waiting on the steps of the church in Collioure, this is no time to call a breakdown truck and wait for major surgery.

Back on the motorway. At about 90mph, a vicious grinding opens up from the very guts of the engine, and the speed drops quickly to 70. The gauges stay steady, the warning lights off. I am thinking that she will seize if I stop now, but if I keep going, maybe she won't. And, hey, we have completed the circuit, the dream has become reality. The vamp from Littlehampton has tramped around the Med.

The grinding noise fades, then comes stabbing back, louder than before. Whatever it is that has dropped into a combustion chamber, an exhaust valve I suspect, has holed a piston and is beginning to disintegrate and sprinkle through into the sump. Is it possible for an engine to take such punishment? Perhaps, just perhaps, we will be left with five serviceable cylinders; and that has been enough before.

How can a machine be so overengineered?

*

Autopista becomes *autoroute*. Popping and burbling, we thread our way through the border controls and down into France. At the first *péage* exit, I pull off. The toll man swears at me for not having French francs, then bows sarcastically when cajoled into taking Spanish pesetas from '*Monsieur Le Marquis*', as he spits. No kidding, he just gobbed on the bonnet. Welcome to the land of *Fraternité*.

We head for the sea. Mature avenues of trees in the soft tungsten beams; yellow stained oncoming headlights; fractured farm buildings with faded murals for Pernod and Michelin.

This is France.

*

And so, 500 miles from Madrid, and hours late, an ageing Englishwoman noses into Collioure and down to its tiny harbour. I am asking a group of teenagers, clustered round a moped outside a café, which way to the church, when the little girl's father, Remi, walks up.

Again the happy fortune of finding one person in a million; he and his wife, Hattie, my friends from Marseilles, who warned about the body parts in the post, were finishing supper in the restaurant across the road and saw the Bentley pass.

'Round here, this square is the *parking*, and join us,' says Remi, and I do.

Fleur has long since been put to bed.

Day 60

Remi phones through to my room in the hotel, above the restaurant.

'Have you seen out of the window?'

'What on earth is the time?' I ask.

'Eight o'clock, but I think you had better look out of the window.' And indeed a farmers' market has set up around the Bentley in the leafy square. I can barely see her for awnings and umbrellas.

Climbing back to my bed, I hear Remi is still on the line.

I say, 'Forget it, there is nothing we can do.'

'No, no, Fergus, it is still early enough to save the day. But soon the buses will arrive. Then all will be lost'. A pause. '*Vraiment*,' he says, and I imagine his Gallic eyebrows raised in emphasis.

It feels like a wind-up, a French plot, but he is right.

I run down to the street. Trestle tables, are being banked up with fruit and vegetables. Sweet stands are filling with confectionery. Our fate is still in flux. The stallholders and barrow boys give me that obstinate refusal which traders the world over reserve for Englishmen in pyjamas. Be it a bond dealing room in the City, the souk in Damascus or this fishing village in the Languedoc, market-makers do not like wedding cars or complete idiots on their turf.

Here are flower sellers, onion-stringers and beekeepers unloading their treasures; mammiferous plyers of Roussillon *rouge*, who press me with an early morning glass; shellfish gatherers, sausage-vendors, *patisserie* and *paté* artists; alchemists in jam and preserves; young girls hawking the local soft, wet cheese.

What to do?

A tactical switch to not understanding a word of French; and there, by the *charcuterie*, is the diminutive village gendarme, who must become an ally. He finishes his baguette, brushing the crumbs wearily from his tunic.

Soon the situation is fluid. The gendarme understands the seriousness of kidnapping. The wine women come over on the grounds that their plonk is delicious. Also, this car evokes sisterly solidarity from the least likely old ladies. Together we begin to set aside crates, mats and weighted umbrella bases. Apologies and smiles are met with grunts and gesticulations, but no one actually resists. The gendarme's presence holds the traders impotent, operetta-style. Gradually, everyone is moved to help, if only to protect their goods from the accident-prone attentions of their neighbours.

When a manoeuvring area is cleared, the populace stands back to watch a *Rosbif* in his nightwear trying to start a Bentley with one piston already gone to the angels. We raise the bonnet, one side, then both, and screwdrivers appear. The small gendarme insists he be the one to sit behind the large steering wheel and turn the ignition key. Churn, churn, nothing.

Just as impatient murmurings begin, Remi arrives, every inch the heroic compatriot. He suggests we all push and we can fix the engine later. French mobs love a leader thrown up by destiny. The mood warms, then crystallises into active assistance. This is the spirit of the barricades. The policeman again takes the wheel, perched on the leather seat with his hands reached wide on the rim; six men seize the front, and another eight or nine the rear, and the crowd shouts 'push' and 'pull'.

In this fashion My Lady does not move for some time. Then, with a mighty, uncoordinated heave, all chance upon a common direction. She springs forward; and the insensitivities of two and a half tons, with no power hydraulics to the brakes and steering, surprise us all. She makes the very most of her moment centre stage.

With me now steering, she rolls out between the stalls and, after one last push, across the street to a little pedestrian precinct where I catch her on the handbrake before she accelerates down to the dockside. We ask permission of a fishmonger to leave her in front of his barrow. '*Devant une belle dame comme ça, on ne peut que s'incliner,*' – one can only bow to a beautiful lady like that – replies the old man. And so he does, to Remi's delight.

I look up at the hotel and see Fleur and her mother, leaning over their balcony. Is that stomach cramp they are suffering from? I bow too.

*

After we have eaten, a light drizzle falls, the first of winter. The stallholders have come prepared, and there is frantic ferrying and holding of forts while they dig out plastic sheets and hooded anoraks.

I sit in the fighting chair, behind the big steering wheel and face the moment of truth. The engine is dead. The soul is gone. The crank sounds sluggish, laborious, but, as in the Syrian Desert, the battery just will not give in. I look down the short slope to the edge of the quay. It would be so easy to slip the handbrake, let her roll and just sink her in the harbour for good.

No sooner has the thought crossed my mind than one of her cylinders fires, and then another. Slowly all five catch on. You can't say she hasn't got heart.

Or that she doesn't love a scene.

I let her warm up, then back her out of the pedestrian zone, popping like a coffee percolator, away from her watery grave and round, up to the top of the castle hill where the parking is legal. She pulls like a train up the incline, better than when there were only five cylinders in Turkey. So a holed piston is preferable to no spark at all.

*

Taking the *autoroute* from the border to Perpignan, in convoy with Remi's Lancia, the Bentley feels comfortable at 70mph. She and I are braced for total failure. If the engine seized it would either lock the rear wheels or smash the automatic gearbox – the same old debate, in a novel guise. I drive with one hand on the gearshift, poised to slam it into neutral. Remi discouraged the idea of his daughter coming with me on this part of the jaunt.

In this way we make it to Perpignan, park and find an excellent fish terrine, roast duck breast and a heady Banyuls red at Le Fournil de Pierre. Fleur tries one of my cans of Libyan lemonade, and she approves. Her bored young brother,

Alexandre, runs away to the lavatory, whence his sister brings reports that he has removed all his clothes. At the threat of no pudding, he promptly reappears, all his clothing on, but with some back to front.

He is three, but he knows his *millefeuilles* like a true Frenchman. They are astonishing. Weightless, six inches high and still hot from the oven, this is the pastry and custard I recalled in Palmyra, unmatched in 8,000 miles.

*

A motorway exit ramp east of Nîmes. The sun has set. Do I go north to Orange, or east to the Luberon? The Luberon was where Her Ladyship first stayed on her own after Ibiza, at the farmhouse of Geoffrey and Elizabeth Kime, near Menèrbes.

Nestled between Avignon to the west and Cannes to the east, these steep, sylvan hills enjoy year-round spring water. It oozes from the valley walls, from a band of soft stone trapped between layers of impermeable rock. The northern slopes of *Jean de Florette/Manon des Sources* country are, if anything, even more achingly picturesque than those films.

So the Kimes live at the head of a valley in one of France's prettiest national parks. Soft country, dove-like woods. Fifteen months ago Geoffrey showed me the ancient entrance to their own spring, tunnelled under the cellars. I also admired his orderly vineyard, in terraces down the narrow valley floor. It would be the perfect rest cure for the company car while I work out how to deliver her to the inspectors at Velo.

But can I descend on them again? This time without warning? With Geoffrey in Paris recovering from leukaemia and Elizabeth expecting their second child?

I have known Elizabeth since we sat together in our first undergraduate history lecture. She had blagged her way into uni without A-levels, having accidentally entered an all-boys sixth form college. She was quite the sexiest, longest-legged, coolest cat on the block. To be honest, any man with an ounce of gumption would have sat next to her the morning I did. But initiative is in short supply among male history freshers at redbrick universities.

She soon rose above that life; you could not say dropped out. Things were dull for a time after she left. Later, I was neighbours with her older sister, Anna, and got to know her parents, brothers and little sister too.

On the other hand the town of Orange could be a more sensible stop, and it is bound to have a covered car park. 'Seville to Orange in a long weekend' has a certain ring to it, too. I could catch the train to Paris with no further worries.

The Luberon is an hour away. The Paris train leaves Marseilles two and a half hours from now. It may stop at Cavaillon, Elizabeth's nearest station, about 9 p.m. It is six o'clock now.

Let's find a mainline station and see what the stationmaster has to say.

*

The stationmaster says Avignon offers a third possibility, as yet undreamt of. Put the Bentley on a train to Paris. With the car dropped off at night, I could take the sleeper up, drive her from Paris-Bercy station the next morning and leave her in the Paris Charles de Gaulle airport long-stay car park for a fortnight or so. Only one problem. Tonight the train for cars is fully booked after the French bank holiday weekend. But the passenger train departing from Cavaillon has space.

On the stationmaster's TV, the French are celebrating a rare Williams-Renault victory at the Australian Grand Prix. Prost had already won the championship after Senna's strange disqualification in Japan, and withdrew because of the rain. But Senna roared on until he ran into the back of Brundle while lapping him.

I pluck up courage and phone Elizabeth.

*

Crescent moon again, wet country lane, gleaming pinhead stars pricked into a black velvet sky.

Menèrbes sits on its luscious cliff face, sable shapes against charcoal. This is the fertile Eden of France, a place to build a monastery, to bear a family, to convalesce. The road up into the hills seems seductively familiar, though I have only been here before by daylight. But the Bentley helps me out. The lame mare has smelt her stable and limps herself home.

There – the fork in the road from Oppède; there – the single-track bridge; there – in the distance, the gateposts; there the wicker gate and, at last, the brown barn doors, lustrous in the headlights as I pull over on the long wet grass. Switch off, lift the latch on the yard gate, crunch over the gravel, turn the heavy front door handle and push.

Elizabeth looks elegant, radiant, her long legs curled up under her on a satin couch, yet somehow not comfortable.

'Have you had a baby?' I ask.

'Fergus,' she says in a strained voice. 'I'm just about to have it.'

Chapter Five: A Kind of Homecoming

East Germany, West Germany, France
Friday 1st December to Sunday 3rd December 1989

Day 61 minus one

Not many cars in East Berlin. A few Trabants are scattered down the sides of the Leipzigerstrasse. This area was bombed flat by the Allies during World War II and rebuilt in an even more monotonous Le Corbusier style than Cairo's Heliopolis. Illuminations, strung across the streets for the fortieth anniversary of the German Democratic Republic, have been extinguished, supposedly to save power but actually to avoid further embarrassment. The land of Marx and Engels is in turmoil and reverting to a market economy.

Tonight the Volkskammer, the GDR parliament, abolished the first clause of the constitution. The Communist Party is no longer the only permitted political organisation.

The spirit of revolution is in the air. The Unter den Linden, the road in front of the Volkskammer, is seething, people craning in the street light, eager for the next piece of news, to think yesterday's unthinkable. They are saying that parliamentarians by the dozen and citizens by the thousand are resigning their Party membership tonight. The optimism is boundless.

An old woman walks her dog – what changes she has seen in her eighty-odd years, from Kaiser Bill to Helmut Kohl. On her left is the symbol of it all, the winding, floodlit no-man's-land between East and West which runs league upon league, from the Baltic to the Black Sea.

I sit down in a pub. I talk to the girl next to me, Annette (Netti) and her husband, Jörg. She is General Guderian's great great niece. Guderian, the tank strategist, surrendered to the Americans in 1945 and was investigated but never charged at the Nuremburg Trials. Who knew he had left a nephew in the East?

Netti and Jörg (I call him George) are East Berliners and in their twenties. She is too pretty to hide and he is better read than I will ever be. These are the people who will elect a new parliament next April; four months to replace a political hierarchy that has reigned for forty years.

My border entry papers say I must be out by midnight. I buy us one last round and leave the Zum Nussbaum pub with minutes to go.

How much longer will Berlin be divided like this?

The Trabi car is a colour beyond Calypso Green. *Ossie*. Off-the-scale brash.

Day 61

Checkpoint Charlie, Friedrichstrasse. The East Berliners stream back the other way through the raised barriers, home. They form a sea of heads, backlit by floodlights, like at the end of a pop festival.

Midnight. Made it.

My employer is the biggest independent manager of European equities on the planet. We are number one in the UK and have happy clients in North America, Japan, the Commonwealth, the Netherlands, Scandinavia, the Middle East, almost everywhere with big pension schemes, huge insurance companies and massive sovereign wealth funds. However, until now, selling into Germany has been considered 'too difficult'. The language, the regulations and the caution instilled into Germans by three financial meltdowns in living memory meant my ambitious colleagues looked elsewhere for glory. Yet pension funds and insurance giants are here too. This was an opportunity for someone who liked a long shot. Me. For eighteen months I have had it all to myself.

Now many people will want in. They may even hire Germans to do my job. But this is my hour. I am stamping my name all over it.

There is no doubting I am drunk.

The stars are out. Clear, dry weather over the whole of Europe. I walk north carrying my suitcases, along the west side of the high concrete Wall to the Brandenburg Gate. This section has not yet been breached. Russian guards still patrol it. At the tribune or viewing platform, which I climbed only six weeks ago to see into the East, I stop. I walk to the spot where, just this May, I knocked my head against the Wall in frustration, doubting it would come down in my lifetime. How wrong I was. How much has changed.

I try it for resonance, as at Stonehenge and the Great Pyramid.

Nothing. Transitory.

I continue northwest, through the top of the Tiergarten park to the old Reichstag, derelict since the government moved to Bonn. This was the escape route of the staff from the Führer's bunker, after Hitler shot Eva Braun and himself and the SS cremated them.

Now I'm angry.

I rage at the flaming waste and the lost humanity of it all. World War, Cold War, Genocide, Fascism, Communism, Dictatorship.

When did Stalin, Roosevelt and Churchill make this bet about whose system would win? Well, it has finally been resolved. Stalin lost.

In an inebriated fury, I walk a mile west along the Strasse des 17. Juni, past the cannon-clad Siegessäule, Bismark's column commemorating victory in the Franco-Prussian war, then another mile and then some more.

Taken with its sister Unter den Linden, this straight-line avenue from the old palace is surely the most magnificent in Europe. London's Mall is just over half a mile; Paris' Champs Elysées–Arc de Triomphe–La Défense triples that. But here is an axis at least a mile more than Paris'. Moscow's Leningrad Avenue is supposedly grand, but it does not exactly lead from Red Square. Or to anywhere. Berlin's marching way sucks you along it, whatever the pain.

History.

And tonight we have drunk many times to history.

Yet Europe must take care. If the architecture of imperial Berlin remains, with its parade grounds, sweeping steps and this triumphal boulevard, what else is still hanging around? This avenue retains a whiff of megalomania.

At Ernst Reuter Platz I hail a last taxi. But the driver tells me that Tegel airport is now closed for the night. So I climb out again.

Mistake. Hotels are absent in this quarter – as yet. They will come, but not tonight. And no more taxis appear.

I am too tired to sort myself out. The suitcase of documents from meetings yesterday with the insurance and banking regulators, the BAV and BAK, is heavy, biting.

I stop in an entrance to rest my arms. Leaning against the door, it swings away from me, unlocked. I tiptoe inside.

It is a building site, the reconstruction of a tall villa. At the top of three flights of stairs, under the roof, is a room with glass in the window and a door I can close. I curl up under a spread copy of the *Financial Times* and shiver fitfully through the night.

*

Düsseldorf airport.

Transit passengers waiting for a connection to Paris. Tegel reopened at 5 a.m. and they changed my Business Class ticket to London for an Economy stopping flight with Air France to Marseilles.

Down in the Luberon the phone rings and rings. No point flying south to rescue a damsel in distress if Elizabeth is not there to unlock the barn.

The phone answers. Yes, Elizabeth is out but will be back home around 3 p.m.

*

Lunchtime at Marseilles airport.

The Provençal air is bright-cut, a Van Gogh sunflower away from wintery Berlin.

Last time I was here, walking through this sparkly car park with no inkling of a circumnavigation, Geoffrey drove the Bentley down from the hills to collect me. The sight of her white coachwork rounding the end of the airport approach road, between the avenues of palm trees and exotic shrubs, was worthy of its own film festival. I wonder if he will be there at home now? I hope to God he's still on the mend. I head for the airport bus station.

*

Sun in the pruned lime tree square. Seagulls like diamonds in the sky. The slope of the hill through the town to the old port, and the Gallic one-way system, give the airport coach problems. At last we reach Marseilles train station, with its showpiece of 1980s municipal architecture: an elevated concrete bus terrace.

The French of Provence have not changed. The attitude on the taxi rank, when asked the way to the Avignon bus, is in direct line of descent from the *tricoteuses* at the foot of the guillotine. French taxi drivers against the world. It is not a viewpoint found on the streets of East Berlin, or Ankara, or even Cairo, where taxi drivers are poets, minstrels by comparison.

The trains are on their Saturday timetable. The bus to Cavaillon leaves an hour and a half before the next train. I need information about wagons of automobiles running from Cavaillon station up to Paris overnight. Aha. One departs from Marseilles at 8:55 p.m., but when does it leave Cavaillon? And what about Avignon – closer to the Bentley and in the right direction for Paris?

Maybe My Lady won't start anyway. We can but try. She and I are on our last warning from personnel.

*

A bus to Cavaillon. Then, after dusk, a hitched lift to Menèrbes.

A second hitched ride, the mile back west on a minor road towards Oppède, and at last I see the half-open barn door in the night, and a white boot glinting in the headlights.

*

Red wine casserole, wood smoke, a fluffy toy dog called Charlotte.

When the Bentley has started we will enjoy a celebratory drink.

Elizabeth is about to put her month-old daughter to bed. She seems to be running a crèche. Other infants lie helpless on the rugs. More than one new mum, hearing that Elizabeth has produced, has come to pool their sanity.

Geoffrey is on the mend and will be down in two weeks. Elizabeth's mother, Susan, flew back to England last week, declaring the coast clear.

'Could you bring in some logs when you next go out to try the engine?' asks Elizabeth.

Apparently My Lady has been driven twice since she arrived, by Lucy, Elizabeth's help. Lucy has discovered a mechanical bent. She suggests she come out to the barn with me next time.

'You have to talk to her a lot,' she tells me, and asks more disapprovingly, 'What do you mean, you think you've flooded her? What on earth's that?'

I try to explain.

Lucy speaks reassuringly about pulling out the choke and warming the ignition. Having managed 15,000 miles since the end of June last year without discovering either of these features, I'm obviously impressed.

We go into the cool night with a torch and round to the wood shed, where the ghostly apparition is nosed into heights of sawn logs.

Lucy's 'choke' is the one-shot chassis lubrication pedal, and the 'ignition warming' is the 'Picnic' position for the key, for listening to the radio. But it takes a girl to suss a girl and these two tricks do have an effect.

My moody car catches several times.

I take in the logs.

Elizabeth's two-year-old, Matilda, was only crawling when I first was here but is now running around with nothing on.

'Fergus might actually never go away,' Elizabeth tells her. 'So there's no danger in turning your back on him for a second.'

*

Fourth trip to the barn. Down into the black depths. Open driver's door, slide across red leather, don't touch the accelerator, turn the key, vroom, a surge followed by a splutter and the engine dies. Nearly there.

Kill time. Open the other garage door and gaze up at the waxing moon.

Back in the driver's seat, the engine springs to life first turn. All is well. Headlights on, gear lever down, steady backwards up the narrow corridor between the bales of wire mesh and the spare panes for the greenhouse. The Bentley is like a barge in a canal lock, or a dreadnought launched tail-first, an incalculable mass gliding gently into a calm lake of darkness. Forwards round the barn to turn, squeaks from the steering and whines on full lock from the belts under the front of that long, slim bonnet.

In the farmhouse, Matilda doesn't want to go to bed. Elizabeth chooses a tape of children's songs and I try to teach an old favourite from it, 'Nellie the Elephant'. It was my first '45', when I was not much older than her. However, it seems children of two can't sing.

Also, I find to my horror that I am unable to say bedtime prayers with a little child. This was so easy when the child was me. I am losing my spirituality.

*

Gearbox failure in sight of my hostess' gateposts. Darkness. Hedgerows loaded with the scent of falling winter dew, a bouquet which northerners cannot auto-effluviate. I am alone with the starry night. So much more relaxed than previous gearbox failures, previous starry nights. There's the Plough, over to the north.

A slip of a crescent moon is setting in the west.

*

Five minutes was all she needed.

Backroads from Menèrbes. Brakes pull to the left. Five cylinder engine shudders every time we accelerate. Nevertheless the driving position is just divine. Stretch out my left leg, pull down the armrest, open the side quarter-light to clear the mist from the screen. Settle down in the fighting chair.

Heading north to Les Baumettes. It's about 8:15 p.m. I have an hour to reach Avignon. The stationmaster at Cavaillon checked for me. Glad he did, Marseilles station was reading the summer timetable when I phoned them. Into Les Baumettes, first wolf-whistle. The brakes, if you can call them that, have warmed up so are retarding less well. The engine runs a little hot, but Lucy sold me some antifreeze, looks like about four litres. That should fill any deficit in the radiator. Best not waste time putting it in now; do it on the train.

The flying wing 'B' mascot is silhouetted against the road and we are holding a steady 55, driving on the right. I am steering a river launch, not a speed boat. Smooth, slightly slack in direction, a hint of wallowing in the troughs of the road but altogether effortless. Twenty-two kilometres to Avignon. Main beam on, fog lights too.

The CD of the Beatles' album is coming up to the theme song. We take a level crossing. Everything works. No clonking from the shock absorbers – not even the CD jumps. Track five, 'All You Need is Love'. John Lennon, 1967.

There's nothing you can do that can't be done,
There's nothing you can sing that can't be sung...

Whenever we reached a destination, this song announced our arrival. It broke the news of our every entrance in Ibiza, it took them by storm in Chianti and Rome. It whispered to the deckhands in Piraeus. It curled toes in Kusadasi. The song was played to the stones of lost civilisations in the wastes of Syria. In Amman and Petra, all we needed was love. This was among the tracks on the beach at Ras Mohammed. It had an airing one night on the Gulf of Sirte. And in the streets of Madrid.

Plenty of middle-class British parents in 1963–1969 tacitly disapproved of pop culture in general, and especially Beatlemania. Lennon's increasingly revolutionary tone was quite frightening, 'Back in the USSR' and being 'Bigger than Jesus'. Nevertheless, despite the cloak of silence, snippets of Beatles songs snuck into the playroom, via visitors' radios or live on early evening black-and-white telly.

We kids picked up many dozens of tunes and lyrics at random, dipping in, by osmosis. It was one long, blind tasting. A decade later, the 'labels' were revealed. Well, actually just one. I couldn't believe it; so many ballads from a single band. It was a game Celina and I played in the car on long journeys – who could remember the most Beatles tunes? Between us, over a 100.

Now here the song is, in the south of France, back among smooth roads, intelligible street signs. The Beatles even briefly had an S1, the Beatles' Bentley, but pink, purple and blue, overpainted with psychedelic plumage. It was auctioned in New York by Christie's this summer.

Bet that one never even had a puncture; and now my breath is fogging between me and the windscreen.

*

Concentration is needed to find the shunting yard (not the station) before 9:15 p.m. It is supposed to be three kilometres this side of Avignon.

Football match at Avignon St Germain. Stop to ask the supporters. Yes, St Germain is here, but no they do not know anything about putting a car on a train.

Then suddenly there are car-on-flatbed-wagon signs, more signs…

The guards realise in time that the lower deck has insufficient headroom for Her Ladyship. The ramp to the top deck is steep, like coming out of a riverbed in Syria. I cannot see a thing, and the five cylinders won't pull. We take a run. The whole world disappears beneath the long bonnet. We could be flying in space, but the wheels stay in the runners and she is aboard. A metal bar is wedged under her front tyres, then another locks the back ones from behind. I climb down. A motorcycle is being tied in place on the lower deck directly beneath the Bentley and the sight of the big white limo flying over this Evel Knievel object adds to the arc-lit surrealism.

*

A *navette* bus takes me up to Avignon main station to catch my accompanying sleeper. I won't see the circumnavigator again until about 8:30 tomorrow morning. They strapped down her aerial to stop it flapping in the breeze. These trains can only be doing forty-five miles an hour, I hope, if they take ten hours to slog up to Paris through the night.

I forgot to put Lucy's antifreeze in the radiator. The frost and wind chill going over the Côte d'Or after Dijon is bound to finish her. Will she be heading tail-first? That might reduce the wind factor.

Well, too late. She is on her own. Only she could summon up a mild night to save her engine block.

Day 62

Paris-Bercy marshalling yard.

Seven o'clock in the morning and not yet dawn.

Dozens of parallel sidings. The frozen tracks spangle white beneath the arc lamps. Hoar frost prickles on the sleepers. An immensely long train of cars stretches away under the floodlights. Beyond the end of the platform, past the bend in the tracks is a single wagon bearing a familiar white shell, somehow built to a different scale.

This sub-zero morning was made to crack cylinder heads. But then we have been through it before in Turkey. The most important thing is to be allowed to wake her in her own time.

The goods yard handlers start to drive the cars off the first wagons. Here comes the bier with my dead archduchess, nudging up to the platform now. I cannot quite see. Is she impeding anyone else? I don't think so.

No, she's not even on this wagon. She must be somewhere.

Brrr! God it's cold! She's bound to have frozen up in her engine.

*

Aha, what's that?

Another, longer line of freight cars.

The handlers have detached the tail of the train. I think I saw, through iced eyeballs, on the last carriage, before it slipped into the night... I think I saw a white roof.

*

Far away, a different train completely, going out of view. She's stopped. Right in the distance, perched up on the same wagon on her own. And she's back to front. Somehow she did manage to turn her back into the wind.

They are changing the points over.

The train is coming down beside me, sweeping in, cars from many quarters, flatbeds marked Fréjus and St Raphael, hot names, slowly they go by; Toulon. Even in this little slipstream I buckle with cold. My poor baby will have to reverse 100 yards along the tops of the wagons. The air is a riot of creaking rolling-stock and wheels thumping over fishplates. There she passes, gliding backwards above me, a heavy icing on her rear window. If she was facing backwards all the way up, there's a chance that she'll be all right. I'm surprised the boot hasn't blown open.

Once again, the carriage slips out of the siding, quite fast. My Lady rolls serenely back into the guts of this huge shunting yard. Still it is dark, though the time is a quarter to eight now. Can they turn wagons round to bring them in faced about? A short toot from the distant engine echoes off the encircling sheds and towers, huddled in Sunday lie-in.

I walk back down my platform. What are they doing now? Her train is creeping closer incredibly slowly. They shunt her wagon into an empty one, they touch, a bang, another echo. A man swings a lantern away between the tracks.

All stops. Signs of life, none. Signs of sanity, also none.

*

Dawn comes up over Paris. Two geese low in the pink sky to the east, skimming the silhouettes of churches, chimneys, cranes, square-topped office blocks and apartments, speak of a guileless time when this was Gaul.

*

Almost all the cars have been moved. A man with a lorry battery on a trolley has just jump-started a Ford Fiesta on the top deck three tracks away, a flyweight sprinting off the flu.

I remember once in the Alps rising in the dark to light candles in the snow under my own Fiesta's sump and putting a rug inside the bonnet to swaddle the rising heat. When the trick worked, the noise was just the same.

That leaves all the cars moved except for those on our wagon. Someone must come with the Bentley's keys soon. Is that him on the deck below? He's playing cat and mouse with me.

I must reach a staircase down before he can find another and come up. Where's he gone? There he is. I have the key. He was keeping it in his pocket. I wonder why.

The key fits, the door opens. Poor frozen soul.

I have to admit I never heard a car sound so dead in my life.

*

She's angry, furious with me.

She is never going to speak to me again.

Oh dear, oh dear.

*

It's been three-quarters of an hour. Footplate men, handlers, cooks, secretaries and yard managers come and go. I've hooked up two lorry batteries in series. They make the Bentley engine churn faster, but it sounds as dead as a beaten carpet.

Come on! London want their car back.

And French National Railways want their wagon back. They have removed the others. A general despair hangs over the last spectators. They shake their heads like the road menders south of Karaman. The guy who has been turning the fan when the starter won't engage asks if I am a member of AlpAssistance. Nope. A locomotive moves like a scavenger, menacing in the background. The siding faces north so not even the sun is going to shine on the Bentley and warm her. The French are giving up.

They take away their second battery.

*

We are alone. No one is left to show off to. Now my little hellcat will pull herself together.

I'm going to wait a few minutes.

Here comes another locomotive. It sidles in like a crab, a hyena, a ragged-winged vulture and grabs the remaining wagons from the next platform.

She nearly went on the first turn of the key. Give her one more rest.

Down the tracks in the misty morning, the railway workers are assembling a new train, moving from wagon to wagon.

It's nine-thirty, eight-thirty in England; I won't make it to London for lunch.

*

She's going! She's going! Ha ha!

She's going, the old girl's done it, she's staggered into life one last time, one last morning, to get back to England. That took an hour and a quarter. Hip hip and jubilee; and no one here to celebrate but me. They've all gone for breakfast or elevenses or lunch, for all I care. Ah! Listen to that sweet music – give or take a cylinder. For a 32½-year-old starter motor, an hour's churning is no mean feat either.

The first of the incredulous Frenchmen returns. He isn't even smiling, just looking stunned. As soon as he comes beside us, Her Ladyship remembers herself and stalls. Then the Bendix clutch does an Aqaba and will not engage, although I turn the fan time after time after time. Then we reverse to the middle of the next wagon and the gearbox packs up. No motion, backwards or forwards. Oh, come on little car, you can de-board this train somehow. Or don't you want to go back to England? I know you are only teasing now. And these guys are not worth the show.

*

As soon as we are clear of the station, the Bentley detects my hubris and calls up clouds of steam from the radiator, made all the more spectacular by the chilly morning. Pull over in the sleepy boulevard. OK, swallow this; three litres of antifreeze and a litre of water. The boiling stops. The leak is still there, but without the pressure of steam, I hope we'll be able to make it. We have seen her recover from the Camargue trick before.

And of course, we've got no petrol either.

Missed it! Missed the ring road gas station. Round we go again, leafy Paris suburbs, don't run out, you can do it…

*

The tank's full, the radiator's settled. The tarmac is slipping underneath us, to the end of the adventure.

The sun slants across the winter *autoroute* to Lille, the frost is off the driving line, crawling back to the verge. There's a haze in the air. These French motorways are so relaxing, so tame. You could do a million miles in a car like this on a road like this. Even the Karaman tyre would wear forever.

This grey northern light reminds me of the morning I took delivery of her, confident in what I had done, as we ventured along the seafront highway at Eastbourne. I didn't know how accurate the speedometer was, and there was a police car doing, according to us, 30mph precisely. I assumed Bentleys, like all cars, had slightly optimistic speedometers, so that the police must be doing 28. I overtook at about 32. Flashing blue light. Pull over.

'That wasn't very clever, was it, Sir?'

*

A squat-wide Porsche 911 Turbo pulls up and holds formation behind my offside wheel arch, looking at the lines, and I know he is mulling those haunches. Her rear three-quarter view is her best. A picture comes back of a beach before Jerba Island, as wide as the sky is high, and only a perfect white dot seen from behind against the sea in the distance.

Flanders fields, where another kind of strength and determination was once recorded and made up into heavy black books of words and drawings and photographs, volume after volume about the Great War, in the libraries of Home Counties prep schools. Now these killing grounds are perfectly manicured, agricultural showpieces, and the woods have all but regrown, a testament to the Common Agricultural Policy.

*

Stop for an excellent motorway lunch, phone home and say 'Perhaps teatime' – I can't believe it, teatime, teatime in England.

It's been so long.

*

The Somme. Ice on the river; the heavy black books showed that too. The covering on the trees is so deep it must be snow; wrong, just the thickest frost, a foot wide in places. Everywhere the east wind has deposited frozen dew on the sheltered sides of trunks, branches, twigs and even stems of grass. Punk hair and hoary fingers strut in pre-Christmas fancy dress. We pass a car from the GDR – the first I have seen in the West. I wonder what he thought of us, and of these battlefields.

One day, forty years from now, the world will look as strange to us ageing Westerners as it looks to Eastern Europeans now.

*

Turn on to the Autoroute des Anglais, under construction, closing the gap from Vimy Ridge to St Omer.

*

Just before the turning north to Calais the earth warms briefly. The Serre River passes under our wheels, an enchanted tableau of white-iced trees but with still, reflective water.

We overtake an aged British sports car, navy-blue, being pulled up towards Calais on a trailer behind a diesel Mercedes. What looks like its new owner is lying down in the back of the Mercedes. We exchange a small salute, like Hind MI24s.

We are coming home.

Do you remember in Turkey last winter, contemplating the crossroads, one way back to London, the other to the Izmir warehouse? When the madness went on? Now it is ending.

The motorway has been built closer to Calais than on the outward leg. I wonder if it goes all the way yet?

It does not.

*

Freezing fog in the kingdom of the wicked witch. The temperature has plummeted again. The wire mesh fences are all but closed shut by blown ice. Frozen condensation has beaded in great sweets of sugar from the top of the Armco barriers.

It would be ridiculous, but we might have to put the snow chains on again. The engine is running so cold the needle is barely off the bottom of the water temperature gauge.

A clean wash of sunlight bathes us, already low in the southwest.

The lines of frozen poplars form a guard of honour, hexed hussars. Our own courageous leading Lady is returning up the valley of the Lys. The French kings took the white three-pointed flower that blooms here in the spring as a symbol of their independence.

What is nobility? It starts with a line, a physical statement or definition. Nobility looks. It says presence, place, position. Guesses have been eliminated. Corners have not been cut. The combination is of strength rehearsed and genius evolved; because underneath the look is the purpose. Beneath her femininity, our noblewoman does not suffer fools, is deadly accurate, can kill with a wink.

But usually that last is not necessary, because nobility encourages, inspires. It says: Be the best of yourself, in repose, which is the beginning.

What else? What is this courage which she has, which dares to push, because it senses the infinite; which makes all other moves look small by comparison; which postulates that spirit is enough? Courage can show self-discipline, determination, holding to an objective – when it no longer seems tenable, when the complexity seems overwhelming, the consequences unbearable; when the potential catastrophes spill like high-speed tape to the floor; when fear leaches bile through the last membrane around the heart; when we force ourselves to wake up and find we are already awake; when responsibility grows lonely.

Sometimes courage says, 'This is all out of perspective, lighten up, don't imagine things to be so serious'. Sometimes it says, 'Live by your wits, let go trying to control the whole, apply a little active intelligence to the parts one by one, as they come at you'. Sometimes it says, 'Lift up thine eyes unto the hills, whence cometh thy salvation'. Sometimes it just says, 'Play the role, sway the room, turn the mob, spin the illusion, for all men's hearts are human'.

But only one heart counts now. The dark-eyed leprechaun's that awaits in London. Courage draws strength from past success. The longer the odds already overcome, the more possible the future seems. I need all the optimism I can find.

All she needs is love, as much as any of us.

The heart of bravery is dark, inscrutable as the warrens of an ancient wasp's nest. If the noble lady foresees a crisis, she will marshal every resource, and in her devilry she will laugh at what shocks others. Courage knows, she remembers, her black core is sympathetic. For she must reproduce before she dies. So her laugh has the same fundament, whether in the face of defeat or greeting victory.

*

Piles of turnips by the road, dogs rootling, hunters walking with rifles on their arms; we hold just under 70mph, fifth cylinder hammering, the red-tiled roofs of the houses with the little whitewashed walls, which have withstood two World Wars. The sign reads 'The Field of the Cloth of Gold, 1520'. Just a flat plough, with the frost lying in the furrows. These acres have been watching nobility come and go since prehistory.

*

Calais. Fluffy blonde candy floss rises from the Trioxide chemical works to drift over the town. The ferry dock has capacity for six boats to load cars at any one time; and huge crawling robot cranes.

They took the ticket! The day shift didn't see that it carried last year's date. Lane Number 1, sailing at two fifteen. Two o'clock now.

The marshal reports into his walkie-talkie, '*Oui, j'ai un autobus et un Rolls.*'

Straight up over the bridge.

We left England on the 16th of August 1988 and today is the 3rd of December 1989.

Sings the radio: '*Il n'y a que les grands qui rêvent*' – only the great dream.

No. Please. We can all dream. It's what you do next.

Two buses embarking in front of us. Water temperature rising. Select neutral and let the fan spin faster.

Can we receive the BBC yet? That will be the cherry on the cake.

Coming up on to the boat. How many boats has it been? Let's see. Dover to Calais, Denia to Ibiza, and back, Brindisi to Patras, Athens to Chios, Chios to Chesme, Aqaba to Nuweiba, Jerba to Tunisia, Tangier to Algeciras, Ayamonte to Vila Real de San Antonio, and back. Eleven, excluding this.

Clunk, we hit the ramp, clunk, clunk-clunk.

Epilogue

Don't judge a girl by her tantrums.

From front to back My Lady had gone through headlight and fog light bulbs and wiring, a burst radiator, perished hoses, a thermostat, fan belts, dynamo bushes and bearings, plugs, points, rotor arms, distributor heads, foaming oil, a broken inlet valve, a suspected valve seat holing a piston, reportedly a cracked cylinder head, definitely a smashed shock absorber, a ripped suspension arm, bent tracking, a flaming tyre, punctures, roasted brake pistons, knackered condensers, grit in the flywheel, a worn crown ring, a sheared Bendix starter drive, a burnt-out regulator, airlocked hydraulics, gearless gearboxes, fluctuations in the water temperature gauge, a dicky microswitch, a part-time fuel warning light, severed CD remote control, snapped driver's seat springs, perished door seals that sucked in dust, window winders that fell off, sinking rear suspension, and a boot that only locked when it was least wished for.

Yet these were but window-dressing, disguise, rag-netting to cover a heart of solid gold. For the Bentley did indeed have a snapped piston gudgeon pin, due to one shattered exhaust valve seat dropping into the combustion chamber, and broken piston rings on three out of the five other cylinders.

She collapsed that December night, as we backed into the garage at home, and did not move for many months.

Velo came to the mews and saw for themselves that she still existed.

I did the bulk of the mechanical work over my own inspection pit, with Bruce dropping by in the evenings to advise and guide.

Fleur, who was already seven, flew up to pat the convalescent at the critical moment.

When all was done, she and I took My Lady over the road to the petrol station where this began, to tank up.

They welcomed us as though we had never been away.

Index

People met or spoken with

Places

Lightning Source UK Ltd.
Milton Keynes UK
UKHW051448120223
416624UK00009B/10